1998

Global Exchanges

Global Exchanges

The Washington Post International Marketing Companion

The Washington Post Writers Group

Edited by T. Bettina Cornwell
Fogelman College of Business and Economics
Memphis State University

Allyn and Bacon
Boston • London • Toronto • Sydney • Tokyo • Singapore

Editorial Director: Bill Barke
Editor-in-Chief, Business: Rich Wohl
Series Editor: Suzy Spivey
Editorial Assistant: Sarah Carter
Cover Administrator: Linda Dickinson
Manufacturing Buyer: Louise Richardson
Cover Designer: Suzanne Harbison

ISBN 0-205-14720-8

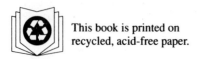

This book is printed on
recycled, acid-free paper.

Printed in the United States of America

10 9 8 7 6 5 4 3 2 1   97 96 95 94 93

Contents

Foreword

Global Exchanges captures the dynamic field of international marketing as it is being practiced today. The articles in this book, drawn from the pages of the *Washington Post*, offer you insights into the fast changing and increasingly complex world markets and acquaint you with the major issues confronting marketers today.

If your reading to date has left you mystified as to what the major issues in the international marketing are, this book can help. *Global Exchanges* is organized into four parts: Introduction to International Marketing, The International Marketing Environment, International Marketing Activities, and The Future and International Marketing. Each part begins with a brief introduction and each part contains vivid examples of international marketing in action.

This book is designed to enrich any marketing course, from principles to international. For readers engaged in marketing activities or those who simply want to learn more about this topic process, *Global Exchanges* provides fascinating examples of international marketing in action.

–T. Bettina Cornwell

Part 1

Introduction to International Marketing

International Marketing is exciting. As with many exciting things there is an element of risk. Some businesses are willing to accept the additional risks inherent in international marketing and some are rewarded. Others are not. We can learn from both successes and failures of international marketing found in the stories presented in this book.

The readings in this first section seek to establish the actors and the stage on which international marketing is conducted. One of the central differences between domestic marketing and international is the introduction of more entities to any marketing endeavor. Very few of the marketing activities (discussed in Part 3) change in the international environment. However, in international marketing more than one government will be involved and perhaps many. Many more "middlepersons" will take a share of the activities and new and different groups not present in most domestic marketing will play a role. Everyone from "doodad exporters" to "Superfirms" is included.

1 The Lure of International Marketing

How Some Firms Become Foreign Success Stories

Report Credits Persistence, Creation of Niche Markets

CINDY SKRZYCKI

For many American firms, cracking foreign markets is Mission Impossible.

Some don't show enough commitment and initiative, bow out too soon, or simply consider themselves defeated before they ever get started. Others are content to concentrate on domestic markets.

Some of that attitude, which put America at a competitive loss in the world, has been changing with the dramatic drop in the dollar. An increasing number of U.S. companies are making drives abroad and finding success as their products become more price-competitive with foreign goods.

Even American car manufacturers finally are stepping up exports to difficult markets such as Japan.

But long before more clement competitive winds began blowing—when the dollar was at its height and choking off U.S. exports—there were companies that not only made dents in foreign markets, but exploited them by emphasizing investment and "intellectual" factors such as technology, innovation, marketing and management.

A study of such success stories was released last week by the American Business Conference (ABC), a coalition of 100 high-growth, midsize companies.

The group also hopes that its report, which is rich in example, will boost its lobbying effort in Washington to supplant restrictive and protectionist measures contained in pending trade legislation with measures that emphasize bilateral trade and multilateral negotiations.

The report, called Winning in the World Market, is a nine-month effort by management consultants McKinsey and Co. to examine how ABC member companies, with average sales of $360 million, managed to increase foreign sales almost 20 percent annually for the years 1981 to 1986. Foreign sales of the ABC companies increased 17 percent annually between 1981 and 1984, while exports rose 15.2 percent.

2

By contrast, a group of 1,453 other U.S. companies doing business abroad had an annual decline in sales averaging 1.8 percent and 10.2 percent in exports during that period.

Even more recently, when the international performance of most companies improved as the dollar weakened in relation to other currencies, the ABC companies outstripped competitors in foreign sales and export growth.

"Much of what we found falls into the category of common sense," said Richard Cavanagh, a partner at McKinsey and Co.

"In general, the same principles of competition—innovation, competing on value, not price, creating and leading in niche markets, and getting and staying close to customers— works as well in Paris as in Peoria," Cavanagh said.

Simple as that sounds, many of the companies that gained footholds abroad do not have the advantages of size, name recognition and the resources of major exporters such as General Electric Co. or IBM Corp.

But they have successfully cultivated niche markets, developed products with singular appeal and adopted attitudes that are decidedly global.

Their stories seem to fly in the face of common perceptions that U.S. companies face insurmountable barriers in entering foreign markets and that they leave home markets only to take advantage of cheap labor and economies of scale.

The president of Electro Rent, which rents and leases electronic equipment, said his company's entry into foreign markets violated most of the classic approaches to international expansion.

"We knew we would lose money for a couple of years, it would take far too much of our time and the markets we were looking at didn't justify the effort," said Greenberg. "Then we promptly went out and developed two major markets."

The company, which has a joint venture in Japan and is about to break into Europe, expects its foreign sales to grow from their current 10 percent level to 25 percent between 1993 and 1995.

Greenberg predicted that sales will be boosted in part by a higher yen, which makes prices of Electro Rent equipment more competitive.

Loctite Corp., a manufacturer of industrial adhesives and glues that does 60 percent of its business in 80 countries, has surmounted different types of obstacles in each of its markets.

In Japan, it was a game of inches. The company first had an ad hoc licensing arrangement, then minority participation, and then a joint venture before it finally was able to create a wholly owned subsidiary.

In France, it was creating advertising that had local appeal.

Loctite's U.S. advertising campaign for Super Glue features a man stuck to the ceiling with his shoes on. To appeal to a French audience, the model became a prostitute in a tight leather skirt (that doesn't fly up) who ends up being stuck to the ceiling by her procurers.

"We learn so much from being involved in foreign markets that we probably generate more business domestically," said Ken Butterworth, chairman and chief executive of Loctite in Newington, Conn.

Besides determination and a global outlook, many ABC companies have innate advantages that ease their entry into foreign markets.

"One reason is their uniqueness. Many of them create their own niche markets at home and abroad. As niche players, they face little or no competition overseas initially. These companies enjoy the benefits of being first movers," the McKinsey report noted.

For example, customers came calling for Cray Research Inc.'s supercomputers. Overseas distributors asked Loctite for appointments. Others have unusual technical advances to offer, such as Millipore Corp., a worldwide producer of products for fluid analysis and purification with annual sales of $443 million. Hasbro Inc. and Dunkin' Donuts have unusual concepts— toys and doughnuts— with mass appeal that they readily adapted to foreign markets.

Outside some of the advantages ABC companies have capitalized on, there are certain approaches and management techniques that characterize their success outside home markets.

Those that started the earliest did the best, Cavanagh noted. "They began as corporate infants to explore international markets," he said.

Loctite had only $1 million in sales while Pall Corp., a $400 million company that makes highly specialized industrial filters, decided to enter the European market when it had only $15 million in sales and the Common Market was still just an idea.

"The big companies in the U.S. never needed to find a reason to go overseas," said Abraham Krasnoff, Pall's vice chairman and chief executive. "Inertia is a difficult thing to overcome."

Once the decision is made, the progression then is to start with a modest but well organized export program.

"The sequence almost always begins with the establishment of an in—country sales, distribution and service network—a requirement for healthy export sales and a prerequisite for long—term success in the local market," said the report.

The point also was made that failing to lay this foundation may be part of the reason U.S. exports have made such a slow recovery since 1985, despite a lower dollar. For example, non-ABC, medium-sized companies had export growth of only 2.1 percent from 1984 to 1986 while 34 ABC companies with an international presence had growth close to 21 percent, the report said.

Most of the ABC companies also find it essential to put foreign nationals in charge of their foreign operations.

"The only way we can do business is where there are no cultural barriers between local management and customers. I believe in establishing a country organization around the right local national; if you can't find the right person, don't do it," advised Ray Stata, chairman and president of Analog Devices Inc.

A review of 562 foreign subsidiaries of ABC companies showed that 86 percent were managed by local nationals, though sometimes finding the right person can take years.

Comdisco Inc., a computer leasing and service company, spent four years finding a Japanese to lead its joint venture operation.

Loctite will launch operations in China with a native of the People's Republic who earned an MBA in Boston.

In addition, many ABC chief executives are natural champions of international ventures, since they often are foreign—born or began their careers in foreign countries with ABC companies.

Besides early entry into foreign markets through exporting, many ABC companies went the joint venture, acquisition and licensing routes.

But most ABC companies—some 80 percent—ultimately have direct ownership in mind. Safeguard Business Systems, for instance, enters into joint ventures with buyback clauses.

Most ABC companies do so well overseas that they graduate to establishing overseas production facilities, with some 80 percent of revenues coming from foreign production last year.

Like Japanese auto makers who are increasingly locating plants in the United—States to insulate themselves against currency swings and the threat of protectionism, ABC companies cite some of the same reasons for manufacturing outside the United States.

Part of the payback from setting up foreign operations is extracting two—way benefits either by gaining intelligence about competitors or keeping on top of new technology, new product applications and manufacturing processes.

Electro Rent's Greenberg said his company's foreign foray was a strategy to hedge technological bets.

"The U.S. and Japan are locked up in a long—term war on many scientific and electronic fronts," said Greenberg. "I wanted to be in both markets."

Loctite's Butterworth said his company "bothered" simply because it is very profitable.

In fact, the financial return for many of the companies, Cavanagh noted, was almost immediate: 64 percent were profitable in the first year and 75 percent within two years.

"It's a series of small, pay-as-you-go smart bets," said Cavanagh. "And it proves you don't have to be big or have deep pockets to compete overseas."

Overall, the experience of ABC companies "may serve to turn conventional wisdom on its head," said William Lilley, president of the American Business Conference.

The group also hopes to use its findings to make headway on the trade front.

"The report should serve to reorient the competitiveness debate away from a single-minded concern about obstacles to international success, toward a view that encompasses the opportunities that exist abroad {and} how our companies exploit those opportunities and what public policies promise to help international growth," said Arthur Levitt, chairman of the American Business Conference.

Other trade experts were less optimistic about companies being able to surmount trade barriers and currency fluctuations.

"An overwhelming determinant of our ability to compete has been exchange rate fluctuations," said Jerry Jasinowski, chief economist for the National Association of Manufacturers. "There is nothing companies can do, in many cases, to overcome enormous swings in rates that have cut American firms out of markets and dramatically increased imports coming into this country."

Noted another trade expert: "Trade barriers are not a mirage. Many of our most competitive industries have been badly damaged by them.

November 15, 1987

The Rise and Fall of Saatchi & Saatchi
How One British Ad Agency Grew too Big too Quickly

GLENN FRANKEL

Charles and Maurice Saatchi liked to tell their colleagues the story of the blind beggar in Central Park who sat on the sidewalk with a sign that read: "I am blind."

One fine morning in early spring, an advertising copywriter passed by on his way to work, bent down and wrote something on the sign. When he stopped by that evening and asked how the day had gone, the blind man replied, "Fantastic. Never done so well. What did you write on the sign?"

The copywriter replied, "I added a few words to make it read: It is spring and I am blind."

Even a beggar needs an adman, or so the Saatchis believed. During two frenetic decades of hyperactive deal-making, they set about to make themselves admen to the world—nothing less than the biggest, boldest, most creative and most profitable advertising and marketing agency that ever existed.

Or, as they themselves put it in one annual report: "It's good to be big, it's better to be good, but it's best to be both."

For a brief moment, some would say, Saatchi & Saatchi Co. was both. Starting only 20 years ago, Charles and Maurice Saatchi transformed their six-man agency on a London side street into the largest advertising conglomerate in the world. Just as the Beatles took American popular music, refined it and brought it back across the Atlantic, so too did the Saatchis lead the British conquest of Madison Avenue with a quintessentially American weapon: the ad.

They did it by a combination of British chic and British cheek. They hit London with a series of stylish, hard-edged ad campaigns— a pregnant man to advertise family planning, a pack of lemmings to illustrate the dangers of smoking, a long unemployment line with the slogan "Labor Isn't Working" to promote Britain's Conservative Party—shaking up an industry that despite its worship of innovation had grown stale and self-satisfied.

By 1979 they were the biggest ad agency in Britain. By 1986 after a corporate buying spree, they were the biggest in the world, operating on five continents and servicing more than 50 of the world's 100 largest companies. Among their clients: Toyota, Honda, Procter & Gamble, British Airways, Colgate Palmolive and Live Aid.

"Charles saw the world as a big supermarket— you go in and buy what you want off the shelf," says a former senior officer at the company, one of many who left on less-than-friendly terms, yet speaks of the brothers with a wary affection. "Everything is for sale. The only question is can you afford the price. Things had to get out of hand—and inevitably they did."

Among the corporate refuse of the '80s, from Boesky to Milken to Campeau to Trump, the Saatchis stand out for many reasons. Perhaps the Saatchis were victim to their own hype, believed too deeply in their own infallibility. Meanwhile a chastened stock market caught up with the incredible game of buy and buy and buy with borrowed money that was the key to their breathtaking annual growth in sales and profits.

Their tale is in large part the story of Britain in the era of Margaret Thatcher, when entrepreneurs armed with cash and insouciance set out to reassert British influence in a changed world. Their climb was one of the most swift, their fall one of the most sudden.

The Saatchis helped pioneer the concept of globalization. Thanks to computers, satellite television and films, they reasoned, markets were shrinking, national identities slipping. If everyone was buying the same products, then everyone could be sold in the same way. And a few large, fearless corporations could practically run the world.

Neither of the Saatchis would speak for this article, and many of their closest associates and former colleagues insisted upon anonymity. Once the darlings of the press, the Saatchis now believe the press has turned vicious and unfair. Yet like those former associates who parted on bad terms, journalists remain fascinated, even when appalled, by the brothers and the world they built.

"They had a terribly low boredom threshold and a momentum they felt they had to maintain— they didn't want to do this year what they did last year," says financial journalist Ivan Fallon, author of, "The Brothers," the definitive British book on the brothers' rise.

"You say your bottom line is to become the biggest in Britain, and then in Europe and then in the world, and before you've even arrived there, you're asking, 'What do we do after that?' You keep forging a philosophy to fit whatever pleases you. And all the time you're succeeding, you reinforce your own view that you're infallible. They came to utterly believe that there were no ceilings for them." Advertising may have been an American invention, but the British have always been masters at image making. A few weeks ago they celebrated the 50th anniversary of one of the most humiliating defeats in their history, the evacuation at Dunkirk, as if it were a triumph, a fable of small boats and brave men. Three generations of Britons believed the myth. They also believed that the gruff, steely voice that entreated them to stand tall during the darkest hours of World War II belonged to Winston Churchill, perhaps Britain's greatest image maker, rather than to the actor who read Churchill's lines over the wireless.

In the 1970s, the British had their chance to assert those skills anew. Like Washington after the Cold War, Madison Avenue had grown uncomfortable with its own vast powers, wary of its own instincts. For all of its explosive growth, the advertising business was still something of a cottage industry— a few giants, but lots of small agencies, and not much attention to bottom lines.

Enter Charles and Maurice. "They arrived at a time when rising American domination had been accompanied by a pervasive blandness and repetition in the actual creative work of advertising," wrote Robert Heller, editor of *Management Today*. "It gave British agencies, mostly new, the chance to become the Greeks to the Romans of Madison Avenue. A rolling tide of brilliant British advertising reset the standard and the style.

"The Saatchis shared in the flood. The difference was that their ambitions were Roman in scope. They wanted an empire."

The Saatchis were born in Baghdad, the sons of an Iraqi Jewish merchant who fled the country with his young family in the late 1940s. Their place of birth was a fact the Saatchis, keen to be seen as insiders, sought to conceal as they made their way up the mountain of British business.

Maurice went to the London School of Economics while Charles, bored, gifted and restless, skipped college and went directly into the ad business as a copywriter. He made few friends, fewer allies, but gathered a small circle of devotees. Eventually he decided that the only way to get where he wanted to go was to open his own shop. And he persuaded his younger brother to join him.

The Saatchis launched themselves with a typically self-engineered attention-getter a two-page ad in the *London Sunday Times* titled "Why I Think It's Time for a New Kind of Advertising." It was bold and arrogant and it cost them a quarter of their start-up money.

They soon became London's hottest ad shop, a place for talented, difficult people. And the most talented and difficult, friends say, was Charles Saatchi himself.

William Muirhead, who now is chairman and joint chief executive of the original Saatchi ad agency on London's Charlotte Street, recalls his first glimpse of Charles Saatchi's witheringly high standards. Muirhead had been dispatched to a client with an ad he had never seen before and didn't quite understand. The client loved it, however, and Muirhead came back pleased.

Charles was not. "Charley said, 'It's crap,' and he ripped it into little pieces," says Muirhead. "I had to call back the client and say, 'You know that ad you really loved? Well, we've done something even better.' That's how Charley operated." Friends say Charles Saatchi bullied everyone—his clients, his employees, but most of all his younger brother. Now 47, Charles remains a harsh, relentless, profane, reclusive, intensely competitive man with a take-no-prisoners approach the adman as existential hero. Maurice, now 44, is a charming, quieter but no less assertive person, the ego to his brother's id.

To outsiders they were Rambo and The Nerd, a carefully honed brother act. Charles had the restless energy, the impulses and the intuition; Maurice, the know-how to translate the raw energy and ideas into a strategy for the '80s.

Charles was the spark, but Maurice handled the cash. He was the one who convinced London's tightfisted financial markets that an ad agency was a good investment, one worth backing with millions in share issues. And while Charles would skulk and hide from clients, Maurice would turn on the charm.

Between the two, friends recall, there was chemistry and there was terror. Sometimes there was blood as well when Charles lit upon Maurice. "They are Cain and Abel," says a former friend. "You have to remember that Cain loved his brother.

"Even in a hysterical rage, Charley could be very funny. I can remember him one day, red in the face, screaming at Maurice: 'I can't believe you came from the same womb as me.'"

Friends say today Charles still brings his pet schnauzer to work each morning, still plays board games like chess and Monopoly as if they were life-and-death struggles, still dominates the psyche of the company with his brooding presence.

But it is at most a spiritual presence most employees these days say they never see Charles Saatchi, who has long made a point of avoiding direct contact with clients and the press. After Saatchi & Saatchi went public in 1977, Charles never attended a shareholders meeting. There has been only one official photo in the past decade.

Both brothers tend to hover on the edge of London's social scene, a world friends say they have never felt part of.

Maurice is married to Josephine Hart, whose career is as a West End theatrical producer. While less reclusive than Charles, friends say, Maurice prefers the privacy of the vast English garden he has designed for the multi-million-dollar country home where he and his family live in Sussex, south of London.

Charles's marriage to Doris Dibley, an American and former ad copywriter, broke up three years ago, but he still maintains houses in London's Mayfair area and in Long Island, still pursues the art collection he and Doris initiated together. It is now considered one of the world's largest collections of contemporary art —worth more than $100 million, by some estimates and a small portion is displayed in a stark, white-walled former warehouse turned gallery in north London. Most of it, like Charles himself, remains behind closed doors, sealed off from view. Among the best and brightest hired by the Saatchis in those early days of the agency were Tim Bell, who started as media director and ended up managing the day-to-day operations of the agency for the increasingly remote Charles; and Martin Sorrell, who did the same on the financial end. Sorrell and Maurice Saatchi together created a management system that monitored the company's financial condition daily and imposed rigid budgets on its new acquisitions yet allowed the new purchases wide-ranging autonomy in conducting business. The system impressed financiers in the City, London's version of Wall Street. They provided the cash that fueled the new acquisitions and made Saatchis the City's top glamour stock.

Both Bell and Sorrell left the Saatchis with bitterness, and their departures are considered among the key reasons for the company's subsequent decline. Sorrell bought a small firm, known as WPP, and began acquiring larger companies until last year he surpassed Saatchi as the world's largest advertising group. Bell has opened his own firm to develop corporate strategies and lobbying campaigns. He is also considered one of Margaret Thatcher's most intimate advisers. Yet friends say Bell, despite the rancor, still stands in awe of Charles Saatchi.

"Tim was great on a surfboard," says Muirhead, "but Charley made the waves."

The Thatcher account in many ways was the key to the Saatchis' reputation and acceptance. They won it in 1978 in typical fashion, according to Fallon—neither brother showed up for the meeting at the Conservative Party's central office. But Gordon Reece, then the party's communications director and a member of Thatcher's inner circle, was eager to import American-style techniques to help defeat the ruling Labor Party and he believed the Saatchis could help him do it.

The best ads were sharp and bitter—a slick, fast-moving television spot depicting everything in Britain moving in reverse, and the famous poster campaigns. One depicted an unemployment line above the simple message "Labor Isn't Working"; another showed a young black man with the line, "Labor says he's black—Tories say he's British."

The ads were aimed not at specific policies or issues but feelings, what Bell called "the emotional meaning" of voting for Thatcher. Labor was caught off guard—every time its leaders criticized the ads, the result predictably was more publicity, which made the Saatchis and the Conservatives look even more clever, and Labor more clumsy. Thatcher won a substantial electoral victory in 1979 and the Saatchi legend was born.

But by then the Saatchis were already moving on to bigger battles. Clever ad-making was not enough. They also wanted to be known as the top marketing company. And so the Saatchis had started buying. The first big acquisition was Compton in 1975, a blue-chip ad agency that was twice as big as they were. The Saatchis convinced Compton's owners that the two companies should merge. They even added Compton's name to their own. But within a few days, the headline in *Campaign,* the London ad weekly with a direct pipeline to Charles, read "Saatchi swallows up the Compton Group." Many of Compton's senior managers left quickly.

After that, says a former employee, the pattern was established. "Charley and Maurice would tell the prospective sellers anything they wanted to hear, invent an ideal version of what life would be like after the deal was signed. And afterward we would just do exactly whatever it was we wanted."

It was the biggest acquisitions binge the London stock market has ever seen. By 1985 the Saatchis were buying companies, most of them American, at the rate of one a month. In the spring of 1986 they paid $100 million for the New York ad firm of Backer & Spielvogel, the largest sum ever paid for an ad agency. A month later they smashed that record by paying nearly $500 million for Ted Bates Worldwide, the third largest agency in the United States.

Bates was the deal that made Saatchi the world's biggest agency, yet it also marked the beginning of the end. Analysts said they paid far too much for Bates and bought a company whose conservative approach to the business was the virtual antithesis of their own. The deal also cost them big amounts of business from major clients upset that Saatchi had grown so large its many little arms were servicing rivals. Procter & Gamble, the Saatchis' biggest client, Colgate-Palmolive and Warner Lambert reportedly removed more than $300 million in business after the Bates deal.

There were other problems. Searching for new worlds to conquer, Charles and Maurice decided that the consultancy business was as ripe for acquisition as the advertising business. As usual they formed a theory to justify the instinct the Saatchis would become a full-service company that could offer clients not only advertising, but public relations, research, even financial services.

Beginning in 1984, they bought a dozen small agencies, only to discover that their expertise in advertising did not extend to the specialized world of consultancies. The new agencies proved a big drain on corporate profits.

The 1987 British general election was also a minor disaster—Saatchi still designed the ad campaign for the Conservatives but played a much reduced role. The brothers resisted Thatcher's plea that Bell, who had just left the firm, be hired on as a consultant to run the campaign. As Thatcher's lead in the polls melted away, she grew more and more panicky and increasingly inclined to blame her predicament on the Saatchi campaign, which looked lackluster compared with the crisp new Labor Party ads produced by Hugh Hudson, director of the movie "Chariots of Fire." Hudson's ads personalized the campaign and portrayed Labor leader Neil Kinnock in the same heroic terms as the protagonists of the film, and included the inspiring Kinnock lines about his coal-mining ancestors that U.S. presidential candidate Joseph Biden later got caught plagiarizing.

Unbeknown to the Saatchis, Thatcher started quietly consulting with another agency, Young & Rubicam, then secretly called in Bell. When it was over, less than a month later, and the Conservatives had won another landslide, the Saatchis accused Bell of attempting to undermine them. Weeks of recriminations followed insiders say Charles Saatchi phoned prominent newspaper editors and businessmen to accuse Bell of drug addiction and criminal wrongdoing before both sides agreed to an uneasy truce. The brothers formally resigned the Conservative account a few months later. Thatcher, Conservative insiders say, was fed up with the Saatchis. By then Charles and Maurice were adrift in even deeper waters. They tried to buy Midland Bank, one of Britain's largest, then Hill Samuel, a smaller merchant bank. In both instances they were rebuffed by the owners but word got out around the City, whose financial mandarins viewed the bids with awe and anger.

"Here they had just paid a ridiculous sum for Bates, had had difficulties with consulting, and the next thing you know, Maurice wants to buy a bank," says Emma Hill, an analyst with Wertheim & Co. in New York.

The drain on cash flow of the massive acquisitions began to eat into profits. After Sorrell left in 1986, the financial monitoring system fell into disrepair.

There was also a deep sense of alienation among newly acquired employees in the United States, where people never really caught Saatchi fever. Clients too sometimes felt unloved or ignored. Charles and Maurice increasingly removed themselves from day-to-day operations and turned them over to subordinates who were said to lack Sorrell's brilliance and Bell's feel-good style of inspiration.

After the Midland Bank fiasco, investors grew wary and the share price of Saatchi stock tumbled. At the same time, corporate spending on advertising was shrinking as British interest rates soared and sales tailed off. Suddenly the dream was over.

It ended officially last October when Maurice announced that the brothers were relinquishing their roles as joint chief executives and appointing French businessman Robert Louis-Dreyfus to sort out the mess. He has been trying to sell off the consultancies, keep investors from bailing out and ward off the takeover artists who are hungrily eyeing the bloody remains like birds of prey after a massacre. Last week Saatchi sold, for only $2 million in cash, plus royalty payments, a Chicago legal consultancy called Peterson that it paid $116 million for only three years ago.

Louis-Dreyfus has quickly forced out a number of the brothers' longtime associates and allies and installed his own people. He has also lowered the company's sights. The new Saatchi image, says an insider hired by the new team, is that of "a company run by mature adults rather than a bunch of young creative guys playing with someone else's money."

The brothers each have accepted a 30 percent cut in their salaries. Maurice is still actively involved but appears to outsiders to have been reduced to a front man, accompanying Louis-Dreyfus when he goes to see fund managers to plead for more time and money, and taking senior clients to lunch. "His name is over the door," says an insider, "and he's not going to walk away from the mess."

Charles still plots and dreams, friends say, but is more reclusive than ever and often deeply depressed. They say he attributes the blame for his downfall to others, never to himself. "Charley is never wrong, he is never ever ever wrong," says a former associate. "It's the investors' fault for getting cold feet. Or it's Maurice's fault for failing to replace Tim or Martin."

Some of the glory remains. Bill Muirhead, the Saatchi loyalist who runs the original Charlotte Street agency, points out that his shop is still the biggest in Britain and last year was voted tops in the business by clients in an independent survey. It won more creative awards than any other firm and was the first agency to place a billboard on the eastern side of the Berlin Wall.

But even as Muirhead recites those achievements, a certain weariness creeps around the edges of his optimism. "It's a very competitive business," he says. "You've got to have an edge all the time and you can't stop competing, because once you stop, you're dead. I don't worry about the big guys. I worry about the guys who are just opening their doors. They're hungry and they want the money and they're ready to take the risks."

Sometimes the nerve endings show. When Paul Cowan, an accounts manager, and seven other staffers left last month and opened their own shop, boasting that they were the true "keepers of the Saatchi creative flame," Saatchis fired back with derogatory comments in the press and threats of lawsuits. It all looked rather heavy-handed and it contributed to another drop in the share price.

What it all comes down to is not just the loss of money, but of something almost as valuable in the ad business aura and mystique. Without those two characteristics, the Saatchis are just another pair of hustling admen, Supermen who lost their capes.

"The Saatchi magic was a huge plus factor, and now it's gone," says author Fallon. "These were the people who could do no wrong. But just as the gilt has gone off the Thatcher image, it has gone off Saatchi image as well. And they themselves are terribly conscious of it.

"They still have basically a very good advertising business. But is that enough?"

July 8, 1990

Major Actors in International Marketing 2

The Multicultural Corporation

ROBERT J. SAMUELSON

"Globalization" is the hottest new business trend. It's one of those fashionable words that people love to use even if they're not sure what it means. But beyond the catchy phrase-making, something is changing. Giant multinational companies are slowly beginning to lose their national identities. They're engaged in a worldwide competition for "the scarcest resource of all—talent," says Christopher Bartlett of the Harvard Business School.

Here are some telltale signs. Between 1985 and 1987, U.S. companies increased research and development spending in their foreign laboratories by nearly 40 percent. In 1988, European companies raised their investment in the United States by 16 percent. For the first time, a major Japanese company (Sony) has appointed an American director. Separately, these are modest changes. Together, they point toward a further breakdown in the autonomy of national companies and economies.

Of course, big companies have long been global. In 1988, U.S. companies had $327 billion invested abroad and about 6 million overseas workers. But most multinational companies have never fit the stereotype of truly stateless enterprises. They have retained their national character. After World War II, U.S. companies invested in foreign markets on the basis of superior technology and products. American companies could make and sell abroad what they had perfected in the United States.

What this meant is that overseas operations tended to remain separate from and subordinate to U.S. corporate headquarters. In different ways, the same has been true of Japanese and European multinational firms. For example, the Japanese advantage lay primarily in superior manufacturing. Costs were low, quality high. So Japanese companies manufactured at home and created huge sales companies abroad. But control remained firmly in Japan.

It is this reality that's now quietly changing. Companies are increasingly disregarding national boundaries and trying to organize their manufacturing, product development and research on a genuinely worldwide basis. Consider some changes by U.S. companies:

Until the late 1970s, Kodak produced a full range of films in plants around the world. To improve efficiency both in the United States and elsewhere Kodak decided to have plants produce fewer films in greater quantities. Finished films are then shipped to different markets.

One of Procter & Gamble's major new products of the 1980s—Liquid Tide, introduced in late 1984—was developed as a joint project by researchers in Procter & Gamble's laboratories in the United States and Europe.

Hewlett-Packard assigns worldwide responsibility for designing, manufacturing and marketing different products to separate plant locations around the world. A division in West Germany handles fiber-optic test equipment. A division in Australia manages computer-aided engineering software.

As these examples imply, globalization hardly occurs in a flash. Despite recent increases, for example, less than 10 percent of research and development by U.S. companies was done abroad in 1987. And many industries aren't affected at all. Cultural differences among nations won't disappear. National or regional companies are more efficient in many businesses. Newspapers may sometimes have foreign owners, but newspapers will never become a truly global industry.

Changes are occurring mostly in industries in which products and technologies are similar across borders. Electronics, chemicals and machinery are three good examples. Because markets in these industries are genuinely global, the companies that maximize total world sales have the best chances of recovering the high costs of developing new products.

Old formulas for overseas expansion no longer work. U.S. companies can no longer grow simply on the strength of superior technology, which has ceased being an American monopoly. Japanese companies can no longer simply manufacture at home and sell abroad. Protectionism and a higher yen are forcing Japanese firms to build plants elsewhere. As for the Europeans, they must expand or risk being overrun by U.S. and Japanese competitors.

The terms of competition are subtly changing, as Bartlett argues in a new book ("Managing Across Borders," coauthored by Sumantra Ghoshal). Companies will increasingly flourish or fail on how well they become multicultural organizations. They will need to create effective cooperation between people of different nationalities. Some U.S., European and Japanese companies already succeed at this. Others are having trouble. More cooperation will be required in the future.

American companies have some advantages. English is the global business language, and Americans are generally accepting of outsiders. But many American executives dislike working abroad, reports management professor Stephen Kobrin of the University of Pennsylvania. Japanese strengths and weaknesses are reversed. Executives go abroad in great numbers, but Japanese companies have a reputation for keeping non-Japanese from positions of power. Bartlett thinks European firms with a cosmopolitan tradition may do best at the cultural balancing act.

Multinational corporations were first popularized as world citizens that would roam wherever business beckoned. It's doubtful that companies will ever quite fulfill this prophecy. As a practical matter, most companies will never completely lose their national characters or allegiances. But the blurring of identities is an irreversible consequence of the growth of global commerce. If unsettling, this trend is not destructive.

What it means for our national well-being is simple enough. The marketplace for ideas and technologies is now worldwide. Companies are the means of transmission. The nations that prosper will be those best able to exploit the best new ideas and technologies—whatever their origin. It helps us if (good) foreign companies become more American and (good) American companies become more foreign. These cosmopolitan corporations are the wave of the future.

August 23, 1989

Brave New World, Inc.:

To Superfirms, Borders Are Just A Nuisance

HOBART ROWEN: JODIE T. ALLEN

Can the power of money accomplish what many centuries of military power could not bury the nation-state?

Yes, says Kenichi Ohmae, one of the new breed of management consultants that has helped propel Japan into its present eminence in the world economy. Astride its new riches, the Asian economic superpower is charting the way into a new world without borders in which nations no longer contend with military might. Instead the battles will be fought between NEC and IBM, between Mitsubishi and General Motors; and the prize will be the fluctuating loyalty of the world-class consumer whose search for the new and best will drive tomorrow's world economy.

The all-important economic vehicle of this future is the corporation, whose function is to serve its customers and its stockholders—but not the state. Thanks to huge trade surpluses, Japan's major corporations are awash in liquidity every day these conglomerates must decide how to invest more than $1 billion in new dollar holdings. By 1988, net Japanese assets outside of Japan stood at an estimated $300 billion, more than the total amount of money recycled by the OPEC countries in the 1970s. "By being a global player, {today's international} corporations can make money in Japan, Europe or the United States," Ohmae said.

Forget the "Japan Inc." model, the partnership of government and industry that some saw as the power behind Japan's economic sprint, says Ohmae. Nowadays, Japanese companies wish government would just get out of the way: "There are no longer any national flag carriers. Corporations must serve their customers, not governments."

Of course, governments, with their manifold constituencies, are not likely to turn over the reins of power quietly to corporate chieftains. But governments are already coming under increasing pressure from international mega-corporations which generate both domestic jobs and export surpluses—the West German government, for example, has found itself both embarrassed and relatively impotent in the face of disclosures of industry sales of chemical weapons technology to Libya. Such pressures may increase if, as Ohmae suggests, corporate interests in Japan decide to establish their own lobbying arm over here to augment their government's already substantial PR effort. Ohmae, an engineer, is director of the Tokyo office of McKinsey & Co., a management consulting firm with multinational clients in every part of the globe. The single motivation of these companies is profit, Ohmae makes clear. National security and national pride belong to an outdated generation. And such governmental concerns as the environment or social welfare appear not to count for much, if at all.

"National borders are disappearing," says Ohmae, who is viewed as something of a maverick in his own country for his calls for sweeping reforms in Japan's land management, education system and work week. "Money is transmitted electronically, and the information network criss-crosses. That reduces to zero the ability to fool people." Governments, at least secular governments, can no longer convince their populations to march off to war or to buy inferior domestic goods if better imports are available.

Ohmae's vision electrified members of the trade and finance establishment gathered to hear him at the Institute for International Economics. It was, as one member of the blue-ribbon audience observed later, "good theater." But it was more than good theater. It jolted an audience, comfortable in dealing with the terms of markets and money, into thinking in larger, less quantifiable terms: Are we really headed toward a corporation-dominated world of the future? Will we like it when we get there? And, if not, is there much we can do about it anyway?

Calls for viewing the global economy as a single unit dominated by large companies are not new: Charles Kindleberger, for one, talked in the 1960s of the dwindling power of the nation-state. But now, as Federal Reserve Chairman Alan Greenspan noted, that possibility seems far more real as economies are increasingly linked through multi-national companies and the sophisticated financial networks that service them. In fact, as the institute's Fred Bergsten observed in an interview, "there is a fundamental tension between markets and governments."

Moreover, the reality of economic interdependence should make the world more secure against war and invasion: If the Japanese enjoy a growing ownership of American assets, they have a stake in the health of the American economy. A new generation of warlords in Japan, should they ever emerge, would find it harder to sell the idea of bombing Pearl Harbor now that Japanese own many hotels and office buildings there.

Ohmae, however, takes this logic one step farther to deny the relevance of the statistics that have alarmed some policy makers by suggesting growing American economic dependence on Japan. The traditional trade accounts, he says, ignore the fact that American companies produce goods offshore that then are shipped back to the United States; these show up as imports. For example, U.S. corporations in Japan have a sales volume in Japan of about $50 billion annually. If those goods were made here and shipped to Japan, that would add $50 billion to the export ledger, he contends.

But this argument is seriously flawed, in political as well as economic terms. First of all, as Bergsten pointed out to Ohmae, few believe that the same $50 billion worth of goods could have jumped Japanese trade barriers if the producers had not set up plants there. (This is not to say that America doesn't have its own trade barriers.) Moreover, goods sold by U.S. companies in Japan create Japanese—not American—jobs, and the innovations in technology and production that grow up around the actual manufacturing process are more likely to benefit Japanese producers in the future.

To be sure, Japanese investment here helps create American jobs, and forces U.S. competitors to meet new competitive standards. So why should America worry?, asked Ohmae. Yes, Japan sends you goods and you send us dollars. But America is the "Greenbacks Empire": Even if Japan won't buy U.S. goods and services, sooner or later the dollars must come home in the form of Japanese investment in buildings, factories, securities, paintings and resorts.

Once the accounting is properly understood—and Japan's corporations must do a better PR job, Ohmae averred—a lot of the "unfortunate and uneducated bashing {of Japan by Americans} will stop."

But Ohmae's taunt provoked, rather than stilled, criticism among some in a sophisticated audience. By justifying the current "{Sony} Walkman-for-real estate exchange" asked Harvey Bale, a former trade official now with Hewlett-Packard, aren't you avoiding the necessity for the United States to increase its own saving and investment and for Japan to increase its own imports? Won't we be poorer in the long run, if we trade away our capital stock?

Moreover, as long as each nation still has its own currency that fluctuates against other currencies, trade patterns can strongly affect both internal price levels and economic growth. "Ohmae would be right," says Bergsten, "only if we moved to one currency, and if financing of trade imbalances were somehow automatic and indefinite." As it is, a precarious arrangement helping to finance the U.S. trade deficit is currently in force. But how long it goes on could be at the whim of the Japanese, Europeans and other investors. Ohmae himself suggested bluntly that a substantial further decline of the dollar could turn off the flow of Japanese money. That would mean that other governments, not our own, would start calling the important shots in our economic policy—and, perhaps our social policy as well.

Governments, of course, inconvenient as they may seem to the international corporation, do more in behalf of their citizens than wage war or erect trade barriers. Governments are the custodians of public goods—things like clean water and air, secure neighborhoods and protection for families from the vagaries of illness, disability, old age and natural catastrophe. Yes, and at least a measure of protection against the harshness of industrial change, too.

Indeed, it was on the sensitive subject of unemployment that Ohmae demonstrated a truly blind spot. There, the "national" question is abundantly present. Jobs don't float across national borders as easily as capital (which accounts for much of the protectionist sentiment in Congress). Fair or not, the impression persists that Japanese targeting of U.S. markets, whether for autos or semiconductors, has cost us jobs.

But the charge is unfair, said Ohmae, suggesting that the United States unemployment rate is bloated by the fact that 25 percent of those without jobs are blacks and Hispanics and recent immigrants—as if that meant that they don't count in calculations of our national interest.

Is a world with no public authority—in which the corporations are the law— "an attractive world?" wondered Jack Sheehan of the United Steel Workers Union. "It sounds like the wild and wooly West."

That's a question worth thinking about because this country may already have ceded substantial control over its internal economic and even social policies. According to Ohmae, U.S. industrial decline has already proceeded to the point where 70 percent of the United States economy is dependent on services, including computer software and know-how. "The most competitive products the U.S. can offer," he observed with a tinge of sarcasm, are the buildings and corporations that Japan can buy up with the highly-appreciated yen. And, in this view, there is little that America can do to regain its industrial might.

The standard economic prescription for righting the U.S. trade imbalance has been to let the dollar fall on international exchange markets until foreign goods become so expensive here that imports decline substantially, while U.S. exports rise because American goods and services have become cheap abroad. We know from the bitter experience of the last few years that there is no magic in the prescription for depreciation, and that a more basic confrontation with our own industrial inadequacies is urgently needed.

So far, Japanese (and many European) companies have managed to keep their market share because they have—through greater efficiency and/or lower profit margins—resisted much of the repricing that the falling dollar was expected to imply. Pushing the dollar lower, says Ohmae, would be a self-defeating strategy.

Well, if currency adjustments don't work as classical economics says they should to reduce the Japanese trade surplus, what about other options? What about stimulating Japanese consumer demand and foreign aid as suggested by the Maekawa Report. That proposal, made three years ago by a high-level Japanese group, recommended raising Japan's standard of living and redirecting its economy from its export-orientation toward more dependence on domestic expansion and tax reform. The essential theme of the report was that as a key player on the international scene, Japan now had an obligation to give to—as well as take from— the global economy.

Won't work, said Ohmae, again surprising his audience, because the Maekawa Report, based on a miscalculation of the savings rate in Japan, generated a superficial boom in consumption. "That kind of bubble could burst at any moment," he argued, saying that statistics already show the beginning of a decline.

Adding it up, Ohmae sees no problem in maintaining the current U.S.-Japanese trade imbalance (as recorded in the traditional way) unless Japan reaches a point where it no longer is willing to accept paper U.S. dollars. If the dollar keeps going down, he suggested, Japan will abandon its supportive role, "and at that point, America becomes another Brazil."

His prescription for the future is for the United States and Japan to drop their adversarial postures, stop worrying about exaggerated trade deficits and surpluses. Relax and enjoy it, he says, and form a "Group of Two" to manage the global economy. "Years ago, territories meant something. Resources meant something. Today, those are very old notions. Economies, such as Singapore, Taiwan, Switzerland and Japan, are people-driven. We have to redefine the role of government, which is no longer so important."

Perhaps not, at least, as far as today's multinational conglomerates are concerned. And it is true, as Greenspan pointed out, that the country that tries to shield itself from global forces of economic change will find itself both poor and isolated. But in the world of the future, there will be not only multinational conglomerates but human needs and values that only governments can protect.

March 19, 1989

Foreign Journal
Embargo Crimps Doodad Exporters

LEE HOCKSTADER

Santa Clauses in red velvet robes. Long-eared rag Easter bunnies. Wicker baskets painted with the Stars and Stripes. Rooster weather vanes, pink birdhouses that say "Welcome," painted wooden eggs.

Chintz, schlock and doodads of every description, the kind of stuff that ends up in bins at Woolworths and on the shelves of gift shops all over America: It all starts here in the work sheds at Ace Baskets, Haiti's largest purveyor of handicrafts.

"It's just rabbits, rabbits and more rabbits," said Jean Bernard Faubert, a partner at Ace, explaining Ace's top-selling creations, more than 500,000 of which are shipped to the United States every year. "We dress 'em for Easter, we dress 'em for spring, for Christmas . . . We dress 'em for any occasion."

But because of a tough trade embargo imposed by President Bush, Ace is now a leading entry on Haiti's endangered businesses list. All the firm's exports to the United States, which account for three-quarters of its business, are banned after Dec. 5. With Haiti no longer receiving shipments of diesel fuel or oil, Ace may run out of electricity even sooner.

"We can't last two weeks," said Victor Boulos, another partner in the firm. "If there's no change, I'll leave the country in December."

"After that, if we have to close down, we'll close down," Faubert said.

With buyers all over the United States and $5 million in sales last year, Ace has been a Haitian success story. Started as a tiny basket-weaving company in 1974 by Boulos, an American-born, Haitian-reared entrepreneur, the firm invested, grew and diversified. Today it employs about 1,400 workers full time and supports thousands of artisans in the countryside by buying and exporting their products. But the company is also a prime example of how dependent Haiti's anemic economy is on the United States and how devastating the embargo ordered by Bush is likely to be. Not only do most of the firm's exports go to the United States, but most of the raw materials for its products, such as wicker, wire, rattan, denim and rag, are imported from the United States.

In addition to the handicraft industry, which employs at least 10,000 and possibly as many as 40,000 people, there are dozens of small assembly plants making clothing, electronics, baseballs and other products for the American market that employ another 35,000. Agricultural exports to the United States, such as mangoes, which are being harvested this week, account for thousands more jobs. All may be lost if the international sanctions stay in place.

The U.S. embargo was announced Oct. 29, about four weeks after a military coup toppled President Jean-Bertrand Aristide, Haiti's first freely elected executive. While the embargo was intended to press Haiti's de facto authorities to reinstate Aristide, U.S. diplomats acknowledged it would also cripple Haiti's economy. The State Department said the suffering it would cause was the responsibility of the coup leaders.

Haiti's business leaders and politicians, many of whom hated Aristide and supported the coup, say the main impact of the sanctions will be on Haiti's indigent masses.

But judging from interviews with workers at Ace Baskets and other job sites, most Haitians seem to understand the intent and likely effects of the embargo and to support it as a means of forcing Aristide's return. They said that if they lose their jobs the blame will lie not with Bush or Aristide, but with the Haitian army.

"Everyone here is for Titid," said Sonia Brun, 29, mother of three, who was snipping loose threads of rattan from a woven basket painted with the stars and stripes.

Titid, or Little Aristide, is the Creole nickname for the ousted president, who was widely popular with Haiti's poor. "After all," she added, "it's not like he got up and left the country on his own. He was thrown out."

Although there have been no layoffs yet at Ace, the company thinks its days are numbered by the embargo. Already, raw materials from the United States have stopped arriving, and the firm's finished products that do not contain American raw materials cannot be exported to the United States. The products that can be exported will have to be shipped out by the end of the month in order to clear customs in Miami by the embargo deadline.

Economists say the danger of layoffs is that each wage earner in Haiti is responsible for feeding about five others without jobs—children, spouses and parents, usually. Businessmen say the main impact will be on the poor.

"If the United States wants to reinstate Aristide in power, they can do it in about a half-hour" by military force, Boulos said. "But why impose an embargo and make 6 million people suffer? This is unjust. You cannot hold 6 million people responsible for a military coup."

But at one of the work sheds out back of Ace's headquarters, Emmanuel Saint-Julus, a wire worker, offered a different perspective. "I'd rather lose my job than not have freedom in this country," he said, taking a break from bending wire into frames for baskets. "You can't sleep at night or go out now because the thugs will get you."

Asked whom he would blame if he loses his job, he said, "the army."

November 18, 1991

Into Africa, Trading Firm
Taps Entrepreneurial Market
Bruce Bradford Builds on Global Goodwill

MARGARET K. WEBB

There are trade missions, and then there are people, like Bruce Bradford, for whom trade is a mission.

The son of a career diplomat, Bradford, 33, spent his childhood in Sierra Leone, the Belgian Congo (now Zaire) and Chad, where he gained an appreciation for what he calls the "heart" of Africa's people. Once he started a career of his own, he said, he wanted to work with them.

After almost 10 years as a trader for such companies as Associated Metals and Minerals Corp. of New York, which stationed him in Johannesburg, and WJS Trading Inc. of McLean, Bradford opened BTB Trading in McLean in January 1989.

His goal, he said, is to foster trade agreements with small businesses and entrepreneurs in Africa, selling them used or reconditioned industrial machinery to improve the quality and productivity of their businesses. In return, BTB looks for opportunities for them to export their products to the United States.

Pursuing contacts made by word of mouth, through his father or with African delegations to their Washington embassies, Bradford has completed deals in Cameroon, Ghana and Zambia, and has projects pending in Chad, Tanzania, Zimbabwe and Angola.

He usually buys first from his potential clients to establish a relationship and then extols the benefits of better, newer machinery. In some cases, he also will supply training on the equipment he sells.

Business in 1989 was "exceptionally good," Bradford said, with revenue of about $100,000. So far this year Bradford has completed five deals, has 13 more in the works and two dozen leads. He has a head start on credibility with Africans, he said, because of his father's reputation.

Except for part-time help from his wife and parents, Bradford works alone, getting a 6 percent or 7 percent commission on sales, which generally run from $10,000 to $100,000 and sometimes more. Forty percent of his business comes from equipment sales, and 60 percent from importing fabric and yarn. Bradford said he soon hopes to import wood products as well.

Bradford specializes in textile, woodworking, agricultural and food-processing equipment.

"In the textile area there are warehouses full of machinery," he said. "It's just so frustrating seeing machinery sitting in a warehouse in North Carolina and knowing how valuable it is overseas."

The largest markets in Africa, Bradford said, are for textile and agricultural equipment. He said many African businesses create printed and batik cotton garments, but, lacking equipment to produce their own cloth, are importing material from the Far East, which increases the final price of the product.

The result is twofold: African businesses cannot easily export their high-priced goods and Africans pay too much for even the simplest garments.

"People are getting charged $15 or $20 for a $4 to $5 shirt," Bradford said. "And in a country where it can really least be afforded."

He said the same problems plague the agricultural industry in Africa.

"There's more money in the ground in Africa than there is in any of the banks," Bradford said of the continent's resource riches. But the technology is lacking to take advantage of them, he said, and it is especially difficult for farmers to get loans from African banks because "they don't consider land an asset."

"Most of the deals I do the commercial trading {companies} would scoff at," Bradford said. "But the developments in Eastern Europe have got a lot of African ministers worried that America is not going to be interested in Africa anymore ... That's why it's so important that small people get involved."

"The potential for small- and medium-size industries {in Africa} is tremendous, but the means to get them to grow is really lacking," said Mark Chona, a native of Zambia who is working in Washington with the Overseas Development Council on a study of economic and political reconstruction in Africa.

"The future small-scale and medium-scale industries will come from that pool of people who are ready but don't have access to the type of information and training and equipment {they need}," Chona said.

"By increasing the capability of the general population—that is when growth will come," he said. "That is our hope."

Bradford doesn't mind that this could be a long time coming.

"Certainly there might be easier places to do business, but Africa comes from the heart," he said. "There's so much good that can be done there, that just doing a little bit, you feel a lot better about yourself."

June 11, 1990

Philips to Buy 25 Percent of 'Channel One' Firm:

Whittle Communications To Get $175 Million

PAUL FARHI

Christopher Whittle, the Tennessee entrepreneur who has generated praise and controversy for his innovative media ventures, has a new Dutch uncle.

Philips Electronics NV, the giant consumer electronics company based in the Netherlands, agreed yesterday to invest $175 million in Whittle Communications L.P. in exchange for 25 percent of the Knoxville, Tenn., firm.

The deal pumps fresh cash into a company that during the past five years has revolutionized the ways in which advertisers reach captive audiences with their messages.

Christopher Whittle, who once owned *Esquire* magazine, is best known for creating "Channel One," a daily 12-minute TV news program containing commercials that are beamed into 9,000 junior and senior high schools.

The company also started "Special Reports," a sponsored-TV service aimed at people waiting in doctors' offices, and has published a line of books, by such authors as David Halberstam and William Greider, that contain advertising.

Executives at Whittle and Philips said yesterday's agreement will give privately owned Whittle Communications the capital to expand its current programs and speed up the introduction of new ones.

Whittle last year announced, but hasn't built, a nationwide chain of as many as 200 private preschools that would be stocked with the latest high-tech gadgets.

Forstmann, Little & Co., a New York investment firm, came close to buying 33 percent of Whittle for $350 million in September.

But the deal fell apart a month later after the two sides could not agree on the company's growth prospects.

The size of Philips's investment indicates that the value of Whittle's company has roughly doubled in less than four years. Time Inc., now Time Warner Inc., paid $185 million for 50 percent of Whittle Communications in 1988.

Although neither company would discuss future projects, both stressed the potential for using the other's products and expertise to create "synergies."

With worldwide sales of $30.8 billion in 1990, Philips is a global concern that makes TVs, compact disc players, VCRs and other hardware products under the Magnavox, Sylvania, Philco and Norelco brands.

It also owns Polygram Records, one of the world's five largest record labels.

A Time Warner spokesman, Peter Costiglio, dismissed the prospect of a three-way venture among Time Warner, Philips and Whittle, saying his company had no plans to contribute any entertainment software to the concern.

Time Warner owns Warner Records, the world's largest record company, a direct rival of Philips's Polygram.

"All of his ideas have a possibility of being very hardware-intensive," said a source familiar with Whittle's plans. He's looking to create whole new alternative forms of media. He's trying to bring {sponsors'} messages to consumers outside the home. That implies a need for hardware."

For example, Whittle Vice Chairman Laura Eshbaugh suggested that Philips' Compact Disc Interactive system, or CD-I, could be used in Whittle's school projects. CD-I combines video, stereo sound and computer memory into a single box.

But a Philips executive, who asked to remain anonymous, tried to downplay the company's involvement in "Channel One," which has been the most controversial of Whittle's ventures.

School officials in several states, including California, have sought to ban "Channel One" from classrooms, saying that children should not be subjected to TV commercials during school hours. School systems must agree to show "Channel One" to students in exchange for receiving free TV equipment from Whittle.

The ties between Whittle and Philips were already tight before yesterday's announcement. Philips has supplied about 270,000 color TV sets, valued at about $200 million, to "Channel One" and "Special Reports" in the past three years, making Whittle one of Philips's largest American customers.

Coincidentally, Whittle Communications and Philips's U.S. consumer electronics subsidiary are both located in Knoxville.

The agreement gives Philips the option to buy up to 33 percent of Whittle Communications during the next two years for an amount determined by Whittle's financial performance.

A banking source familiar with Whittle said Philips ultimately could double its initial $175 million investment.

Time Warner will hold 37 percent of Whittle after yesterday's deal is completed. Associated Newspapers Holdings PLC, a British publishing company, will see its stake reduced from 33 percent to 24.6 percent, and Whittle's personal stake will shrink from 11 percent to 8.5 percent—a share worth nearly $60 million based on the price paid by Philips. The balance of the company is owned by 60 limited partners.

Table 1 • A Boost for Whittle

Company: Whittle Communications.

Revenue: $207 million (fiscal 1991)

Headquarters: Knoxville, Tenn.

Main Operations:

"Channel One": Brief news program with commercials, shown in 9,000 schools nationwide.

"Special Reports": Video program and magazine on health issues distributed in doctors' offices.

"Larger Agenda": Non-Fiction book series carrying advertising.

Whittle Owners:

Associated Newspapers Holdings (England)	24.6%
Chris Whittle (founder)	8.5%
60 other limited partners	4.9%
Philips Electronics	25%
Time Warner	37%

Source: Associated Press, company reports.

February 6, 1992

Hungary's Little Shops of Dreams:

A Few Energetic Entrepreneurs
Buying State-Owned Stores

PETER MAASS

Like a mother cooing over her ugly baby, Laszlo Gyorfi stood proudly the other day in front of a store that only its new owner could love.

The cement walls were chipped and unpainted, the neon "Food Shop" sign was falling apart and the faded products in the display windows seemed as old and battered as the two-lane highway a few paces away.

But none of this dented the dreams of Gyorfi, who less than an hour earlier bought this chunk of urban blight for about $100,000 at one of Hungary's first auctions of state-owned shops.

As six or seven workers unsure about their next paychecks watched, Gyorfi swept through his new domain like a spring storm and poured out some of the bright ideas on his drawing board: paint for the walls, soft light bulbs to replace the glaring fluorescent tubes, special promotions and discounts, 24-hour service seven days a week, quality foods and new shelves to display more products.

"It will be more visual," he said, sounding like the inspired commercial artist that he is.

Energetic people like Gyorfi, 47, bear the future hopes of Hungary and Eastern Europe. Reviving the region's moribund, post-communist economies depends on many factors, and few seem as important as forming a new class of entrepreneurs to help invigorate cities like Vac, which lies along the Danube River about 30 miles from Budapest.

One of the hopeful signs for the region's future is the fact that adventuresome capitalists like Gyorfi are emerging, most notably in Poland and Hungary. Newspapers here often recount startling tales of entrepreneurial spirit, such as the small company that is renting a now-vacant Soviet nuclear missile silo to grow mushrooms.

The well-intentioned Hungarian government would like to send an army of Laszlo Gyorfis marching onto the economic battlefield. It is trying to do that by selling off 10,000 small state-owned shops and restaurants at public auctions that began last month.

But the sell-off is turning out to be a bust. According to Erno Racz, a director of the State Property Agency (SPA), which is in charge of the sales, most auctions have failed to draw bidders. There was no other bidder for the shop that Gyorfi bought, and only one of the six other shops for sale at the auction attracted an offer.

The explanation tells a lot about why the rebirth of capitalism in Eastern Europe is taking longer than expected. Hopeful plans are running into a heavy burden from the Communist past and occasional mistakes by the new democratic governments.

Most of Hungary's 10,000 shops are located on land whose ownership is unclear, and, as a result, only the rental rights are being auctioned. Few entrepreneurs seem willing to shell out money just to get the privilege of paying rent without real guarantees against eviction.

The ownership squabbles are among national and city authorities, neighborhood committees, company directors, trade unions and workers. Because ownership equals money and power, nobody is bowing out and forgoing their claims so that the shops can be sold outright as soon as possible.

There are 2,000 shops being sold that can be purchased with a clear title. But interest in them is only lukewarm because the prices are too high. Parliament passed a law last year instructing the SPA to start the bidding at prices reflecting market values. SPA accountants, afraid of violating the law or being accused of selling state assets too cheaply, are erring on the high side.

Even if an entrepreneur is willing to buy a shop at the SPA's price, lining up bank loans is difficult. Squeezed by an overhang of bad loans from the Communist era and a government attempt to control 30 percent inflation through a tight monetary policy, the banks are not taking any chances. Entrepreneurs with solid credentials or substantial collateral can arrange loans, but few others can.

Gyorfi, for example, used his country cottage and French passenger car as collateral for a six-year loan with 22 percent interest. And even with collateral, the crucial factor that swayed the bank was his previous experience managing a state food shop.

Gyorfi expects to triple sales within a few months of the store's metamorphosis from a Communist clunker, and its location may make the difference: It is at a highway intersection with a stoplight, just a few hundred yards from a riverside leisure center.

Some of the shop's workers will be replaced, although Gyorfi evaded that issue on his visit to the store.

"What will happen to my colleagues?" timidly asked Janosne Szekeres, 50, the store manger who knows her own days are numbered.

Gyorfi looked past her as he artfully replied, "We'll talk about that later."

May 28, 1991

GATT, a Litmus Test for World Relations:

Trade Negotiations Crucial to Issues of Global Cooperation, Both Economic and Political

STUART AUERBACH

The end of the Cold War and the current Persian Gulf crisis have dramatically raised the stakes for global free-trade talks that were designed to push the world of international commerce into the 21st century.

The final six days of the talks start tomorrow in Brussels, and the results could do as much as the events in the Middle East to determine the character of international cooperation and competition in a world without an East-West divide, according to top-level public officials and experts in international politics and commerce.

"It is a highly significant test of the willingness of countries to accept international responsibility," said a senior U.S. Treasury Department official. "In effect, this is the first test of post-Cold War economic cooperation," said C. Michael Aho of the Council on Foreign Relations.

"The implications ... have grown well beyond trade. They go to the ability of the big industrial nations to cooperate in the mid-1990s," said Robert D. Hormats, vice chairman of Goldman Sachs International Corp. and former assistant secretary of state for economic affairs. "If they fail in trade, it will be difficult for them to cooperate in the Persian Gulf and on other political and strategic issues.

"The whole basis of the new world ... is that the Americans, the Japanese and the united Europeans would work together to create a better economic order and a new world political order."

The issues on the negotiating table are wrapped up in the arcane language of a post-World War II institution called the General Agreement on Tariffs and Trade, known as GATT. The negotiators' goal is to promote the buying and selling of everything from corn to printing presses to insurance across international boundaries.

When the negotiations began four years ago, the Berlin Wall still stood and the idea of a rapidly uniting European Community was still a dream. Then, the goal was to take a system that had increased world trade fiftyfold—in the process lifting the wealth of nations and individuals—and expand it into new areas that take a growing share of global commerce, such as advanced technology, international finance and overseas investment.

These areas, uncovered by GATT, amount to one-third of all trade, about $1 trillion. Without those changes, the ability of a free-trade compact to enlarge the global economy in the next century the way it did in the past is being called increasingly into question. "GATT may become an organization where its rules are honored more in the breach," said Alan Oxley, former Australian ambassador to GATT.

For all the emphasis on the future, the negotiations, called the Uruguay Round because they were launched in that South American nation, are foundering over an issue that evokes the past protection of farmers. Bitter differences between the United States and its Western European allies have developed over government price support for farmers, which is a bedrock question for European politicians. With the farm trade talks deadlocked, negotiations have ground to a halt in other key sectors.

Facing the possibility of failure or continued stalemate, U.S. Trade Representative Carla A. Hills now talks about possible lost benefits, including $4 trillion she says the world economy would gain over 10 years from increased trade flowing from an agreement. A failure of the talks, she said in an interview, would intensify existing trade frictions, encourage simmering protectionism and create "instability" among emerging democracies in Eastern Europe and South America that need free trade to get their economies moving.

Political Concerns

There is more at stake, however. A senior European official also acknowledged that the transatlantic trade differences are threatening to spill over into the political arena and could undermine continued cooperation in the Persian Gulf.

Hills underscored the point: "The very act of drawing into collaboration" in the gulf and on future foreign policy problems "is going to require us to have trade tranquility. It will be difficult to generate the international cooperation that we need to deal with tomorrow's problems if we are at each other's throats on economic and trade issues."

The ties between political cooperation and international trade rules have been heightened by a new view of national security that values economic strength as much as bombs and missiles. Furthermore, the growth of a nonmilitary Japan as an economic superpower and the end of the Cold War have created multipolar power centers in the world, replacing the superpower rivalries that dominated global politics for the past 40 years.

Moving in concert with these developments, the political map of Europe has been redrawn by the decline of communism and the speedy movement of Western Europe into an economic and political union dominated by a unified Germany. The Soviet Union's former East European allies are reaching out to Western political and economic ideals, presenting new challenges to established systems such as GATT.

GATT, along with the World Bank and the International Monetary Fund (IMF), are the multilateral agencies created under U.S. leadership after World War II to manage and expand the world economy.

Instead of working in GATT with the United States to forge a new world order, however, former U.S. trade representative Michael B. Smith observed, "The Europeans are being obstinate, the Japanese are not doing anything."

Hills said the Japanese could exhibit the kind of leadership role equal to their economic power by agreeing to end their outright ban on imports of rice. "They could lead by example" in the GATT talks, she said.

Rivalry's Role

Kendall Myers, a European specialist at Johns Hopkins University's School of Advanced International Studies, said neither Japan nor a Western Europe led by a united Germany is ready to assume the global leadership role that the United States held for the past 45 years.

"These three power centers {Japan, Western Europe and the United States} would like to be able to get together and tell the world what the new order will be," said Myers. "But there is so much rivalry between them that they cannot get together."

Facing the possibility of no agreement, or a lesser accord than envisioned, Bush administration officials led by Hills have backed away from the "Apocalypse Now" scenario for the future of world trade that they had been painting in past months.

But Hills still maintains that U.S. industry, farmers and Congress will not accept a package of GATT reforms that includes only minimal liberalization in agriculture, investment and trade in services as well as protection against the piracy of patented products.

If the 107 nations meeting in Brussels fail to come to a broad agreement, Hills said the United States "will try very hard to manage trade frictions and to negotiate trade liberalizations where we can."

"There will be another day when there may be more political will" among trading partners to make needed concessions, said Hills. "If I can't get it," she added ruefully, "my successor will."

Standing Firm

Other administration officials believe that the United States should stand firm on President Bush's prescription that no deal at Brussels would be better than accepting a bad deal. A senior administration official said this would demonstrate to Congress that the administration is looking out for U.S. commercial interests and demonstrate to Western Europe and Japan that the United States expects them to make the kind of concessions that go with their new political and economic strength.

"For 40 years, we've been paying all the bills," the official noted.

But Enriques Iglesias, head of the Inter-American Development Bank and the foreign minister of Uruguay when the trade talks were launched, said the losses from a failed round of trade talks will be most profound for developing countries and Eastern European nations that have just broken from communism.

"To put a brake on expansion of trade is to put a brake on the expansion of the world economy," he added. "Today, we need growth and expansion in the world more than before."

Canadian Ambassador Derek H. Burney questioned whether the big three in the talks—the United States, Germany and Japan—really need the Uruguay Round and suggested that they would be hurt least by the trade frictions that are likely to accompany its failure. Recalling Canada's national animal, Burney said: "The elephants don't need the rules the same way the beavers do."

In 1948, 23 nations reached the General Agreement on Tariffs and Trade; since then, more than 100 countries have accepted it. Two-thirds of world trade falls under GATT rules. The agreement is administered by a secretariat that is headquartered on the banks of Lake Geneva.

The Principles

GATT's guiding principles include trade without discrimination under most-favored-nation principles; using tariffs rather than import quotas to protect domestic industries; providing a stable, predictable basis for trade through negotiated tariffs at fixed minimum levels; and settling disputes through negotiations and, as a last resort, dispute settlement procedures.

The Uruguay Round

The Uruguay Round of GATT talks, named for the South American country where the round began four years ago, is the eighth in a postwar series of talks that have lowered tariffs and increased world trade.

Major Issues: Agriculture

Farm issues have been the linchpin of the talks. The United States and 14 other nations want cuts of 75 percent to 90 percent in government subsidies for exports and special payments to help farm production, and reduced barriers to foreign agricultural goods. But Western European nations are offering a 15 percent cut in production payments, and no reduction of export subsidies or trade barriers. The Bush administration has said it would not sign an agreement without sweeping agricultural trade changes.

Services

In talks to bring banking, telecommunications and other services under GATT rules, the United States rejected a deal to let Europe keep its telecommunications markets closed to foreign companies while the deregulated U.S. market stays open. Europe wants audio-visual services exempted from GATT to preserve limits on foreign programs on its radio and TV networks. Australia and Canada want entertainment industry exemptions to preserve their cultures. No one appears to want air transport and ocean shipping covered, and the U.S. maritime industry kept shipments between American ports out of the free trade agreement.

Intellectual Property

Piracy of patented products has moved from blue jeans to high technology with the growing economic importance of computers, costing U.S. firms $60 billion a year in lost sales. Third World nations many of which make little effort to stop product counterfeiting, are resisting GATT rules against trade in pirated products, arguing that they will impede their technological development and increase the cost of needed medical supplies to their poor. U.S. firms back domestic laws against piracy and some favor raising the threat of trade retaliation to pressure other countries to enforce laws against piracy.

Investment

Developed nations oppose rules seen as discouraging foreign investment, especially requirements that foreign companies buy components locally, produce only for export and keep foreign exchange earnings in the country. Third World nations oppose such changes, saying the rules don't hurt trade and are vital for their national development.

Textiles

Industrial nations' quotas on cloth and clothing imports, largely from developing countries, are to be phased out, although the extent and pace remain to be negotiated. This is the price industrialized nations are paying to the Third World for agreements on intellectual property and investment rules. The U.S. textile industry opposes the changes.

Subsidies

The United States backs tough rules against government subsidies to industries. Japan, South Korea, Hong Kong, Singapore and other Asian nations want to make it harder to impose penalty duties on subsidized goods, which they see as harassment based on their export success. The gulf is so wide that there may be no agreement on this issue.

Tariffs

The talks aim to cut tariffs by one-third. The United States opposes Europe's 15 percent tariff on semiconductors Japan, Canada and the United States have no such duties but the Europeans want to reduce it to only 9.2 percent.

December 2, 1990

U.S., German Officials Need to GATT Together

HOBART ROWEN

It seems fairly obvious that the U.S.-German economic and strategic relationship is critical not only to both countries, but to the rest of the world. America is still the leading global power—if creaking around the edges—while Germany once again is emerging as the powerhouse in Europe.

In the post-Cold War era, they need to cooperate to assure peace. But despite the friendship that has existed since the end of World War II, the lines of communication appear to be faulty.

What German Chancellor Helmut Kohl seems not to comprehend is just how important the current round of trade talks, known as the Uruguay Round, is to the United States, still the world's largest exporter of goods and services.

Fast-rising exports have prevented the U.S. economy from suffering a recession much worse than the one it has gone through in 1991-92. Further export penetration of global markets in the years ahead is the one decipherable economic policy that unites Republicans and Democrats.

Successful completion of this round of talks, designed to liberalize and extend world trading rules, under the aegis of the General Agreement on Tariffs and Trade (GATT) therefore is a "must" on the Bush administration's agenda.

I suspect that Kohl, like most Europeans, does not fully understand the pressures under which President Bush is operating in the current political campaign. He has been accused, justly, of bending too easily to the protectionist and insular challenges of presidential candidate Patrick Buchanan.

Bush cannot afford to accept minor concessions purporting to lower farm subsidies, as floated last week by the French. Kohl, of course, would be happy with any deal taking the GATT issue off the agenda of the seven-nation economic summit, which he will host in July. But for Bush to settle for anything less than a substantial elimination of excessively high European protection of its agriculture would be taken as yet another sign of political weakness. This would then play to the Democrats' charge that Bush says one thing and does another. On the other hand, "the American-built system" based on the GATT and other international monitoring agencies may not survive in the post-Cold War era, especially if there is a serious recession, according to W.R. Smyser, a visiting professor at Georgetown University. In a new book, "The Economy of United Germany," Smyser says: "The

American government is no longer in a position to decide and to structure a new system unilaterally, if indeed, it ever was. The German view will be more important than ever."

Axel Krause, author of "Inside the New Europe," makes the point that Europeans are disturbed by Bush's recent reference to an "iron curtain of protection" descending on Europe, and what they see as a drift toward "managed" American trade with Japan. While Americans talk of fears of "Fortress Europe," Krause says, the Europeans raise the specter of "Fortress America."

All this makes the upcoming Camp David meeting next weekend between Bush and Kohl highly significant. It will cover a wide range of issues, including the American role in post-Cold War Europe and the responsibility of Western powers to finance reforms in the former Soviet states.

Kohl no doubt will point out that Germany is encountering economic problems of its own—at least according to German standards. On Friday, officials announced that 1991 fourth-quarter GNP was down 0.5 percent from the third quarter. But for the year as a whole, GNP growth was up 3.1 percent. From an American point of view, the German economy is still in sound shape. And German officials, to the concern of their neighbors in Europe, still pursue a high-interest-rate policy.

Regardless of what the sanitized post-Camp David briefings by Bush and Kohl suggest, the tendentious GATT issue will dominate the private conversations of the two leaders. Kohl made a clear commitment—at the Houston economic summit in 1990—to get France's President Francois Mitterrand to modify his country's intransigent stand against reducing agricultural subsidies. But Kohl hasn't delivered on that promise.

The real bitterness among American officials centers on Mitterrand. Nonetheless, they view Kohl as the key player, the only one in Europe who can save the GATT round. "The president {Bush} has a lot riding on free trade," a senior administration official said. "{We don't} want a failure of the GATT round on top of the problems that we've been having with Japan and Canada. And our European friends need to take this seriously."

Administration officials believe Europe is so caught up with European Community affairs that if the issue comes down to choosing between the GATT talks and cementing the feeling of "union" that came out of the recent European summit in Holland, Europe will let GATT go down the drain, triggering costly global trade wars.

"Kohl would rather keep Mitterrand's friendship at this point," one well-informed Washington insider told me. "The Germans are always afraid of being too bold, afraid of being criticized for being dominant. Kohl wants to make sure that he has Mitterrand on his side instead of against him."

Historically, French diplomats have brilliantly played "the German card," manipulating German officials to be responsive to a French agenda. This frustrates those German business executives who understand quite well that German manufacturers will be among the principal losers if the GATT talks fail.

The pro-GATT, anti-Mitterrand argument has been privately laid out to Kohl by—among others—his coalition partners in the Free Democratic Party. But as a politician, Kohl weighs that argument against the insistence of some others that the current decade will be "the decade of Europe," and success in Europe will be a more important source of economic growth for Germany than GATT.

According to New York investment banker Jeffrey E. Garten of the Blackstone Group, even the German business community does not present a solid front for a strong global trading system.

Increasingly, German trade is concentrated within Europe, he points out: "Individual German businesses don't have time for transatlantic or Far East affairs in a way that matches their words. Their minds are preoccupied with the massive changes taking place in Europe, and making sure that they are placing themselves in a strong competitive position against the Japanese and American firms who are entering the community."

As Americans read the signals coming from Germany, Kohl has already made his decision by choosing the future of France, as defined by Mitterrand, over the future of the global system, as defined by other trading partners who want to restore rationality to agricultural subsidies. In fact, says Robert Hormats, vice president at Goldman Sachs & Co., GATT may rank only fourth among current German priorities, behind the rebuilding of a united Germany; continued efforts to build a strong and united Europe; and a broadening of Germany's geopolitical role in the East.

Yet, Kohl is said to be seeking a way of getting the GATT issue put behind him, so that it won't dominate the Munich economic summit. But the only way in which Kohl can get the issue resolved is to put pressure on Mitterrand to make a deal with the Americans, the Cairns Group (of agricultural nations) and the principal Third World countries.

That's what Kohl must do to continue to get U.S. support for his country's priorities, including Germany's lead role in Eastern Europe and among the former Soviet states. Otherwise, he risks a serious break with the United States.

May 15, 1992

Gatt Forum Says U.S. Increasingly Uses Trade Laws to Limit Imports

STUART AUERBACH

The United States came under sharp criticism in a leading international trade forum for being overly zealous in using its unfair-trade laws to block some imports.

In a general expression of worry about a U.S. slide toward protectionism, the General Agreement on Tariffs and Trade cited Washington for a sharp increase in "antidumping" actions and for high tariffs on a selected group of products.

The Geneva-based GATT also suggested that one of the President's major economic initiatives, a North American free trade agreement, could hurt other countries while helping the United States, Canada and Mexico.

But the 103-nation GATT, in its second review of U.S. trade practices in two years, gave the U.S. administration high marks for its strong support of the ongoing Uruguay Round of global free trade negotiations and for resisting pressures from industries such as textiles and footwear for further restrictions on imports during the recession.

The study noted that footwear and textiles, along with sugar, glass and medical and pharmaceutical products, were among a small group of products already subject to high U.S. tariffs.

Both the North American free trade pact proposal and the United States' use of its laws against allegedly unfair trade practices have touched raw nerves among some of America's major trading partners. Asian nations such as South Korea, Singapore and Thailand, which became prosperous through exports to the United States, fear that any preferential treatment given Mexico under a free trade pact will hurt them.

Canadian ambassador to GATT Gerry Shannon, whose country is fighting U.S. charges that it subsidizes cut-rate lumber sales to the United States, said these trade laws have become "instruments of choice for U.S. industries seeking protection," the Associated Press reported. Shannon said the laws were administered "arbitrarily and capriciously" by U.S. agencies.

While the GATT report didn't go that far, it noted that the United States is one of the most frequent users of these laws and that the Commerce Department agrees with most industry complaints.

Under a series of trade laws, the U.S. government can restrict imports in retaliation for government subsidies by other countries, for the "dumping" of goods at artificially low prices or for other countries' barriers against U.S. exports.

Shannon also criticized Washington's use of "managed" trade agreements, in which countries agree under pressure to limit exports. "Our concerns over managed trade are not simply rhetorical. The effects are real and damaging," the news agency Reuter quoted him as saying. An example of this would be "voluntary" restraints by a number of countries on their sales of steel in the United States.

According to Reuter, Shannon was joined in his sweeping attack on U.S. trade policies by Roderick Abbott, a European Community representative to GATT.

Despite its critical comments, the GATT review concluded that "the U.S. market was generally open."

While GATT has reviewed trading practices of 16 other nations since 1989, including Japan and Canada, the world trade body clearly held the United States to high standards as "the world's largest single trading entity."

"The United States has a major responsibility for maintaining and reinforcing the faith of the international business community in the open, liberal multilateral trading system," the report said.

The report was issued at a time when GATT is facing the greatest crisis in its 45-year history, with five years of negotiations to strengthen the rules of free trade near collapse over the demands of the United States and other countries for an end to European agricultural subsidies.

President Bush personally tried to break the stalemate Tuesday with a letter to European Community President Jacques Delores, but a senior U.S. trade official said yesterday that it was unclear whether the White House initiative had been successful.

Rufus Yerxa, the U.S. ambassador to GATT, accepted the report as "a good exercise," but called it "an understatement . . . of the contribution of the United States to the growth of world trade."

He cited figures showing the United States as the largest importer in the industrialized world of cars, steel, textiles and consumer electronics.

Yerxa also called "a bit extreme" GATT's concerns that a North American free trade agreement would hurt other nations by diverting sales to the United States to Mexico and Canada. He said regional arrangements in Europe, Latin America, North America and Asia "make political and economic sense" and, if properly structured, can foster free trade.

March 13, 1992

Is the Group of Seven an Irrelevance Today?

HOBART ROWEN

In the space of 24 hours last week, the German Bundesbank raised interest rates and the Federal Reserve Board moved in the opposite direction.

The reasons for these contradictory economic policies were clear.

Facing recession, the Bush administration and the Federal Reserve are pursuing lower interest rates to help restore growth. The Germans, enjoying a boom and facing rising budgets to pay unification costs, are acting to choke off a perceived inflationary threat.

At a meeting three weeks ago in New York, just ahead of those moves, the Group of Seven leading industrial nations said that currency rates were about at the right levels, and it was prepared to respond in appropriate fashion to maintain stability.

But financial markets, as they watched the U.S. dollar slide in response to the interest rate changes despite intervention, wondered whether the G-7 could deliver on its promise to help maintain stability, or whether the divergent underlying trends spelled a weakening of the economic coordination process.

For the latter half of the 1980s, world financial markets had been accustomed to a strong effort by the G-7 (and its predecessor, the G-5) to achieve stable relationships among their currencies through coordinated intervention, when necessary.

"But the G-7 no longer has enough muscle in the market to set any sort of exchange rate bands or zones," according to Robert Hormats, vice president of the investment firm Goldman Sachs & Co. and a former State Department official. "Therefore, the G-7's market credibility is much less than it was two or three years ago." Some go even further, dismissing the G-7 as irrelevant.

German central bank President Karl Otto Poehl and U.S Treasury Undersecretary David C. Mulford, two of the key G-7 policy makers, disagree. In separate interviews, each contended that given the dramatic events of the last several months—involving war, recession, and gyrations in oil prices—exchange rates have remained remarkably stable.

In a conversation from Bundesbank headquarters in Frankfurt, Poehl said that the exchange markets "reacted in a very calm way" to the interest rate changes, "although we intervened a lot" to accomplish that. Mulford added: "When you look back at this period {some months hence}, there is a strong probability that you will see that despite all of the elements of uncertainty and tension, they were managed impressively by the G-7."

Poehl stressed that the present divergence in underlying economic conditions among the major G-7 members "makes coordination and cooperation more urgent than ever before. The question is, what do you coordinate?

"Some people think you have to have stability of exchange rates at all costs. That is not our concept of coordination, nor is it the concept of others. We have very different economic situations in the United States and Germany. So coordination doesn't mean and cannot mean that we all have to do the same things at the same time. It is more important that we pursue prudent policies that lead, finally, to a stable system," Poehl said. "What happened last week is not a contradiction of the cooperative process. It would be very bad if coordination prevented any country from doing what is necessary for stability at home. First of all, we have to keep our own house in order—all of us." Poehl made clear that Germany felt compelled to boost interest rates despite incurring the wrath of its European partners—which, incidentally, he thinks is misplaced because "they stand to benefit from the German expansion."

Others are less sure than Mulford and Poehl that coordination is working. There are increasing global economic tensions, outside the G-7 process, relating to trade and contributions to pay for the gulf war. Critics see the possibility that strains will continue and deepen if the interest rate spread widens between the United States and Germany.

Treasury Secretary Nicholas F. Brady, who is pressing the Fed to lower interest rates still more to battle recession, took pains to emphasize in congressional testimony last week that "we don't have a policy of a weak dollar." The Treasury argument is that lower interest rates don't automatically result in a cheaper dollar.

C. Fred Bergsten, director of the Institute for International Economics, supports the Mulford view that the G-7 can remain effective, even if the dollar—as Bergsten expects—goes down. Nonetheless, the perception among many sophisticated traders and analysts is that the best the G-7 can do for now is to slow the pace of the depreciation.

As Poehl's remarks implied, techniques of coordination may have to be more subtle, and perhaps less ambitious, at a juncture when key countries pursue what each believes to be the requirements of its own national policy.

Count Otto Lambsdorff, head of the Free Democratic Party and a former German economics minister, said central bankers today "pay more attention to domestic strategy and less to creating a regime of exchange rates that must be defended against the market."

The principal concern expressed by financial markets, as they contemplate the lessened influence of the G-7, is the prospect of a global recession, touched off by high European interest rates, beyond the power of any international force to moderate it. Many Europeans feel that Germany should have raised taxes to squash an inflationary potential before boosting interest rates. But Chancellor Helmut Kohl didn't mention a tax boost until he could blame it on the $5.5 billion extra contribution Germany is making toward the costs of the gulf war.

The bottom line is that the G-7 may have to take a back seat for a time. Mulford suggests that the G-7 process, given Brady's preferred ways of operating, "may be less visible, but that doesn't mean the process has atrophied." Nonetheless, today's perception of the G-7—among financial market players it tries to influence—is one of weaker leadership.

The coordination process worked best when it was managed by former Treasury Secretary James A. Baker III, a visible and influential wheeler-dealer, with the help of other strong finance ministers. Markets acknowledge that because of diverging economic trends, today's G-7 managers have a tougher assignment than they did under Baker. But collectively, they look less fearsome.

February 10, 1991

U.S. Ambassadors Making Business Their New Business:

Effort Planned to Boost American Trade in Asia

WILLIAM BRANIGIN

Years ago, American cars were a fairly common sight in Southeast Asia. Now, except for the wheezing relics that still ply the roads of such relative backwaters as the capital of Myanmar and southern Vietnam, they are hard to find. And even in those places, they are rapidly being replaced by shiny new Nissans and Toyotas.

The abandonment by American automakers of potentially lucrative markets in Southeast Asia reflects a mindset that U.S. government officials and businessmen say is shared by many American companies: a preoccupation with domestic sales at the expense of exports. At the same time, they say, efforts to remedy the situation by prying open the Japanese market may amount to barking up the wrong tree.

"The growth market in Asia for automobiles is Southeast Asia, not Japan," said Michael Dunne, an American automotive consultant at the Bangkok-based Southeast Asia Management and Investment Co. "Between 1988 and 1990, Thailand's auto market grew by 40 percent per year." Compared to growth in the U.S. car market in the range of 1 percent to 2 percent during that period, he said, "that's phenomenal."

Indeed, said Robert D. Orr, the U.S. ambassador to Singapore, "we spend so much time trying to open up the Japanese market that we almost totally overlook the fact that the Japanese are everywhere selling their products. They consider the world as their marketplace."

In an effort to awaken American companies to trade opportunities around the region, Orr and four other U.S. ambassadors are making an unprecedented tour of the United States this month. The group, including the envoys to Indonesia, Malaysia, Thailand and the Philippines, is to visit Portland, Chicago, Detroit, Atlanta, Houston and Washington during the 11-day trip starting Saturday.

"We hope it will have a consciousness-raising effect," said a U.S. official in the Philippines. "The ambassadors will be the barkers to get people into the tent."

At the core of the trip is a perception that the United States needs to increase its competitiveness in the world marketplace.

"It's so difficult to talk American business people into exporting," said Orr, a former governor of Indiana. "They're so addicted to our great big beautiful market."

Although U.S. exports have been rising in recent years, he said, they accounted for only 7.2 percent of GNP in 1990, compared to an average of 19 percent among major competing nations.

"If we were to double our exports, there wouldn't be a recession right now," Orr said.

Together, the countries that make up the Association of Southeast Asian Nations (ASEAN)—Indonesia, Malaysia, Thailand, the Philippines, Singapore and Brunei—represent a market of 320 million people with a growth rate that has averaged 7.25 percent over the last two years. And the market is relatively open.

"Market access is just not the problem that it is in Northeast Asia," said one U.S. commercial officer in the region. Whereas non-tariff barriers and other protectionist mechanisms often discourage U.S. companies from trying to penetrate markets in Japan and South Korea, he said, "it's not that difficult to do business here."

Still, he added, developing trade relationships with Southeast Asia requires an investment of time and effort that some American firms seem to ignore.

"We still get a lot of U.S. companies that think they can do it all by mail," the official said. "The good news is that the market is open. The bad news is that it's not an automatic sale. If you want a long-term relationship, you have to build it."

Generally, U.S. government and corporate officials say, it is not the American industrial giants such as IBM and Exxon that need coaxing to venture into the Far East, but the smaller "middle class" of corporate America.

According to Jack Hanlon, co-chairman of the Investment Promotion Committee of the American Chamber of Commerce in Thailand, 80 percent of U.S. foreign investment is done by no more than 100 major firms. "The rest have no inkling or interest in foreign investment in the exotic tropics," he said. "I think it's just xenophobia on the part of the U.S. businesses. It will take a tough, uphill fight to get small businesses to take advantage of their opportunities here."

A prime example of lost opportunity is what many U.S. businessmen regard as Detroit's neglect of its export markets. With economic prospects looking fairly bleak after the communist takeovers of South Vietnam, Cambodia and Laos in 1975, General Motors and Ford virtually pulled out of Southeast Asia, leaving the field open for the Japanese.

"Years and years ago, you used to see American cars all over the place," a U.S. business executive in Manila said. "Where did they all go? The American automakers concentrated on the U.S. market and they neglected the rest of the world. It's their own fault."

Certainly, the U.S. auto market dwarfs those of Southeast Asia. The United States produces 6.5 million new units a year, compared to about 300,000 in Thailand and Indonesia, 200,000 in Malaysia and 50,000 in the Philippines. However, Dunne said, "if you look at the whole region, it's a very attractive place for investment." China's market is about 700,000 new cars a year and Taiwan's is another 500,000, he noted. "Add all this up, along with the vast potential for growth, and there's every reason for American automobile manufacturers to be more aggressive out here," Dunne said.

Today, Japanese companies control about 90 percent of the market for commercial vehicles and 85 percent for passenger cars throughout Southeast Asia, Dunne said. U.S. companies have less than 1 percent of the market share, with European manufacturers making up the rest.

"American automakers always have an excuse for not competing," Dunne said. "Meanwhile, the Japanese just eat it up. Local partners are not thrilled about being dependent on the Japanese. They'd like to work more with Americans."

Part of the problem is that, like the Japanese, most Southeast Asians drive on the left side of the road. The exception in ASEAN is the Philippines, but even in that former U.S. colony the automobile market has long since succumbed to the Japanese onslaught.

Dominating the protected Philippine market are car and truck assembly plants controlled by Nissan, Toyota and Mitsubishi. The latest entry is a South Korean firm, Kia, which has begun assembling a model called the Kia Pride.

In Malaysia, a Mazda model called the Telstar is assembled by Ford, which owns 25 percent of Mazda. But the bulk of the market is held by a Malaysian car, the Proton Saga, the only indigenous auto in the region. Although it uses a Mitsubishi Lancer chassis, the body is Malaysia's own design and about 60 percent of the content is locally made.

Ford's strongest presence in the area is on Taiwan, where the company eventually hopes to make cars for export to mainland China.

Other U.S. automakers also are starting to take a second look at the region. Chrysler opened an office in Thailand in 1990 and hopes to launch its Jeep in the country in 1993.

In an effort to boost its meager market share, General Motors has set up offices in Hong Kong and Thailand, a joint venture in Shenyang, China, and wholly owned subsidiaries in Taiwan and Indonesia.

According to American officials, some of the best opportunities for U.S. business in Southeast Asia lie in such sectors as computers and peripherals, food processing and packaging machinery, aircraft and avionics, telecommunications gear, health care and pollution-control technology, management services, and oil and gas equipment.

Relatively low labor costs and a growing pool of technicians and middle managers make the region attractive for foreign investment. However, new investments by U.S. firms in recent years have been lagging behind those of Japan, Hong Kong and Taiwan.

The major obstacle to increased American trade and investment in Southeast Asia, U.S. officials say, is intellectual property rights. The worst offender in the region is Thailand, where the counterfeiting of everything including designer watches, videotapes and computer software is a growth industry. But problems exist elsewhere as well. In the Philippines, for example, it is estimated that only 5 percent of the software sold in the country is legal.

For many companies, the new frontier in the area is Vietnam. Government efforts to attract foreign investment, a cheap and relatively well-educated labor force and the prospect of new offshore oil discoveries have fueled intense interest by Asian and European businessmen. American firms have been lobbying Washington to lift its economic embargo on the country so that they can compete, especially in the oil sector.

Within ASEAN, the United States has been running trade deficits with every country except tiny, oil-rich Brunei. But the total deficit with ASEAN of nearly $7.4 billion for the first 11 months of 1991 is small compared with the $66 billion deficit in U.S. trade over the same period with the rest of East Asia and the Pacific. The figure includes negative balances of S9 billion with Taiwan, $11.6 billion with China and nearly $39 billion with Japan.

In its efforts to promote exports, the U.S. government maintains foreign trade offices that offer various services to American firms at nominal cost. But the facilities are relatively modest compared to those of some foreign competitors.

"The South Koreans have as many trade offices overseas as we do," a U.S. commercial officer said. "Worldwide, we are generally outgunned by our trading partners."

Thailand

Economy and trade: The kingdom's economic boom—9 percent real GNP growth in 1990, 7.9 percent last year and up to 8.5 percent projected for this year—has put a strain on infrastructure that has somewhat slackened the pace of foreign investments. In the first 11 months of 1991, Thailand ran a trade surplus with the United States, importing nearly $3.4 billion worth of U.S. goods and exporting $5.6 billion.

Investment climate: Still, the projects keep rolling in. In 1988 and 1989, Japanese investment reached nearly $10 billion a year. New U.S. projects in 1991 were valued at $1.1 billion.

Malaysia

Economy and trade: Gross domestic product grew by 10 percent in 1990, 8.6 percent in 1991 and is forecast at 8.5 percent this year. In the first 11 months of 1991, the country ran a trade surplus with the United States of $1.9 billion.

Investment climate: In recent years, the top investors have been Taiwan, Japan and Singapore.

Products: The country is the world's largest exporter of semiconductors—and one of the world's top exporters of room air conditioners and videocassette recorders.

Philippines

Economy and trade: After zero growth in 1991, the economy is projected to expand by 3 percent this year. Trade with the United States showed a surplus in the Philippines' favor of $1.1 billion.

Investment climate: A liberalized foreign investment law took effect late last year, but kidnappings of Americans tend to discourage new U.S. investors. The bulk of U.S. investment came from companies already established in the Philippines.

Labor costs: While still cheap by U.S. standards, labor in the Philippines has become costlier than in some competing countries, with basic blue-collar wages in Manila now starting at $5.12 a day.

Singapore

Economy and trade: America's leading trading partner in Southeast Asia, the city-state bought $8.1 billion worth of U.S. goods in the first 11 months of 1991 and exported $9 billion worth to the United States. Economic growth reached 8.3 percent in 1990, but dipped to 6.5 percent last year and is forecast at 6 percent this year.

Investment climate: With labor in increasingly short supply in the island state of 2.8 million people, Singapore has been moving into high-tech investments and a "triangle of growth" concept with Malaysia and Indonesia.

Indonesia

Economy and trade: Economic growth last year reached 7 percent and is projected at 5.5 percent this year. U.S. exports to Indonesia have risen from less than $1 billion in 1985 to $1.9 billion in 1990.

Investment climate: Indonesia is the giant of ASEAN and has been attracting massive investments, an estimated $70 billion from 1989 to 1991. U.S. private investments have grown from less than $1 billion to about $2 billion.

(Special correspondent Mary Ray Magistad contributed to this article.)

March 20, 1992

The Era of Globalization 3

Planet of the M&Ms

Joel Glenn Brenner

"THE EASIEST WAY TO GROW"

"How many hours did you spend on those charts?" John Mars demanded.

The normally reticent CEO was touring Mars Inc.'s French pet food factory, where he'd encountered a new manager who had hoped to win praise for an elaborate presentation on the unit's marketing strategy. Stunned by his boss's outrage, according to someone who was present, the manager replied, "Two, maybe three."

John's face beamed beet red. "We do not waste our time on charts," he roared, ripping up the manager's carefully drawn graphics before a room full of Mars executives. "If you'd spent half as much time thinking about strategy as you have on these charts, we just might get somewhere."

Scenes like this one occurred in factory after factory around the world as John and Forrest Jr. struggled to expand the operation without altering their father's prescription for success. But unlike him, the sons fled from innovation. For years, they hesitated to trust their own ideas.

This caution was best illustrated by the company's reluctance to introduce new products. Launching a new consumer product in America is enormously expensive, but the payoff is even more enormous if you succeed: Favored products can become virtually invulnerable. The new CEOs of Mars, however, didn't want to gamble on innovations.

John Mars makes no bones about this. After all, he points out, most new concepts fail. He sums up the brothers' basic strategy this way: "The easiest way to avoid a lot of these failures is not to launch new products. The easiest way out is to grow through global expansion." George Greener, longtime head of British operations, says that the 1970s health scare over sugar consumption had a lot to do with the brothers' attitude. "The entire United States was saying sugar promotes tooth decay," he says. "It's no wonder they were afraid to invest hundreds of millions of dollars" in product innovation. (Today's health-conscious consumers are more concerned about fat content than sugar content—a boon to the confectionary industry.)

From his base in England, Forrest Sr. had started a push to the Continent, opening pet food plants in France and Germany, but it was his sons who carried out his lifelong dream. They took Mars global long before it was fashionable. There was no grand design to the expansion; Mars entered new markets as opportunities arose, sending in one or two associates to scout out product potential and organize distribution. Over time, as sales expanded, the brothers boosted their investment, until the new unit became self-sufficient. Today, their efforts can be seen, and tasted, in 70 business units from Helsinki to Hong Kong.

The lack of bureaucracy makes some things at Mars—like hiring new associates—very easy. For example, when David Badger, head of Eastern European expansion, was in Prague scouting out business opportunities in the summer of 1991, he arranged for a tour. Within a day, he had hired his tour guide to work as a Mars associate, helping to establish the business in Czechoslovakia. Milada Novakova, a 25-year-old university graduate with a degree in engineering and a good command of English, has since become the cornerstone of Mars's operation in that country.

Novakova's case is not unusual. Mars units are overseen by managers of many backgrounds and nationalities; on average, they speak at least three languages, and most speak as many as five or six. There are Japanese running Japanese offices and Frenchmen running French offices. But there are also Britons running U.S. offices and Germans running Spanish offices.

Individual units rarely advertise their American origins, preferring instead to let each business unit blend into the local environment. "We're one of the few truly international companies managed by international people," says Phil Forster, who oversees products worldwide. Forster speaks four languages himself and has lived in at least as many countries. At one point, he brags, foreign-born Mars executives outnumbered Americans 2 to 1, although the ratio has evened out some in recent years. (In contrast, most of Nestle's managers are from Switzerland, where the company is based.)

Unlike Coca-Cola or General Foods, Mars Inc. has never established an international board of directors to preside over its global operations. Instead, each individual business unit is connected to McLean mainly through its products and principles and through the shared experience of top managers transferred from country to country. The brothers rely on local talent to get products into the marketplace. And although they traveled the globe, carrying the culture from one country to the next and broadly overseeing local decisions, for years that was the extent of any corporate involvement. While keeping its operating units independent, however, Mars's strategy has been to make its key products as multinational as possible. As overseer of all Mars brands—which number more than 100 worldwide—Forster often asks managers to defend why their products shouldn't become global. It's the opposite of the approach taken by many American executives, who ask managers to demonstrate why a brand deserves to be marketed abroad.

The corporate philosophy behind the Mars approach is known to associates as "the transfer of best practice," meaning simply that what works in one country will work in another, as Forrest Sr. proved so long ago when he took the Milky Way overseas. Following in his footsteps, John and Forrest Jr. preach that if Americans eat Uncle Ben's rice, so too will Pakistanis. And if an advertisement is a success in Britain, it will also be effective in Brazil.

From pet food to candy to rice, all of Mars's best-selling brands are sold around the world. But the company manufactures dozens of local products too. In Australia, for example, Mars makes millions on sauces and spices. In Germany, the company recently started selling freshly made pizzas in grocery stores, an enterprise Mars hopes will become as popular in Germany as Domino's is in the United States.

The "best practice" approach is in sharp contrast to that of Mars's top international competitor, Nestle SA, which routinely enters new markets by acquiring local food companies or by signing joint-manufacturing agreements, often outspending Mars on the front end by hundreds of millions of dollars. Before entering a new country, the Swiss giant will map out its marketing plan and schedule mass production, always bringing in its own Swiss or German managers to oversee the market. The strategy has made Nestle the world's biggest food manufacturer, with 1991 worldwide sales of $33.6 billion.

But Mars associates believe strongly in their entrepreneurial style. And in any case, as former associates point out, the Mars culture left its owners little choice. An acquisition of any size would have required Mars to assimilate hundreds of new employees into its no-frills, hard-working environment. It was much easier, these associates say, to recruit locals who were open to the Five Principles than to teach those principles in the aftermath of a takeover. In addition, the brothers were reluctant to spend the vast sums necessary to buy a business, fearing they would stretch the company too thin or force it into debt.

"Once we become like P&G, Nestle or General Foods, we're dead," says Forster. "We don't buy and sell, we build."

Shootout at the Chocolate Factory

The strategy seemed perfectly suited to Mars, and the brothers stuck to it with admirable tenacity. But like any business strategy, however successful, it came with a downside. And in July of 1988, Hershey showed Mars just what that downside was.

By that summer, the company was well on its way to becoming the empire Forrest Sr. had always envisioned. Mars products were being eaten in more than 30 countries, and annual sales had topped $9.5 billion, still well behind Nestle's at $25 billion, but four times the sales of its closest American competitor, Hershey. The founder himself, meanwhile, had "retired" to Las Vegas in 1974, where, at the age of 70, he created a new firm, Ethel M Chocolates, to make expensive, liquor-filled candies. Ethel M employed just 45 people, but the old man ran it on the same principles he'd used to build Mars. He watched over his workers from an apartment above the factory, constantly reminding them of their responsibility to quality and efficiency. Then, on July 22, Hershey shocked the confectionery industry by acquiring the U.S. candy division of British giant Cadbury Schweppes. Bolstered by such brands as York Peppermint Patties, Mounds and Almond Joy, Hershey's share of the U.S. candy market surged to 21 percent, eclipsing the 18.5 percent held by Mars. For the first time since Forrest Sr. had gained control of his father's Chicago company, Mars had lost its title as America's candy king.

Mars executives say now that Hershey's move came as no surprise tothem. The prior year, they say, the brothers had passed up the same opportunity, leaving the door wide open for their American rival. Nevertheless, the merger struck a nerve.

Focused as it was on global expansion, Mars had made only one significant acquisition: DoveBar International Inc., a family-owned Chicago company that had taken the country by storm with its hand-dipped ice cream bars. Mars had introduced only a handful of new candy products in the United States over the years. The company's last successful launch was Kudos, a chocolate-and-granola bar that hit the market in 1987. Before that, there had been Twix, Skittles and Starburst, all launched years earlier and, so far, achieving only mild success.

But if Mars was to overtake Hershey, John and Forrest Jr. decided, they would have to make fundamental changes in the business. For 15 years, the brothers had struggled to measure up to their father's expectations while adhering faithfully to his management gospel. Now they'd have to rethink the way he did things.

Two months after Hershey's Cadbury coup, John and Forrest Jr. made a small acquisition of their own: They bought Forrest Sr.'s company, Ethel M. Former Mars associates say that John and Forrest Jr. were looking for an opening into the upscale candy market, the one place Hershey wasn't. But there was more to it than that. By taking control of their father's company, they seemed finally to erase his omnipotent shadow.

And they put more trust in a man named Alfred Poe.

The Empire Strikes Back

Al Poe and Mars Inc. clashed right from the start.

Hired in the early 1980s for a top spot on the Kal Kan marketing team, the 32-year-old Poe was one of the company's youngest recruits. But it was more than just his youth that set him apart.

At 6 feet 4 inches, Poe towered over most of the other executives. Aggressive and boastful, he loved to recount the story of his rise from Brooklyn's low-income housing projects to Harvard, where he earned his MBA. One of the company's few black managers, he laced his speech with street talk that contrasted sharply with the Mars brothers' genteel manner. And to top it all off, there were his flamboyant trappings: a stylish wardrobe and a sable brown Porsche 944.

Yet it was precisely because he was different that, in November 1988, Poe was tapped to help Mars reclaim its candy crown. He became the head of marketing at M&M/Mars. Two years earlier, at Kal Kan, Poe had made a couple of remarkable recommendations. Because the U.S. pet food division was struggling, Poe and others suggested that the recipes be changed and that the higher quality European formula be used to make the company's dog and cat food for the American market. To coincide with the changes, Poe suggested that Kal Kan adopt the brand names—Pedigree and Whiskas—that had been so successful abroad. He believed that by folding all the dog food products under one umbrella brand and all the cat food products under another, the company would need just two marketing campaigns to sell the whole range of chow, and the increased name recognition would benefit all products.

Few in the company thought the brothers would go for these changes. Forrest Sr. would have never considered such an outlandish idea. Everyone knew that a brand was sacrosanct; it represented just one kind of product.

But what if Poe and his allies were right? Kal Kan controlled just 7 percent of the U.S. pet food market, and it was losing ground fast. The advantages of such cost savings would be tremendous in the long run, so the brothers took the chance. They renamed their dog food line Pedigree and their cat food line Whiskas.

Critics inside and outside the company blasted the change as too risky and expensive. But consumers weren't buying criticism, they were buying pet chow. And the deluge of advertising caught their attention, which was exactly what Poe was hoping for. The results were phenomenal. By 1989, Kal Kan's market share had nearly doubled. And so it dawned on the brothers Mars: If many different varieties of dog food could all be marketed under the same name, the possibilities for expanding the company's other key brands became endless.

In 1989, spurred on by Poe's success, executives of M&M/Mars launched the biggest blitz of bonbons since the Great Depression. Snickers branched out into Peanut Butter Snickers. Kudos suddenly became Butter Almond Kudos and Cookies and Creme Kudos. Skittles, Starburst, Combos and Twix all burst out in new flavors. Even M&M's got a face lift, with three new varieties—peanut butter, almond and mint.

Other sweets also made debuts. P.B. Max, a peanut butter and cookie combination; the solid dark-chocolate Dove candy bar; and the coconut-filled Bounty bar—which was marketed only in Canada and Europe—were introduced to compete head-on with Hershey, makers of the Reese's Peanut Butter Cup, the Hershey bar and the Mounds bar. The Mars marketers also resurrected—in a new, improved version—a bar called Forever Yours that had been pulled from the market in 1979 because sales hadn't met expectations. This time they called it the Milky Way Dark. And they unveiled the revolutionary lower-in-fat Milky Way II.

Poe's formal responsibilities were limited to the M&M/Mars division, but his ideas sparked innovation in all sections of the company. In 1989, the makers of the

DoveBar created an ice cream version of the 3 Musketeers. Snickers and Milky Way products soon followed.

Last year, Kal Kan introduced Pedigree Puppy Food. It also launched premium, high-profit items, including Pedigree Choice Cuts and a premium line for cats, Whiskas Chunks & Gravy. Kal Kan's most ambitious launch has just gotten underway, with a new line of nutritious vet-recommended pet foods called Expert.

Uncle Ben's also readied several new products. A fast-cooking brown rice and a microwave rice were introduced nationally. The Long Grain & Wild Rice line received several new blends, as did Country Inn rice mixes.

To match the product innovations, Poe and his team of marketing managers beefed up ad spending in 1989 and 1990 and added a few twists to the company's standard marketing approach. For example, Poe persuaded Mars to pay more than $2 million for the worldwide rights to the Rolling Stones song "Satisfaction" to promote the Snickers bar. (Snickers hadn't been advertised in years; it was such a hit that Mars had just let it sell itself.)

The company also increased its visibility by signing on as a sponsor of worldwide sporting events such as World Cup soccer, the Asian Games and the Olympics.

And in a coup that stung Hershey, Mars entered into an agreement with the Walt Disney Co. to become the only supplier of candy and snacks to Disney World's Magic Kingdom, Epcot Center and Disney-MGM Studios, which have a combined draw of more than 60 million consumers a year. Along with the contract, spearheaded by Poe, Mars and Disney rolled out a multimillion-dollar, multimedia Halloween sweepstakes called "Mission from Mars." The 1990 ad campaign was one of the company's most ambitious marketing events in years.

The very title "Mission from Mars" was a departure from standard company practice: Forrest Sr. had never emphasized the Mars name over the brand name. Poe's group pushed on. They launched Mars's first-ever umbrella ad campaign, which showed people of all ages eating Mars and Milky Way bars and used the theme, "Making Life a Little Sweeter—Mars."

Poe believed it was time for the company to start thinking like the huge corporation it had become. Seen as a visionary by some and a pain in the neck by others, he believed—above all—in change. It was his ticket up the Mars corporate ladder. But it turned out to be his ticket out as well.

"It's Their Company"

Over the years, Poe had been courted by dozens of corporate headhunters, all of them attracted by his dynamic style and his status as one of the top-ranking black men in business. But he had ignored their generous offers. After all, at Mars he was earning more than half a million dollars a year. He had been given free rein to explore his creative ideas, to buck the company's conservative traditions and to use all the marketing power he could muster to overtake Hershey.

Then, last spring—just as Mars was poised to recapture the number one spot—the Mars brothers announced new responsibilities for the company's sales personnel and called for the Uncle Ben's, Kal Kan and M&M/Mars divisions to coordinate their sales efforts for the first time. The restructuring—which had been discussed for more than three years before being implemented—was one of the most sweeping changes to take place at Mars in 30 years. Under the new system, it would be up to sales to achieve the company's bottom-line results each quarter—a responsibility that once belonged to Poe and other marketers like him. Sales would also take over all advertising campaigns, leaving marketing with the somewhat amorphous task of building business over the long run.

John and Forrest Jr. signed off on these changes because they believed that the marketing managers were becoming too powerful and the sales division should shoulder more responsibility. As head of marketing, Poe had spoken out against the shift in power, saying it would ultimately hurt the company's brands. But when the brothers asked him to oversee the transformation, he obliged. They told him it was a promotion.

Until he saw Mike Murphy backstage at San Francisco's Moscone Convention Center in August, Poe even believed it.

Poe and Murphy were among a dozen executives preparing to address the 2,500 sales associates gathered at the convention hall to be told of their new assignment. Poe had spent every summer weekend and most of his nights preparing for the historic meeting, an uncharacteristically glitzy affair complete with a theme song, stage show and a rare address by the brothers. But it was Murphy who was being congratulated in the corner by his colleagues. It seemed the longtime M&M/Mars manufacturing vice president was being promoted to head the Kal Kan division, replacing the president who had announced early retirement. It was the job Poe had always wanted.

"I spent four years with Kal Kan and three years with Pedigree—I'm the best in the business in pet care," he says. "I wrote the master plan in 1986 that {Kal Kan} is using now. That is common knowledge. And when they gave that job to Murph, I said, 'Okay, I see how this works.' "

Three months later, Poe quit his job to accept a position with the Campbell Soup Co. as president of Vlasic Foods.

Ironically, Poe's departure came just weeks after Mars learned that it had officially regained the lead from Hershey. A survey by A.C. Nielsen showed Mars with 28.2 percent of the U.S. candy market, compared with Hershey's 26.2 percent.

Poe's seemingly abrupt resignation rocked McLean, which had advertised him as the future of the company, the next general manager of the M&M/Mars candy division. Mars general counsel Ed Stegemann, in explaining Poe's decision, says he really isn't sure why Poe left and suggests that he took the job because his wife wanted a change.

From his new post, Poe laughs at that notion. Campbell's "made me an offer I couldn't refuse," he says. "Here, I can be my own boss. That is the selling point—that someday, I have the chance to be the CEO."

It's a sentiment echoed by other former Mars executives who, like Poe, left the company in the last decade to pursue other paths to the top. "The brothers really don't know how to delegate," says one former executive. "Sure, they give you responsibility. But they keep the authority. In the end, you realize, you'll never make your own decisions."

Poe says he was given the sales force job because the Mars family was uncomfortable with his radical style. And although he was told he would someday become head of M&M/Mars, he says he came to understand that there wasn't enough room in the executive suite for his ideas and those of the Mars family.

Ed Stegemann scoffs at this notion. "Sure, {the brothers} have the final say on business decisions, but that doesn't mean they control every little part of the business. They're open to ideas—you just have to prove your case . . . It is their money."

In the past year, half a dozen top executives with an average tenure of 25 years each have left Mars Inc. In interviews with several of them, there was a recurring sentiment: It's not that we don't love Mars and respect the company and appreciate what the brothers did for us, it's that they don't know how to share power.

"In the end," says Poe, "every discussion that I couldn't win ended on, 'Well, it's my rubber ducky.' Not, 'What if I trust you and you are right.' "

Most of these executives left over disagreements about how to expand the business. Turnover at Mars has traditionally been low, so this wave of defections raises serious questions about whether the family is holding on too tightly.

Virtually everyone at Mars agrees that the brothers can be difficult to work for. But those who stick around seem to accept the pressure from the top. It's their company," says Mike Stefanos, head of Dove International. "They own it. That's how a family business works."

Who'll Put the M on the M&M?

Executives may come and go, but the planet Mars remains. And its essence can be found at the company's factory in Hackettstown, N.J.

Picture thousands of newly candy-coated chocolates spilling onto a conveyor equipped with tiny indentations, each the perfect cradle for a single M&M. As the conveyor shakes, the rainbow of naked candy shells settles in for a ride toward the printing press. The printer's top roller is covered with the raised type of tiny M's, which are coated with edible white dye. But this roller doesn't print the M on the candy; it would crush the delicate shell. Instead, it transfers the print of the M onto a second roller with a smooth surface. That roller passes over the centers of the speeding candies below and transfers the still-wet imprint onto the shells with just the right amount of force—not too much to crush the candy, but enough so that the M comes off, legs intact.

It all happens at the rate of 200,000 M&M's a minute; 100 million M&M's every eight hours. And 99 times out of 100, the machine hits its target perfectly.

Perfecting the equipment that prints the M has taken thousands of hours of engineering. The process is so important to the company, I was told, that no outsider had ever before been invited to observe it.

Secrecy, tradition and obsessive perfectionism united to protect a family name: The M&M factory symbolizes the tremendous legacy that is Mars Inc. But it's a legacy whose future is unknown.

Can Mars protect its culture from the corrosive effects of growth and time? Retain top managers if the road to the top stays blocked? Innovate enough to compete and grow, while sticking to an essentially conservative strategy?

Most important, given the dominant role of the Mars family to date: Can it successfully transfer leadership to the next generation? All together, John, Forrest Jr. and Jackie have 10 children and two grandchildren, and, at any one time, as many as half a dozen Mars offspring are likely to be working in the company. Although they're outwardly treated no differently from other associates, it's clear, say managers, that someday this generation will assume control. But how and when the brothers will pass the baton is anyone's guess.

That's "the big unknown," says former top executive Claude Eliette-Hermann. Senior executives have tried for years to get an answer to that question, he says, but the family is playing it "very close to the vest."

Eliette-Hermann, who ran the company's pet food operations for 25 years and is still highly regarded by Mars, left the company for just that reason. "I had gone as far as I could go," he says from his new post as president of Chanel SA in Paris.

Former associates maintain that Forrest Jr., now 60, has been trying for years to retire and leave the company in the hands of brother John. But, they say, his desire for control is too great; he just can't let go .

Some associates are concerned about the company's future. They say it won't be as easy for the brothers to simply walk away as their father did, because this would leave Mars Inc. in too many hands. And the statistics on family businesses are alarming: By the fourth, fifth and sixth generations, it seems, they almost always fall victim to sibling rivalry, greed and tensions between the family and the firm.

The rumor in the industry is that John, Forrest Jr. and Jackie are forbidden—as a condition of their ownership—to sell any part of Mars. But whoever inherits their stock, one industry leader says, may do whatever he or she pleases with the business. The family would not comment on this.

Of the 10 grandchildren, Jackie's three children are said to have shown little interest in the business. Forrest Jr.'s oldest daughter, Victoria, has been working in England in pet food operations. His daughter Pam, according to Ed Stegemann, is running the Mattoon, Ill., pet food factory and doing "a damn good job." Linda

Mars, John's only daughter, has been working to develop new markets abroad. Al Poe thinks that John's 22-year-old son, Mike, who graduated from Duke in 1991, could be the one to run the company someday. But Phil Forster and others in the company believe that John's eldest son, Frank, is the chosen heir.

Frank's early career looks a lot like those of his father and his father's father. The 31-year-old Yale graduate has built his own business in the suburbs of Phoenix, where he manufactures Styrofoam packaging specially designed to keep chocolate products from melting in the heat. He sells the packaging to two Mars divisions, along with other packaged goods companies. He lives in a sparsely furnished apartment with his German wife, Antje. He tells friends he's "just an average guy." And he's squarely in the tradition of the secretive world he could inherit: He doesn't talk about the future of Mars.

April 12, 1992

'Global Offices' on Rise as Firms Shift Service Jobs Abroad

JOHN BURGESS

Call the new toll-free reservation number for Jamaica's Wexford Court Hotel and you may notice that the agent who answers speaks with a Jamaican accent.

That isn't surprising, because the hotel's booking office for American guests is located on the sunny Caribbean island itself, and your call has seamlessly and at no cost to you gone international, routed across the waters by satellite.

You've heard about the "global factory." Meet the "global office."

In the 1980s, American manufacturers became increasingly willing to set up their assembly lines in foreign countries where employees gladly accept lower wages, a trend that has moved many blue-collar jobs out of the United States.

Now, rapidly advancing communications technology and growing sophistication among low-cost foreign work forces are creating a similar mobility for some white-collar office jobs. The Wexford Court, for instance, formerly booked rooms through a reservation center in Miami.

Many economists have played down the importance of manufacturing jobs in America's long-term economic vitality, emphasizing instead the vast growth in the service sector. But with this trend, questions are arising as to whether even these jobs are anchored in American soil.

Not long ago, U.S. insurance giant Cigna Corp. announced plans to open a $5 million medical claims processing center in the Irish town of Loughrea, creating about 200 jobs there. Texas Instruments Inc. has put a software development facility in Bangalore, India, linked by satellite to headquarters in Dallas. And Chicago publishing house R.R. Donnelley & Sons is sending manuscripts to Barbados to prepare them for printing in the United States.

Although the trend is low-key to date, many analysts expect it to gain momentum. "You will see service jobs being done where the best, most economical service people exist," predicted Richard M. Wolf, executive vice president of Robert E. LaBlanc Associates Inc., a telecommunications consulting firm in Ridgewood, N.J.

Around the world, developing countries like Jamaica are lobbying hard, with tax incentives and start-up assistance, to attract to their shores service companies from the United States and other industrialized countries. With workers who may earn only a third of going rates in the United States, they hope to handle such labor-intensive operations as data entry, software development and telemarketing.

The trend hasn't escaped the notice of wary U.S. labor unions. As they see it, companies can now flip a few switches and send abroad jobs once held by their members. "As office work becomes more electronic," said Dennis Chamot of the AFL-CIO's department for professional employees, "it becomes easier to move." He calls the trend "quite serious" but says that so far it is more potential than real.

One of the earliest types of service work to go abroad was data entry. In the early 1970s, for instance, the legal research service Lexis, owned by Mead Data Central Inc. of Dayton, Ohio, began bundling court documents onto airliners and flying them to centers abroad where key-punch operators typed them into computers. The resulting magnetic tapes were air-freighted back to the United States for use on Lexis' on-line service.

Today, as costs fall, more and more material is traveling across borders electronically, reducing the turn-around time substantially. Rates charged by the Intelsat satellite network for international calls are now about one-thirtieth what they were 25 years ago. And the first transoceanic fiber-optic cables and privately owned international satellites are entering service, which is expected to lower costs further over time.

American Airlines has become one of the Caribbean's largest players in this field. In 1984, it set up a subsidiary called Caribbean Data Services that today employs about 400 people in Barbados and 650 in the Dominican Republic, processing data for the airline and, on contract, for other U.S. companies.

Every evening, thousands of used American Airlines tickets are flown from airports around the country to New York, then south to Barbados, a tiny English-speaking island state about 250 miles off the coast of Venezuela. There, keypunch operators enter information from the tickets into computers, after which it is transmitted electronically to American's headquarters in Dallas.

"Due to modern satellite communications," said Lawson Nurse, director of American operations at the Barbados Industrial Development Corp.'s New York office, "there's no particular advantage to doing the thing, say, in New York and beaming it to your computer in Dallas. It's just as easy to do it in Barbados."

About 1,000 Barbadians currently work for a collection of foreign-oriented data processing centers on the island, earning their country about $10 million a year in foreign exchange. The government views the industry as vital to economic development and is building a $1.5 million air-conditioned facility to lease to foreign data processing operations and is helping to train Barbadian citizens in computer skills.

Now Barbados is angling for its first jobs in what many countries see as the next frontier in service job mobility, telemarketing and toll-free services. Ahead of it in that race is Jamaica, using a $10 million satellite facility that was opened last year as a joint venture between American Telephone & Telegraph Co., the British communications company Cable & Wireless and a Jamaican telecommunications company. Built around a 50-foot satellite dish in Montego Bay, it is operated by a company called Jamaica Digiport International. For now it has four clients doing data processing for foreign operations and three hotel groups, which use or are planning to use it for reservations at hotels, including the Wexford Court. It is working on getting its first telemarketing and airline reservations.

A significant barrier to success in this field, however, is a human one, spoken accents.

Foreign data processors are anonymous cogs in a company's machine and are never seen by its customers. But operators act as personal representatives and many American companies seem reluctant to assign that task to people who do not speak like true-blue Americans.

Charles Ruppman, chief executive officer of telemarketing firm Ruppman Marketing Services Inc. of Peoria, Ill., says that accents are a crucial consideration and have helped in past years to bring many telemarketing centers to the Midwest, where a comparatively neutral form of English is spoken.

"You start one in the Deep South or you start one in the Bronx and you obviously aren't speaking a universally accepted dialect of the language—or in Jamaica or Barbados," Ruppman said.

Nurse of Barbados said that to be successful, telemarketers must have clear diction, understand all the different regional accents of the United States and be skilled in computer operation and salesmanship. But he suggested that these are not insurmountable barriers.

The big draw is lower wages. Barbados says its wages are about a third of those in the United States. For American, this helps to yield annual savings of $4 million to $6 million over what it would cost to do the same work in the United States.

But American also says it has found that even at lower prices, Barbadians do better work. Keypunch positions may be welcomed by foreign workers as if sent from heaven, while to many Americans they may seem like dead-end jobs that should be quit at the first chance.

The news isn't all bad for American workers. International toll-free calls coming from Europe and Canada have helped pump up sales of U.S. catalogue sales companies. And some U.S. companies are finding that the United States is the better place to do work that they had previously handled offshore.

Lexis, for instance, found over the years that it was suffering delays as it shipped documents abroad and cleared them through customs, and that the accuracy of material punched by foreign operators was not always high.

As a result, Lexis has in recent years been transferring jobs back to the United States, according to Kathryn Downing, senior director for legal information publishing. It now handles about a third of its data entry operations in South Korea, China, the Philippines and Jamaica. The rest goes to three centers in the United States.

April 20, 1989

Adjusting as Preeminence Slips

Globalization Produces American Beneficiaries as Well as Victims

PAUL BLUSTEIN

Bad, bad, worse, worse—that's how the 1980s had begun for Inland Steel Industries Inc., recalled Frank W. Luerssen, Inland's chairman. But on a winter morning in 1984, Luerssen beheld a sight that convinced him the company could make it after all.

"My spirits rose to the heavens," Luerssen said. "It was the answer to the maiden's prayer."

That sight was in Himeji, a city in southwestern Japan. What Luerssen saw was a technologically dazzling factory that churned out one giant roll of steel after another—steel of extraordinarily uniform smoothness, strength and malleability— at a speed approached by not other plant in the world.

Heading back to Tokyo on the bullet train in the afternoon, Luerssen and his colleagues excitedly began discussing the possibility that with help from the Japanese, Inland might be able to build a similar facility in the United States and sell the highest-quality steel in the country.

Luerssen's quest for his company's salvation 6,500 miles from its Chicago headquarters is a good symbol for the changes that swept through the American economy during the last decade. The trade deficit, the inflow of foreign capital, the nation's mounting indebtedness— to many Americans, these are meaningless abstractions. But at Inland Steel, they reshaped a giant corporation.

By the mid-1980s, Inland—like the U.S. economy as a whole—depended on foreign capital for its growth. Its most important expenditures for plant and equipment during the decade were financed by foreigners—an ironic twist, for it was Inland's severe losses in the face of foreign competition that forced the company to turn abroad for financial help. Inland was both a victim and a beneficiary of the globalization that has transformed the American economy, creating disturbing uncertainty about the country's future.

Ten years ago, nearly 24,000 people worked at Inland's steelmaking facility, the Indiana Harbor Works, a 2,000-acre site in gritty East Chicago, Ind., at the southern tip of Lake Michigan. Today, 15,000 are employed there. The No. 3 Open Hearth Shop, a 1950s-vintage structure longer than four football fields that once housed massive steelmaking equipment, now shelters a sprawl of rusting machinery waiting to be cut up for scrap. Four blast furnaces, which in 1980 were busily converting iron ore, limestone and baked coal into molten iron, are now silent, sooty 100-foot-tall relics.

In those days, both Inland and its employees were riding high. "I thought I had the world by the butt," said David Ramos, a former machine operator at the Indiana Harbor Works, who was making $12.75 an hour plus generous benefits at the beginning of the decade. He lost that job in Inland's 1982 layoffs, and since then he has been unable to find work paying even half of what he used to make. Ramos, now 31, earns $5 an hour as a security guard; his family of six has gone on food stamps to survive. He said that at times he has been so depressed and irritable that, to spare his wife and children, he has driven off in his van and simply stayed in a field for a week.

About 55 miles east of the Indiana Harbor Works is a scene that reflects a very different sort of change. On the site of a cornfield near the little town of New Carlisle, Ind., workers are putting the finishing touches on a steel mill a half-mile long and 10 stories high. According to industry analysts, it will be the most technologically advanced of its kind when it starts operating early next year.

The I/N Tek mill, a close replica of the one Luerssen saw in Japan, is a joint venture of Inland and Nippon Steel Corp. Japanese lenders provided two-thirds of the $470 million required to build it. Another Inland-Nippon joint venture is under construction at the same site; together, the two facilities will employ about 430 people, perhaps one-third of the staffing required for plants of comparable output based on earlier technologies.

Like all foreign investments, they come at a price: The bulk of the operating profits will flow to the overseas investors, improving the living standards of Japanese rather than Americans. Still, they represent a source of job growth and a boon for Inland.

The Inland story has produced winners and losers. Among the clear losers is the United Steelworkers of America, whose membership in steel plants shrank by nearly half over the last 10 years and was forced during the mid-1980s to accept reductions in wages and benefits— "givebacks," in the jargon of collective bargaining—to preserve jobs and help keep the industry afloat.

Among the clear winners are Inland's customers—and ultimately the consumers who purchase steel products such as automobiles, refrigerators, appliances and office furniture. The price Inland charges for steel fell by 26 percent over the last 10 years in inflation-adjusted terms. At the same time, the quality of the company's products improved considerably. Had foreigners not forced Inland and other U.S. steel companies to compete more aggressively, consumers would not have benefited nearly so much from the lower cost and higher quality of the steel in the products they buy.

Inland is a company coming to grips with the slippage of America's preeminent position in the world economy, making adjustments that seemed almost unthinkable at the outset of the 1980s. John L. Selky, an Inland executive, recalled how the dinner conversation often began during the negotiations with Nippon Steel over the building of the I/N Tek joint venture: "The Japanese would give this little preamble, saying that in the '60s, the U.S. steel industry had helped them and given them equipment and technology. Now they realized it was time for them to reciprocate. They felt it was important to help America.

"It made you feel a little disappointed that we hadn't kept up with the technology in the '70s," said Selky, who now heads I/N Tek. "You knew what they were saying was true. You hated to hear it. You knew why they needed help in the '60s; it was because they had been demolished in the '40s. We didn't have that excuse."

Decade Opens with Optimism

The sky was gloomy and overcast, but the speeches were sunnily optimistic at the Sept. 19, 1980, dedication of a giant blast furnace at the Indiana Harbor Works.

"A larger share of a market with continuing growth prospects clearly is within our grasp during the years ahead," declared Frederick G. Jaicks, then Inland's chairman.

A new decade had dawned, and Inland was bullish on steel—much more so than most other steel companies. It had plowed more than $1 billion into plant and equipment during the latter half of the 1970s, culminating in the construction of the new blast furnace, while some of its rivals had begun to slowly disinvest from steelmaking. Inland, the sixth-largest U.S. steel company at the time, had always been a maverick, proud of its reputation among Wall Street analysts as perhaps the smartest and best-managed company in the industry. Yes, the company had found it necessary to buy Japanese technology to build its new blast furnace, but that just showed how farsighted Inland was. Let the rest of the industry diversify into businesses like oil and financial services, Inland's executives reasoned; they were determined that their company should maintain its steel identity, because they were convinced they had an edge.

But before long, Inland was struggling not only to maintain its commitment to steel, but for its very survival. In 1982 the U.S. economy slumped into a deep recession, and Inland lost $119 million, its first full-year loss since the Great Depression. More disturbing, the company's fortunes did not improve much when the economy began to recover. In 1983, Inland lost another $117 million, and in 1984, $41 million.

The root of the problem was hardly a mystery. It was explained regularly, and loudly, by the company's main customers, like Ford Motor Co.; Whirlpool Corp., the appliance manufacturer; and Steelcase Inc., the office-equipment maker. All felt compelled to buy imported steel.

"We were hearing just incredible stories from our customers about the imports' product reliability," recalled Robert E. Powell, who was Inland's vice president for sales at the time.

The imported stuff was easier to form into auto bumpers, refrigerator panels and desk drawers, the customers said. It did not break as often in their presses. It did not have as many scratches, and it could be painted more readily. It did not cause them to shut down their assembly lines so often.

Imported steel had long enjoyed a cost advantage over domestic steel. That gap was growing wider during the first half of the decade as the U.S. dollar kept rising against other currencies, making foreign products cheaper. West German steel, for example, which had cost just a few dollars a ton less than the U.S. product during the late 1970s, undersold American-made steel by about $170 a ton in 1984.

With imported steel far outstripping the U.S. product in both price and quality, companies like Inland were getting clobbered. The import share of the U.S. steel market soared, from 16.3 percent in 1980 to 26.4 percent four years later. The figure would have risen higher but for a federal import restriction program that went into effect in October 1984 and has remained in force.

Like other American steel companies, Inland had never put much of a priority on quality. The U.S. industry had always been obsessed with producing the maximum possible tonnage. With the market dominated by a relatively small number of companies, all they had to do in high-demand years was churn out the steel and count the profits.

The new reality was driven home with a vengeance by Bob Powell, the sales vice president, who in July 1985 delivered a blunt speech to several hundred Inland managers. "At the most critical time in our history, we stink by most standards," Powell said. "We've done a poor job and we're paying for it." He asked: "Would you fly in a Boeing 747 with 8 percent slivers? Would you tolerate a new automobile with rust, or mixed steel in your child's swing set?"

The speech provoked both hostility and soul-searching, Inland officials recall. "People who worked for me came up to me later, saying, 'How could you let Bob say that about us?' " said Joseph D. Corso, a senior manager at the Harbor Works. "We had always thought of ourselves as simply the best steel company. All of a sudden, we were thinking of ourselves as the best of the worst."

By that time, Luerssen, who had assumed the Inland chairmanship in 1983, had decided that the company needed to adopt a dramatically new strategy aimed at making itself a producer of world-class-quality steel for the consumer-durables market. "Our feeling was that unless we were able to accomplish that, there was a question whether we should continue in the steel business," Luerssen said.

Managers and foremen at the Indiana Harbor Works harped on the need for improving quality, even sending blue-collar workers to customers' plants so they could see firsthand why the product had to be better. The company sank more than $100 million a year into modernizing its plant—a sum not quite equal to the pre-1981 pace of investment, but considerable nonetheless.

But by 1985, the financial drain on the company was becoming crippling. Inland was forced to sell its Chicago headquarters building and a prized Willem de Kooning painting, which fetched $900,000.

The white-collar managerial team was drastically reorganized, and "everybody was convinced they were going to lose their job," an Inland official recalled. More than 1,000 salaried positions—about one-fifth of the total—were cut. At the 1985 stockholders meeting, Inland announced that it would permanently close almost one-third of its steelmaking capacity at the Harbor Works, a move that cost 900 more blue-collar jobs.

Losses for 1985 totaled $178 million. If the "best of the worst" was to improve, it would need outside help.

Initial Talks with Nippon Stall

Nippon Steel, the world's largest steelmaker, is internationally renowned for its technological prowess. So when its chairman, Eishiro Saito, met with Inland's top executives in November 1983 and casually mentioned that his company might be interested in doing "something significant" with Inland, Luerssen quickly followed up.

Two months later, Luerssen and four other Inland executives traveled to Nippon's Hirohata works. The object of their visit was a facility that Inlanders soon thereafter dubbed "Star Wars"—a computer-controlled steel mill that rolls remarkably high-quality sheet steel in a fraction of the time required by more traditional rolling mills.

John Selky recalls the high hopes with which an Inland delegation approached Nippon in early 1984 with an urgent proposition to form a joint venture using the Japanese company's technology. "It was our naivete," Selky said. "We were expecting an immediate answer." The cautious, consensus-minded Japanese almost never give immediate answers to such proposals, but Inland insisted on one, and so the answer came: not interested. But a few months later, Nippon contacted Inland to reopen discussions. Nippon decided it needed a way to serve the growing number of its customers—the Japanese auto companies—that had established plants in the United States.

Still, negotiations dragged and produced some unpleasant experiences. Nippon engineers were dispatched to the Indiana Harbor Works in 1985, looking for ways to make sure that the plant could produce steel of sufficiently high quality to feed into the proposed joint-venture rolling mill. The foreign visitors' presence galled the steelworkers. "There was a lot of resentment," recalled John Mazany, who was then a mechanic at the Harbor Works. "There would be graffiti on the walls— pictures of atomic bombs, or, 'Remember Pearl Harbor'—when the guys knew they {the Japanese} were coming through."

The agreement to build I/N Tek was finally signed in July 1987 . By then, the steel business was recovering smartly, thanks in part to the decline of the dollar, which lowered the price of American steel compared to its foreign competition. Inland, now a much trimmer company than it was at the start of the decade, eked out a $19 million profit in 1986, then made $145 million in 1987 and a record $262 million in 1988.

To staff I/N Tek, Inland chose more than 100 steelworkers from the Indiana Harbor Works and sent them to Japan for training. The new plant's operations plan is strongly influenced by Japanese management theories and involves a heavy degree of worker participation in decisions.

Inland owns 60 percent of I/N Tek and Nippon holds a 40 percent share. To pay for the bulk of the facility's cost, three Japanese trading companies are providing loans totaling about $330 million.

That means that an estimated $25 million to $35 million in interest payments will flow each year to Japan before the partners earn any profit; and of each dollar of profit the venture earns, 40 cents will go to Nippon.

Are such arrangements good for the United States? Many economists argue that the nation has become overly dependent on injections of foreign capital, because U.S. savings are too meager to bankroll the investment necessary to keep the economy growing. American living standards would be substantially more likely to rise in the future if the United States had been able to finance its own investment instead of becoming indebted to foreigners.

Still, the fact that foreigners have been willing to provide capital has helped enormously in sustaining the expansion of the economy that has now continued for seven years. Just ask Jeff Forsythe whether he is better off.

A steelworker at the Indiana Harbor Works, Forsythe was laid off for most of 1986—right after he got married—and for much of 1987 and 1988 as well. "I just about lost the house I had bought, and it seemed like we wouldn't stay together," he recalled.

Now Forsythe, 29, has a job at I/N Tek, where he is earning about $35,000 a year. "All I know is, I got a job and I'm making money," he said. "Whether the money comes from Japan, England, Russia—it don't matter to me. I get a paycheck. That's what matters."

December 11, 1989

4 Issues in International Trade

24 Nations Agree to Curb Use of Export Subsidies

OECD Sets New Trade Rules Covering Developing Nations

STUART AUERBACH

After eight years of negotiations, the world's richest industrialized nations have agreed to U.S. demands that they curb the use of government aid and subsidized bank loans to promote export sales to developing nations, Bush administration officials announced yesterday.

The agreement by the Organization for Economic Cooperation and Development (OECD), the 24-nation group of industrialized nations, set new rules limiting the use of aid and cut-rate loans to promote exports of a wide array of manufactured products.

John D. Macomber, president of the Export-Import Bank of the United States, estimated that subsidized financing by other industrialized countries costs U.S. companies between $4 billion and $6 billion in lost overseas sales each year. In Asia alone last year, he said, Ex-Im Bank officials counted more than $1 billion in contracts that U.S. companies lost because rivals from other countries sweetened their deals with grants of government aid and subsidized, cut-rate financing.

Besides hurting U.S. exporters, Macomber said, the use of aid programs to promote exports cuts into the pool of money available to help the poorest nations, which need the aid most.

The new rules do not apply to agricultural sales or to the use of credits for military hardware.

The Reagan and Bush administrations, hewing to a free-market philosophy, have opposed the use of mixed credits (the melding of aid and cut-rate loans) and tied aid (offers of foreign aid targeted to specific purchases). But under pressure from Congress and U.S. companies, the Ex-Im Bank and the Agency for International Development (AID) have used a specially appropriated "war chest" to counter subsidized financing by other countries. Recently, for instance, AID and the Ex-Im Bank joined to offer low-cost financing that helped American Telephone & Telegraph Co. match a Japanese bid on a major telecommunications contract in Indonesia. AT&T won the contract.

Under the new rules, that kind of subsidized financing would not be allowed, Macomber said, forcing companies to compete for contracts on merit.

In recent years, cut-rate financing has played a role in the sales of telecommunications networks, power generation equipment, railroad engines and cars, airplanes and airport control systems in Asia, North Africa and the Middle East.

More recently, Spain, Italy and Portugal have begun using tied aid and mixed credits to win contracts in Latin America, said James R. Sharp, executive vice president of the Ex-Im Bank.

Under the new rules, the use of cut-rate loans and tied aid would be banned from the richest of the developing countries—those with a per capita income of more than $2,465 a year. These include nations such as Mexico, Brazil, Venezuela and Gabon.

Industrialized countries still could give the large majority of middle-income developing nations cut-rate terms in financing as much as 35 percent of a particular sale. But tied aid would be allowed only if market-rate financing was not available or if a project did not generate enough money on its own to cover operating costs and interest payments.

The 40 poorest developing nations—those that need the help most—will be able to deal in tied aid and get half of any loans at cut-rate prices.

November 6, 1992

Trade Accord Sets 'Voluntary' Auto Purchases

PAUL BLUSTEIN AND STUART AUERBACH

After a late-night negotiating session, Japan and the United States today reached an agreement aimed at easing tensions over automobile trade.

According to Japanese officials, the accord includes "voluntary" plans for Japanese automakers to more than double their purchases of U.S.-made auto parts by 1994.

Although complete details were not immediately available, Japanese press reports this morning said that Washington and Tokyo had settled on a goal of approximately $19 billion in purchases of American auto parts by 1994, more than the Japanese auto companies had originally offered but less than U.S. officials were seeking.

The agreement was hailed by President Bush at a press conference this morning as a major accomplishment of his visit to Japan, which he has billed as a mission to break down barriers and expand opportunities for U.S. exports in the world's second-largest market.

The Japanese automakers' plans to buy more American-made parts could produce a substantial amount of business for U.S. firms. But the accord is not enforceable, and it is not expected to come close to wiping out the $30 billion-plus U.S. deficit with Japan in autos and auto parts. The auto pact also includes measures that would make it easier for America's Big Three automakers to sell their cars in Japan, although American cars are held in such low esteem by Japanese consumers—U.S. brands currently hold less than 0.5 percent of the Japanese market—that the results are not likely to produce much of a boost for Detroit.

Among the steps to help U.S. auto sales is an agreement under which American cars could be imported without having to be subjected to certain time-consuming and costly safety-inspection requirements that apply to almost all new cars sold here. The Japanese authorities have agreed to accept U.S. certification that the cars meet adequate safety standards.

The agreement followed several weeks of tough wrangling that intensified during Bush's visit as trade negotiators from both sides staged late-night and early-morning negotiations that grew contentious at times. Japanese officials expressed strong private resentment over what they considered to be constant American

72

demands for more concessions, but they relented on a number of points because they want to give a boost to Bush, whom they view as less protectionist than his political opponents.

The Bush administration view was conveyed to the Japanese in tough but friendly terms today by Treasury Secretary Nicholas F. Brady, who filled in for the recuperating Bush at a luncheon speech. "If we are to expand our economic ties, we must face up to the economic tensions that threaten our relations," Brady said. "We must reduce the trade imbalance between us—not through managed trade, through gimmicks or artificial devices, but simply by gaining true and welcome access to your markets."

Despite that disclaimer, the plans by the Japanese auto companies to expand purchases of American-made parts involve a considerable amount of government intervention in favor of U.S. firms. But officials and other trade experts here said the pact falls well short of managed trade, which would entail enforceable targets.

In another accord unveiled Wednesday, Bush—anxious for ways to buoy the recession-bound U.S. economy—won Prime Minister Kiichi Miyazawa's commitment to join in a program called "Strategy for World Growth," essentially aimed at using the Japanese economy as a locomotive to help lift growth in the rest of the world.

The program appears to be aimed at inducing Tokyo to adopt stimulative measures—such as interest rate reductions—later this year if growth flags.

Brady has been prodding Japan and Germany since last March to put less emphasis on fighting inflation and more on increasing growth. The Treasury is hopeful that lower interest rates abroad will make it easier for the Federal Reserve Board to cut rates further in the United States, and it is also hoping that such a move—by boosting the purchasing power of Japanese consumers—would increase sales of U.S. and other foreign goods into Japan.

In the most significant portion of the strategy, the two leaders agreed that Japan will monitor the progress of recent interest rate cuts and increased public works expenditures, to assure that the expected results are realized. That phraseology would surely be used by U.S. officials to badger their Japanese counterparts for more stimulus if growth starts to fall substantially below the officially projected 3.5 percent, after inflation, for 1992.

Bush and Miyazawa also issued language apparently aimed at nudging the dollar down a bit further against the yen. A lower dollar makes U.S.-made goods more competitive vis-a-vis Japanese products.

The two leaders agreed that recent exchange rate movements were consistent with current economic developments, suggesting that their governments will not intervene—at least not for a while—if the dollar continues its recent steep descent.

The announcement of the strategy was somewhat unusual in that it involved only two members of the Group of Seven industrial countries. But a senior U.S. official said that Brady is planning on jawboning European members of the G-7 next, notably Germany, whose interest rates have been going up of late. The issue will surely be raised at a meeting of the G-7 finance ministers on Jan. 25, the official said.

David Mulford, the Treasury undersecretary for monetary affairs, is already in European capitals in an effort to explain the new policy to Germany and other members of the G-7, the official said.

After a meeting Wednesday morning with top officials of the Ministry of International Trade and Industry, business executives accompanying Bush were despondent. They said the had forcefully described to MITI officials how Japanese business practices and government regulations keep them out of the country, but got little response.

"It was a nothing meeting," said Joseph T. Gorman, chairman of TRW Inc. "It was a frank exchange of views from one side—our side."

On Wednesday, four of the five largest Japanese auto companies announced revised plans to increase their purchases of U.S.-made parts, along with additional plans to try to sell about 19,700 U.S. cars in Japan through their dealer networks. The increase in parts purchases, to $17.8 billion by 1994, would represent more than a doubling of the 1990 level.

Toyota Motor Corp. said it hopes to sell about 5,000 General Motors Corp. cars—mostly Saturn models—in Japan, and buy a total of $5.28 billion in U.S.-made parts by 1994, for both its transplant operations in the United States and factories in Japan.

Honda Motor Co. plans to sell 1,200 Jeep Cherokees and buy $4.94 billion in parts by 1994; Mitsubishi Motor Corp. plans to sell some 6,000 Chryslers and buy $1.6 billion in parts; and Mazda Motor Corp. plans to import 4,500 Fords and buy $2.3 billion in parts.

January 9, 1992

Tariffs not the Key to Japanese Market

Loyalty, Long-Term Company Relationships Needed to Open Trade

PAUL BLUSTEIN

Making the Japanese market more receptive to U.S. goods is a lot more complicated than it sounds?

In an obvious reference to Japan, Bush said recently that his trip to Asia is aimed at "breaking open markets that shut out American products."

Robert A. Mosbacher, the outgoing commerce secretary, likewise vowed that the mission will help knock down trade barriers, chiding Tokyo for "not allowing U.S. goods into Japan."

It is an image of a Japan that, in the words of French Prime Minister Edith Cresson, is "hermetically sealed"—a nation where foreign products are still blocked by a combination of tariffs and legal restrictions, and where government officials use their bureaucratic powers to block would-be importers. It suggests that all that is needed is some tough, pointed demands for Tokyo to change its laws and regulations and adopt U.S.-style free-trade policies.

But the problems facing most American and other foreign businesses here have little to do with tariffs, import restrictions or bureaucratic obstructions.

Tokyo does maintain protectionist barriers against some agricultural products, such as the near-total ban on imported rice. But in manufactured goods—the area that economists say is most important because it involves high-skill jobs—Japan has virtually dismantled its once-high wall of tariffs and quotas; and much of its trade bureaucracy is engaged in promoting imports, not discouraging them.

The chief factor making the Japanese market difficult to penetrate now, even for foreign companies offering high-quality products and service, is in substantial part the deep-rooted corporate practice of Japanese firms to maintain tight linkages with one another, according to a broad consensus of experts that include foreign critics, business executives and Japanese officials.

Much more than U.S. firms, Japanese companies forge semi-permanent ties with their suppliers, customers and distributors. They stick together partly because of a cultural affinity for group relationships, and partly because the Japanese say they believe—with some justification—that such stable alliances provide economic payoffs by fostering long-run strategic thinking and mutually beneficial cooperation.

In many cases, these bonds involve keiretsu affiliations—membership in corporate "families" such as the Mitsubishi, Sumitomo and Mitsui groups. But even when no formal keiretsu is involved, ties between Japanese firms tend to be hard to break.

"It's bureaucrats—but not bureaucrats in the public-sector sense," said David D. Baskerville, vice president for Asia at Siecor International Corp., a maker of fiber-optic cable, which has achieved considerable success in Japan. "Business people here are slow to admit any outsider. They've got long-term business relationships, and they're comfortable with them."

Many American companies fail to realize how much extra effort is required to overcome this obstacle, Baskerville said. To illustrate the point, he said that even when Siecor manages to gain, say, 5 percent of a customer's business based on superior quality and price, it must "fight like hell" for more, because "there are some {customers} who think we should have only so much. They'll say, it's only fair" to competing suppliers who have loyally served them for years. In the United States, by contrast, Siecor will often lose a contract if its price ranges half a percent above a competitor's, Baskerville added.

So although Japan is readying a number of trade concessions there are reasons to doubt whether these moves will contribute much toward the goal of generating job-producing American exports.

One step that Tokyo is reportedly considering, for example, is a modest tax rebate for Japanese who buy imported cars. The trouble is, most of the benefit would likely go to European luxury carmakers such as Bayerische Motoren Werke AG (BMW) and Mercedes-Automobil-Holding AG, which far outsell American autos here.

In short, the problems of improving access to the Japanese market have become much more subtle and difficult to solve than they were 10 to 20 years ago, when Tokyo still maintained major formal import barriers.

Japan has virtually no more room to lower its tariffs; they are already among the lowest in the world. And to an extent little appreciated by foreigners, the famed Ministry of International Trade and Industry (MITI) has largely dropped its anti-import activities.

In contrast to its prior role as the mastermind of Japan's export juggernaut, MITI now channels considerable energy into easing trade tensions by cheerleading for sales of foreign products. Last year, the government even began offering tax credits for Japanese companies that increase imports, plus low-interest financing for foreign companies that export to Japan.

One recently announced MITI program does hold some promise, U.S. trade experts have said, because it is aimed squarely at increasing the number of American companies forming the sort of long-term tie-ups with Japanese firms that are common in Japan.

Under the program, dubbed the Business Global Partnership Initiative, MITI summoned 40 of Japan's largest companies and told them to produce "voluntary" blueprints of how they planned to raise their purchases of U.S. goods, with an emphasis on forging stable supply relationships.

But American officials say they want to see concrete results before they will be convinced the program can work.

The American Chamber of Commerce in Japan has acknowledged, in a report last June, that the Japanese market "has become much more open in the past five years." On a volume basis, imports rose 45 percent from 1986 to 1990, and the $48.58 billion in imports into Japan from the United States in 1991 exceeded the amount that America exported to Britain, France and Italy combined.

But Japan still has a long way to go, in the view of the American Chamber and many other observers.

Edward Lincoln, an economist at the Brookings Institution, noted that the manufactured goods imported by Japan currently total about 4 percent of gross national product, compared with 8 percent in the United States and 10 percent-plus in Western European countries.

Some analysts contend that the Japanese business mind-set is so unusual that, despite the lack of formal barriers, the market will never be truly fair or open, at least not in the way Americans use those words.

Clyde V. Prestowitz Jr., a former U.S. trade negotiator and author of a book on Japan titled "Trading Places," noted that in the United States a "fair" system means that a customer awards business to whoever offers the best terms.

"In Japan . . . fairness has a lot to do with loyalty," Prestowitz said. "If I've been dealing with you for 20 years, and some guy comes along and offers me a 5 percent price break, it isn't 'fair' for me to switch to him. The idea that a Toyota dealer would sell anything other than Toyotas is distasteful, not only to Toyota, but to the public at large. Any Toyota dealer that would sell Fords at the same time must have something wrong with him. In that sense, the Japanese market is not open, and it never will be."

Other analysts argue that there are ways to change even this deeply entrenched pattern.

Even though many big Japanese companies dispatch buying missions to the United States, the real problem is that few Japanese or U.S. companies are willing to make the commitment to forge Japanese-style long-term ties, said one American businessman with long experience in Tokyo.

"Procurement officers at Japanese companies are afraid to deal with newcomers, especially foreigners," the businessman said. "All these guys have heard the stories—'Company X didn't deliver.' And if a supplier company doesn't deliver, it's the procurement officer's fault."

So what is needed, this businessman said, is for top Japanese executives to make it clear that they put a very high premium on developing stable relationships with foreign firms, and to reward subordinates who do so. A handful of Japanese companies—Nippon Telegraph and Telephone Co. bought $465 million of foreign products last year—have implemented such policies as part of their import promotion programs.

As for U.S. companies, "we've done a terrible job," the businessman said. "Our understanding of this country hasn't changed since the Occupation {after World War II}. Now we're asking for a quick fix, and these relationships take a long time to develop."

January 4, 1992

Customs Rules Civic Engines are 'Foreign'

Honda Says They are Made in Ohio and Should be Duty-Free

WARREN BROWN

When Honda Motor Co. invested $670 million in a plant in Anna, Ohio, to build small engines for its Civic hatchback cars, the company said the step proved its willingness to function as an American business.

But now the U.S. Customs Service contends that the engines for 91,000 of those cars, which were assembled in Canada and shipped to the United States in 1989 and 1990, were Japanese products.

The "foreign" designation, which could strain already tense trade relations between the United States and Japan, means that the Civics should not have qualified for duty-free status. If the ruling stands, Honda will owe the U.S. government $17 million.

The Customs Service ruling, officially issued yesterday, illustrates the growing confusion in determining the nation of origin of a car in a global auto market.

Under the 1988 U.S.-Canada Free Trade Agreement, cars shipped across the U.S.-Canadian border are exempt from duty if at least 50 percent of the monetary value of their components comes from Canada or the United States.

U.S. Customs officials yesterday declined to detail their reasons for sticking a foreign label on the 1.5-liter, four-cylinder engines. But Honda officials said the designation apparently stems from the Customs Service's belief that only about 10 percent to 15 percent of the engine's value, the engine block or casing, comes from North American materials and labor, which would mean that the engine could not be counted toward the overall North American value of the cars.

"For the 2,000 Americans who work at the engine plant, this is a baffling result," said Al Kinzer, manager of the Ohio engine plant for Honda of America Manufacturing Inc.

"We know these are American engines. We make them in Ohio from aluminum ingot and molten iron. We don't understand Customs rules that don't count basic manufacturing processes such as the casting and machining we do at our engine plant," Kinzer said.

Canadian officials apparently don't understand the Custom Service's interpretation of the 50-percent rule, either. Canada last week ruled that the Ohio engines are "American."

"We have the ridiculous situation that U.S. Customs is trying to disqualify an American product that Canada has already accepted as American," said Scott Whitlock, executive vice president of Honda of America Manufacturing.

Whitlock said Honda will appeal the Custom Service's ruling.

March 3, 1992

Part 2

The International Marketing Environment

International marketing takes place in the very dynamic world environment. This world environment is typically divided, for scrutiny and better understanding, into categories such as the economic, cultural, political and legal environments. These environments plus the business and natural environment are examined in this section.

Although each culture will have its own idiosyncratic business practices, perhaps none is as intriguing as Japan's. Therefore, the business environment readings of Part 2 focus on Japan as a case study of one complex business environment. The first two readings represent a *Washington Post* series on Japan's keiretsu and the last article is an example of one person's response to the Japanese business environment.

The final readings of this section are devoted to the natural environment. Corporate environmental responsibility as well as corporate response to opportunity are highlighted in these articles. Also, the article on Greenpeace underscores the need of international marketers to consider the role of activists and other non-business groups that influence world opinion.

5 Differing International Business Environments: Japan as an Example

Japan's Corporate Connections Create Challenge for U.S. Businesses

PAUL BLUSTEIN

Now that Soviet communism has crumbled and American-style capitalism looms triumphant, let us turn to Page 654 of "The Japan Company Handbook."

On that page can be found a glimpse into a system that is proving a more formidable challenger to the U.S. economic model than communism ever did.

Listed there are the major shareholders of NEC Corp., one of Japan's premier high-tech companies and the world's largest maker of computer chips. And what is striking is how similar most of their names are. Among the shareholders are Sumitomo Life Insurance Co., Sumitomo Trust & Banking Co., Sumitomo Bank Ltd., Sumitomo Marine & Fire Insurance Co. and Sumitomo Electric Industries Ltd., themselves all giant companies.

The family resemblance is no coincidence. NEC and the Sumitomo companies belong to what the Japanese call a keiretsu. The word, meaning corporate group, defines the unique organization of Japan's economy. The keiretsu system links already powerful companies, banks and insurance firms into even more powerful groups that can dominate markets in good times, drive out competition in bad times, and provide protection from the kind of hostile takeovers and stockholder demands for quick profits that plague many American industries.

A small but colorful example of keiretsu cooperation: Go into a bar full of salarymen—white-collar workers—from a Sumitomo keiretsu company, and the beer they'll be drinking almost surely will be Asahi, brewed by a Sumitomo-affiliated company. Go into a bar full of Mitsubishi keiretsu salarymen, and the beer will be that of the Mitsubishi group brewer, Kirin.

Although most Americans have barely heard of it, the keiretsu system represents probably the single most potent threat to U.S. firms in the global battle for sales, profits and jobs. The extensive and stable alliances that Japanese companies form with each other enable them to adopt long-term strategies of market conquest that their American competitors can't afford to match.

The keiretsu system also is one of the most important obstacles to foreign companies trying to penetrate the Japanese market—at least in the opinion of the U.S. government.

Arguing that keiretsu members collude against outsiders, Washington is pressuring a reluctant Tokyo to ferret out and crack down on such practices.

Whatever the outcome of that dispute, the keiretsu issue is crucial to understanding the Japan Inc. of the 1990s and the future course of U.S.-Japan economic rivalry.

In the view of a growing number of experts on both sides of the Pacific, the network of long-term links among Japanese companies is emerging as the key to what sets Japan's economic system fundamentally apart from that of the United States.

Many of the other features that characterized the Japan Inc. of the past are diminishing in significance. Tokyo's tariffs, quotas and other legal barriers to imports have been sharply reduced. Even the legendary Ministry of International Trade and Industry has lost much of its power to steer the nation's industrial development, because Japanese companies have grown too big and rich to be influenced much by the ministry's subsidies and research programs.

"Keiretsu is the bedrock of the way Japan competes internationally," said J. Michael Farren, the U.S. undersecretary of commerce for international trade. "A lot of the other {U.S. vs. Japan} issues have been corrected; we've cut through the mush. Now we're down to bedrock."

New Era of Competition

The difference between Japanese economic bedrock and U.S. economic bedrock is looming especially large these days. As communism fades from the world scene, a new era of competition is dawning between disparate models of private enterprise.

Ultimately at stake, according to Kenichi Imai, a professor at Tokyo's Hitotsubashi University, is "a struggle for leadership in shaping the economic systems of the century to come."

This struggle will undoubtedly involve the systems of many countries besides the United States and Japan—an obvious example being Germany, which has its own distinctive corporate structure that lies somewhere between the other two. The struggle also will revolve around issues such as how much government should intervene in the economy and how much power workers should have over their jobs.

But nowhere does the struggle seem more sharply defined—or momentous— than between the keiretsu-dominated structure of Japan and the every-company-for-itself mode that prevails in the United States.

Not that the prevalence of keiretsu means that competition between companies is absent in Japan. On the contrary, some of the fiercest rivalries anywhere in the world can be found between companies like the Sumitomo group's NEC; Mitsubishi Electric Corp., a Mitsubishi group member; and Toshiba Corp. of the Mitsui group.

Nor are keiretsu rigid, isolated clubs that deal exclusively with fellow members. Members of one commonly do business with members of others. Indeed, keiretsu dividing lines are sometimes hard to distinguish because of mixed allegiances. Today's groups are much more loose and flexible than their pre-World War II ancestors, called zaibatsu, which were centrally controlled by powerful holding companies and were mostly closed to dealing with outsiders.

But keiretsu-style connections pervade Japanese industry, and they are based on practices alien to most U.S. companies. The stock of a typical Japanese company is held by scores of allied firms, creating a vast web of interlocking ownership. Moreover, Japanese manufacturers maintain extraordinarily close ties with their suppliers and distributors.

Nothing comparable exists in the United States. Giant conglomerates such as Philip Morris Companies Inc. or Minnesota Mining and Manufacturing Co. (3M), which own scores of subsidiaries in a variety of different businesses, might appear similar to the keiretsu, but they are not even close.

U.S. companies such as these are ultimately single entities with their own boards of directors and stock that is held mainly by the investing public—individual investors, mutual funds, pension funds and the like.

They fall far short of matching in size or scope a keiretsu like the Mitsubishi group, which includes Japan's largest heavy-equipment maker, fifth-largest bank, largest chemical company, biggest auto and property insurer, third-largest electric machinery maker, fifth-largest trading company, biggest beer brewer, fifth-largest automaker, second-largest camera maker, and biggest glassmaker—and in a broad sense, thousands of those companies' distributors and suppliers as well.

Even Japanese officials, who are normally loath to highlight disparities between the Japanese and U.S. systems, see keiretsu practices as creating major new economic fault lines in the post-Cold War world.

"The real choice now seems to be not between 'capitalism and socialism,' " wrote Eisuke Sakakibara, a top official of Japan's Finance Ministry, in a book published last year.

Sakakibara, who holds a PhD in economics from the University of Michigan, made a startling admission: Japan, he wrote, is so different from the United States that it shouldn't be deemed "capitalistic," even though it is a "market economy" based on competition.

What makes Japan "noncapitalistic," he said, is the mutual share-holding pacts that Japanese companies maintain with fellow keiretsu members and other corporate allies. Because of these pacts, companies are totally controlled by management and their business partners; investors—the capitalists—are powerless.

Whatever the terminology, the ramifications are far-reaching. Particularly, strong evidence suggests that the keiretsu system provides Japanese industry with an incalculable competitive edge. It also is a much less open system than America's, one in which insiders flourish and newcomers—notably foreigners—find gaining access to be exceptionally difficult.

"Which system is 'better,' I don't know," Sakakibara said in an interview. "But I personally like the Japanese system."

The Japanese Edge

Would your company ever sell its holdings of NEC stock?

The question elicited a pained sigh from Tatsuki Matsui, spokesman for Sumitomo Trust & Banking. After pondering the question for a while, Matsui arrived at his conclusion: "inconceivable."

Sumitomo Trust is a "stable shareholder" of NEC, as are most other Sumitomo group companies and some additional firms from other keiretsu. From 60 percent to 70 percent of the stock in publicly traded Japanese companies is held by stable shareholders.

Most of them would no sooner sell their stable holdings than you would sell your grandmother's diamond engagement ring. For the most part, stable shareholders have stoically held on even during the Tokyo stock market's dramatic drop of 1990-91.

Stable share holding, the cornerstone of the keiretsu system, is no mere cultural curiosity. It is a practice that gives Japanese companies "a tremendous advantage" over their competitors, said Robert Zielinski, a Tokyo-based financial analyst with Jardine Fleming Securities who this year coauthored a book on the subject.

With the bulk of their companies' shares in friendly hands, Japanese executives can forget about pressures to keep stock market investors happy. Unlike U.S. managers, they don't have to worry about producing constantly rising earnings and higher dividends.

The result is that a Japanese company "can sacrifice its profits by lowering prices to gain market share," Zielinski said. "It can endure years of losses if necessary to drive a competitor out of business. It can spend heavily on new machinery because it doesn't have to spend the money on dividends."

In the United States, companies enjoy no such mutual support and protection against pressure from investors. And while American shareholders may wield little clout as individuals, managements have learned that it is unwise to ignore the shareholders' collective power, especially since the advent of the takeover boom. U.S. corporate executives often find themselves at the mercy of capricious investors who are inclined to dump the stocks of companies that report disappointing quarterly profits. Companies whose stocks are cheapened often then become the target of a hostile takeover. Many experts believe that as a result of this unsettling financial environment, American managers tend to shy from long-term strategies that might hurt short-term profitability and cause their company's stock to fall.

But in Japan, such problems rarely distract management from pursuing an ever-bigger slice of the market, which helps account for the fact that Japanese companies are often admired for their long-term visions and yet reviled for being "predatory." The explanation is less sociological, Zielinski said, than it is "an inherent part of the Japanese system."

Shareholder Interests

The system does not rate shareholder rights highly, as Texas oilman T. Boone Pickens discovered when he made his highly publicized—and unsuccessful—effort to gain control over Koito Manufacturing Co., an auto-parts maker belonging to the Toyota Motor Corp. keiretsu.

Despite acquiring more than a quarter of Koito's shares in 1989, Pickens wasn't allowed a single seat on the company's board of directors. He complained he was being discriminated against as a foreigner.

But in Japan, it's almost unheard-of for an outsider to become a director—even an "independent" person representing shareholder interests, much less a corporate raider. A typical company's board consists entirely of its top executives and a representative or two from a fellow keiretsu company.

Most Japanese executives are unapologetic, saying their system does a better job than the United States of balancing the rights of investors, managers, workers, communities and the nation.

"We don't have to worry about hostile takeovers, and we don't have to worry about short-term profit," said Susumu Kitazawa, a senior manager in NEC's corporate planning department. "I think this system is truly beneficial."

Few experts, if any, would go so far as to suggest that the stable share-holding system deserves primary credit for Japan's postwar economic miracle. Too many other factors have played important roles.

One element that has made a major contribution is the willingness of Japanese consumers to save a high percentage of their money, which has helped provide industry with an ample pool of funds for building factories and machinery. Another factor is Japanese employees' group-oriented work ethic, which is ideally suited to high-quality manufacturing.

Another is the Ministry of International Trade and Industry's policy of nurturing key industries, which many scholars consider to have been particularly effective during the 1960s and 1970s. Still another is the government's emphasis on fostering a stable, low-inflation economic environment that helps boost business confidence. But few experts, if any, doubt that Japanese companies behave just as Zielinski says they do. In surveys, Japanese managers tend to put increasing market share at the top of their list of priorities. Several notches down they usually put earning maximum profits or boosting their company's stock price. U.S. managers tend to do the opposite.

More importantly, Japanese managers put their money where their priorities are.

They spend staggering amounts of the shareholders' money on research, plants and equipment—about $700 billion last year, a sum greater than the U.S. figure despite the fact that Japan's economy is only three-fifths as large. This year, even though interest rates have risen and the stock market is depressed, Japanese firms are continuing to plow considerably more money into long-term capital spending than are U.S. firms.

In their pursuit of market share, they are willing to endure relatively low profitability. From 1984 to 1989, the earnings of Japanese companies were a slender 2.48 percent of total assets, well under half the rate for American firms.

Out of this lower pot of profits, they pay shareholders a relatively miserly portion—the average figure is about 30 percent—in dividends. U.S. companies pay about half of their profits in dividends.

Long-Term Attachments

All of this might suggest that stable shareholders care nothing about earning a return on their investments. The fact is that they do care, but these particular investments offer something besides dividends and capital gains.

In many cases, these investments serve as symbols of long-term attachments. They are investments by suppliers in their customers' stock, by banks in their borrowers' stock and by companies seeking to maintain myriad other sorts of alliances.

Sumitomo Life Insurance, for example, is both NEC's largest shareholder and the only insurance company whose sales representatives manage to gain access to NEC's offices for the purpose of peddling insurance policies to NEC employees.

Sumitomo Bank is NEC's "main bank." This means that NEC, as one of its most important customers, can count on the bank both to take the lead in providing loans to bankroll the company's growth and stand ready to organize a bailout should business go sour.

Unlike the United States, where companies like Pan American World Airways Inc., Eastern Air Lines and Southland Corp. (owner of the 7-Eleven convenience store chain) have undergone spectacular bankruptcies, a main bank will avoid at almost all costs the blow to its prestige that would result from a major client going under.

During the late 1970s, when NEC made a giant competitive leap by investing hundreds of millions of dollars in semiconductor plants, Sumitomo Bank, along with two other Sumitomo lenders, provided one-third of the loans.

Moreover, NEC knew it could depend on the bank to come to the rescue should its strategy encounter problems; Sumitomo had saved Mazda Motor Corp. from bankruptcy after the 1973 oil crisis by installing a new management team and providing financing for the development of a new engine for Mazda cars.

"The terms on which we borrow from Sumitomo are the same as the terms provided by other financial institutions, but I think the existence of the main bank provides strong support in a mental sense," said NEC's Kitazawa. "We don't have to worry about a shortage of funds to finance a long-term strategy; even if we get into difficulty, we know our main bank will provide assistance without fail."

Stable shareholders hang on to their shares through thick and thin for reasons other than customer relations, however. A company that behaved in such an un-Japanese way as to sell off massive amounts of its stable holdings would become murahachibu—an outcast from Japan's corporate club.

"The others would sell its shares. There's an implicit contract," said Yoshitaka Kurosawa, a professor at Nihon University.

Much is at stake, after all, in the stable share-holding system. It arose in the years after World War II almost entirely for one reason: Japanese companies wanted to protect themselves against being taken over.

At the end of the war, the U.S. military occupation ordered the zaibatsu disbanded for their role in powering the Japanese military machine. Nearly 70 percent of Japanese corporate stock ended up in the hands of individuals, and the threat of takeover suddenly loomed for companies that had never had to contemplate such a fate.

So companies began accumulating each others' shares, in some cases by swapping stock in cashless transactions. They went on a final binge of buying in the early 1970s, because the government was opening the economy to greater investment from abroad, raising the scary prospect of foreign takeovers.

By the time foreign companies were legally allowed to buy Japanese firms, virtually all of the targets of opportunity had become safely ensconced in the cocoon of stable share holding.

October 6, 1991

Inside Japan Inc.
Cozy Ties Foster Political Friction

PAUL BLUSTEIN

Yoshiyuki Oguro, a soft-spoken 52-year-old with graying hair and slim build, is a foot soldier in the system that underpins Japan's competitive mastery.

Oguro is a director at one of the 200 companies belonging to the Nissan Motor Co. keiretsu, or corporate group. For 30 years, he worked at Nissan, but in 1989, in a move common among keiretsu companies, the giant automaker sent him to work at Kasai Kogyo Ltd., a Tokyo-based maker of sun visors and other products used in car interiors. Nissan owns about a quarter of Kasai Kogyo's stock and buys slightly more than 60 percent of its products.

People like Oguro are the human glue that bind keiretsu members together in a corporate structure that sharply distinguishes Japan's economy from America's. Cementing inter-company links is a vital part of corporate life in Japan because the keiretsu system is the foundation of Japanese industry—and a principal source of its economic might.

Unlike American companies, which tend to form limited ties to other companies, most major Japanese firms maintain long-lasting connections with scores of other companies. These powerful groups provide their members with mutual support and protection, better equipping them to overwhelm foreign competition in global battles for market supremacy.

In the aftermath of communism's collapse, as differences between free-market economies are coming into clearer focus, the keiretsu system is emerging as a potent alternative to U.S.-style capitalism. But the system raises questions about fairness and openness.

Consider what would happen if, for instance, an American company tried to beat Kasai Kogyo at getting Nissan's business. Could it?

"It would be difficult, I think," Oguro said. He cited the fact that Nissan, after many years of dealing with Kasai Kogyo, has gained complete faith in the quality of the company's products.

But to critics of the Japanese system, the reliability of products like Oguro's sun visors explains only part of the reason that foreign companies encounter frustrations selling to companies such as Nissan. The intimate ties between suppliers and customers lie at the root of what the critics see as a grossly insular and cozy market.

How reasonable a chance do outsiders have, critics ask, when most important companies have fortified their connections with practices like exchanging executives?

U.S. trade negotiators are leading the charge and in doing so they are going well beyond earlier U.S.-Japan trade battles, which focused on the sort of complaint lodged previously against governmental regulations such as tariffs and quotas.

Now they are mounting a diplomatic attack on the very fabric of Japan's corporate society, something the Japanese government might not be able to fundamentally change even if it wanted to. Nevertheless, in Washington's view, Tokyo must loosen keiretsu ties because, the argument goes, the system is operating as a potent, invisible barrier to foreign goods.

"Where it really matters is in the procurement offices of Japanese corporations, where there is a propensity to buy from only a couple of suppliers, frequently from within the group," said Joseph Massey, assistant U.S. special trade representative for Japan and China. "These kinds of exclusive supplier relations are a significant problem for competitive companies outside the network, both American and Japanese."

U.S. officials acknowledge that the keiretsu system affords Japanese industry some clear advantages. Japanese managers can make an all-out effort in seeking to capture markets with high-quality, low-priced goods because, as keiretsu members, they don't have to worry about earning high profits to satisfy investors.

The majority of their companies' stock is held by "stable shareholders"—friendly companies that care about maintaining business alliances rather than making a killing on their investments.

But a more competitive system is one thing, U.S. officials say. A system that unfairly restricts the flow of imports is another.

Japanese officials argue just as vigorously that the U.S. complaints are largely unjustified. Keiretsu, they say, are genuinely open to foreign companies—TRW Inc., the Cleveland-based diversified auto-parts company, is an oft-cited example—that make the effort to develop the relationships and gain the confidence of customers.

In any case, they said, some U.S. companies are just as difficult for outsiders to sell to. General Motors Corp., for example, decades ago bought many auto-parts companies and now gets about 70 percent of its components from in-house suppliers. Toyota Motor Corp. makes about 27 percent of its parts in-house. "Which system is more closed?" asked a Toyota spokesman.

There is, however, little doubt that gaining entry into the charmed keiretsu circles is an exceptionally daunting task. The practice of swapping executives like Oguro is just one of the ways in which those inside maintain their mutual connections.

Many keiretsu stage regular meetings of member company presidents. The presidents of the 30 or so major Mitsubishi group companies, for example, are known as the Kinyokai, or Friday Club, because they gather for lunch on the second Friday of each month.

By all accounts, the discussion at these meetings often revolves around social and political topics, and when the subject turns to business, members are careful to steer away from anything that might smack of the hatching of a conspiracy.

But the meetings underscore how group harmony is promoted at all corporate levels and in all sorts of places, from restaurants to bars to golf courses.

Some keiretsu publish group magazines and newsletters such as Sumitomo Quarterly and the Mitsubishi Monitor. Mitsubishi even maintains a matchmaking organization to help men from one group company meet women from another. It's called the Diamond Family Club and in 20 years has produced 1,600 marriages.

'Exclusionary Effects'

Even the harshest critics of keiretsu do not claim that presidents' lunches or dating clubs make a major difference in corporate purchasing decisions.

But these practices, augmented as they are by mutual share holding and exchanges of personnel, reflect the emphasis that the Japanese place on anshinkan, a word that means "peace of mind" or "feeling of confidence."

In group-oriented Japan, it is especially important to have anshinkan concerning the people and companies you are doing business with. The trouble is, this clubbiness has a dark side.

Peter Young, director of international business at Guardian Industries Corp., a Michigan glassmaker, recounts the story of a meeting he held in Tokyo in May to deliver a sales pitch to the purchasing manager of a major Japanese company.

"We've got a problem," the apologetic purchasing manager said, according to Young. Guardian's glass is highly competitive, the man said, but if he were to buy from Guardian, his current Japanese glass supplier would be incensed—and the ramifications could be serious. "The company we currently buy glass from would tell its keiretsu sister company to stop selling us a crucial raw material," Young quotes the purchasing manager as saying. So, no sale.

There is evidence suggesting that Young's experience is a common one. Robert Z. Lawrence, an economist at the John F. Kennedy School of Public Affairs at Harvard University, found in a recent study that in industries dominated by companies with the tightest keiretsu affiliations, imports tend to be abnormally low.

The study doesn't constitute hard proof of anti-import discrimination by keiretsu, but "it is consistent with the position that there are exclusionary effects," Lawrence said.

Many Japanese officials, executives and academics contend that foreign critics such as Lawrence misunderstand how keiretsu function.

The critics, they say, fail to grasp two vital points:

Closeness between suppliers and customers boosts efficiency. "Have you read 'The Machine That Changed the World?' " is a question often asked of foreigners these days by Japanese officials and industrialists.

The book, published last year and based on a five-year Massachusetts Institute of Technology study, lionizes the keiretsu supplier system as a vital part of the "lean production" method that has enabled Toyota, Nissan and other Japanese automakers to overwhelm their U.S. and European competitors.

As the book points out, Japanese automakers and their keiretsu suppliers feel that they have a major stake in each other's success. So in buying steering wheels for a new car model, for instance, Japanese auto manufacturers don't simply hand a group of competing suppliers a design and place an order with the lowest bidder, as their U.S. competitors are wont to do.

Rather, the auto companies expect their keiretsu suppliers to help design the steering wheels and constantly improve them; the price is subject to frequent negotiation based on both companies' intimate knowledge of the other's needs and problems.

"We don't just say, 'Reduce costs 5 percent,' " said Koichiro Noguchi, a Toyota purchasing executive. "We work together with them to identify wasteful parts of the production process."

According to the MIT study's authors, the system works considerably better than the Western model because "suppliers don't have to constantly look over their shoulders" for fear of being dropped for a lower bidder.

"Instead, they can get on with the job of improving their own operations with the knowledge that they will be fairly rewarded for doing so," the study said.

Keiretsu are highly varied and loosely organized. "It is very complex even to decide which company belongs to which group," said Ryutaro Komiya, an economics professor who is currently director general of the Ministry of International Trade and Industry Research Institute. "For instance, the newspapers say Sony belongs to the Mitsui group. But Sony people don't think so."

The keiretsu issue, Komiya concluded, is "essentially a bogey."

Keiretsu lines sometimes are blurry. Kasai Kogyo, for example, sells not only to Nissan but to an affiliate of Honda Motor Co. as well. Mitsubishi companies hold chunks of Mitsui and Sumitomo company shares, and vice versa.

Hitachi Ltd., the giant electronics company, is a member of three different keiretsu—the Fuyo, Sanwa and Dai-Ichi Kangyo groups. Still other companies have such divided loyalties that they are deemed independent; an example is Nippon Steel Corp., the world's largest steelmaker.

But the complexities shouldn't obscure the main issue—which is that stable, group-oriented links "are pervasive in Japanese industrial organization," and that their impact is profound, said Michael Gerlach, a professor at the University of California at Berkeley.

Gerlach's research shows that while some companies such as Sony Corp. and Nippon Steel are less firmly attached than others are to a major keiretsu, virtually all large Japanese firms maintain essentially the same sort of relationships with groups of stable shareholders, closely-knit suppliers and customers, and a "main bank" that stands ready to provide emergency financial help if necessary.

What is more, these links "are part of a larger family of relationships," Gerlach said. In Japan's electronics industry, for example, a company's main bank is usually the main bank of its biggest suppliers as well.

Plain common sense suggests that foreign criticism of these links are not entirely misplaced, the Nihon Keizai Shimbun, Japan's leading financial daily, editorialized recently.

Keiretsu may enhance Japanese companies' productivity, the newspaper said, "But such relationships have obviously hampered free and fair competition among firms here."

Which System Will Change?

One evening last May, a jet-lagged Charles H. Dallara sank back in a chair shortly after arriving in Tokyo for trade talks and reflected on the problems he was encountering as lead U.S. negotiator on the keiretsu issue.

U.S. officials were making progress with the Japanese on a number of other contentious trade disputes, but very little on keiretsu, said Dallara, who has since left the position of assistant secretary of the treasury for international affairs.

"An issue so fundamental to the structure of the Japanese economy," he said wearily, "is something that their government just finds very difficult to deal with."

U.S. negotiators are always voicing frustration about the problems of getting Japan to change its ways, but the keiretsu issue may prove to be in a class by itself.

Part of the problem is that Washington itself can't figure out how to alter such an ingrained system.

The United States is urging Japan to strengthen its notoriously lax antitrust enforcement on the grounds that keiretsu companies allegedly work together to keep competitors out.

Washington also wants Tokyo to change various rules to boost the power of individual stockholders, who have virtually no clout under Japan's stable share-holding system.

But even if Tokyo were inclined to yield on every point—which it is not—the measures proposed by Washington would result in only modest change in the influence of keiretsu.

In the meantime, some of Japan's toughest critics are questioning whether the keiretsu system requires a more drastic response. Their theory is that Japanese companies are effectively playing under such different rules, and responding to such different cues from the market, that they should somehow be restricted from freely playing on U.S. turf.

A sign of this hardening view came recently from Rep. Richard A. Gephardt (D-Mo.) who, when he introduced a new trade bill aimed at penalizing Tokyo, said:

"In my view, the keiretsu system lies at the heart of the incompatibility" between the Japanese and U.S. economies.

But others say it is unfair to single out Japan on this score, because some other countries, especially in Europe, have systems with keiretsu-like features. Germany, for example, has a main-bank tradition in which banks own stock in their borrowers, and companies establish loose alliances with other borrowers from the same bank group. "We really have two economies that are at two extremes of what is perhaps a continuum," said UC Berkeley's Gerlach. "Japan is at one end. But the U.S. may be at the other extreme, along with other Anglo-Saxon countries including the U.K. that have a strong history of antitrust enforcement, a strong notion that stockholder rights are important and a belief that long-term business relationships are bad if they're anti-competitive." Germany, Italy and France fall somewhere in the middle, he said.

How a country positions itself involves some tough trade-offs. The keiretsu system "is likely more efficient, more productive over the long term," Gerlach said. "On the other hand, as long as the system remains one in which insiders have the advantage, there's going to be a perception that it's a system in which everyone doesn't have equal access."

Learning From Each Other

So which system will "win?"

In the struggle to shape the economic systems of the next century, will Japanese-style efficiency prevail at the expense of American-style openness? Or vice versa?

Japanese officials are acutely aware that their nation depends for its prosperity on maintaining good relations with its trading partners, and they recognize that the biggest of those trading partners—the United States—will insist that Japan move at least part of the way toward the Anglo-Saxon model.

Eisuke Sakakibara, a senior official of Japan's Finance Ministry, said that the United States should not try to force fundamental changes in the way Japanese business works. But, he acknowledged: "The system has some characteristics of a club society, and it has to open up."

Already Japanese auto and electronics companies are trying to bring more foreign companies into their keiretsu supplier networks, although their requirements for quality and delivery are stringent.

In one recent example, Nissan announced that the Japanese subsidiaries of Texas Instruments Inc. and Garrett Turbo Inc. would join its 200-company network of primary suppliers. Three other foreign-owned firms had been admitted earlier.

But the United States, too, may undergo some substantial changes in its industrial structure as a result of the relentless, withering competition U.S. companies are encountering from Japan.

A number of U.S. companies, impressed with what they have seen of the keiretsu system, are emulating some of its aspects.

"I think a lot of American companies are going to move in the direction of having a close relationship between customer and supplier," said William Franklin, who heads the Japanese operations of Weyerhaeuser Co., the giant lumber and paper company.

Weyerhaeuser is one of the small but growing band of foreign firms that have been able to penetrate some of the keiretsu. The company has grown to admire how its keiretsu partners "don't flop around depending on what the price is today," Franklin said.

As a result, he added, Weyerhaeuser's U.S. operations have been "moving very definitely" in the direction of more stable bonds with suppliers and customers.

"I think it's much more likely that we {Americans} will become more that way," Franklin said, "than that they will become less that way."

(Special correspondent Yasuharu Ishizawa contributed to this report.)

October 7, 1991

Regions:

Tending to the Care and Feeding
of Foreign Businesses

JANET BRAUNSTEIN

Jim Hettinger landed the big one with a good fish story.

In March 1984, after more than six years of sniffing around for a U.S. plant site, Japanese auto parts giant Nippondenso Co. sent a team to scout the Fort Custer Industrial Park in Battle Creek.

Battle Creek's Hettinger already had scouted the Nippondenso team and learned its leader was an avid fisherman.

So he couched his sales pitch for Battle Creek in a story about a fisherman who "gets lost on a lake in the fog. But when the fog burns off, he can see where the other boats are. That's where the fish are schooling."

Hettinger, president of Battle Creek Unlimited, a nonprofit corporation created to build and run the Fort Custer park on part of a shuttered military base, repeated the story several times during the Nippondenso visit.

The team went back to Japan, and Hettinger waited. And waited.

Nippondenso's decision came at 6:30 one morning in August, five months later. The telex message read: "We have decided to catch a trout where you have said the fish are schooling."

Hettinger's predecessor at Battle Creek Unlimited had begun courting Nippondenso in the late 1970s. By the time Nippondenso selected Battle Creek as its site, the town best known as the home of Kellogg cereal was already home to one of the nation's largest concentrations of Japanese automotive suppliers.

A dozen Japanese firms in Fort Custer now employ more than 2,000 workers. About 200 Japanese executives and engineers have settled in Battle Creek, a city of 92,000 residents 130 miles west of Detroit. They send their children to the town's schools and share bowling leagues and golf tournaments with their American employees and co-workers.

Nippondenso Manufacturing U.S.A. Inc. was the biggest fish of all. Its 800 workers—soon to be more than 1,000—build automotive air-conditioning and heating components for Mazda, Honda, Toyota, Subaru-Isuzu, Ford, Chrysler, Mitsubishi and General Motors.

"I thought I'd lost them many times," Hettinger said, but over the years he had learned that "chasing Japanese investment is a long-term project. It takes them five years to make a decision and they implement it overnight."

Americans, though, "decide overnight and take five years to implement it." Fortunately for Battle Creek, the town had a head start.

In the early 1970s, the federal government's decision to close most of the Camp Custer U.S. Army base threatened to severely damage Battle Creek's economy.

To fill that hole, then-Mayor Frederick Bridges formed Battle Creek Unlimited on the theory that foreign companies doing business in the United States eventually would need to produce in this country. Long before dozens of other American cities began tripping over themselves in the scramble to lure Japanese investment, Battle Creek's leaders were learning where to find potential Japanese tenants and how to attract them.

"The first thing that impressed me was the hopelessness of what we were trying to do" in overcoming Michigan's reputation as a state with foul weather and surly unions, Hettinger said.

They emphasized Battle Creek's location between Detroit and Chicago, a strong local work ethic, the family-oriented small-town atmosphere and their town's willingness to "welcome all who settle here." It worked.

Paul Williams, a member of Battle Creek Unlimited's marketing team, also is the Lakeview public schools superintendent in south Battle Creek. He encouraged Japanese families to move into his district, and then he opened a Japanese-language Saturday school. "We're trying to be good hosts," Williams said.

In the late 1970s, when Hettinger made the first of his 12 trips to Japan on behalf of Battle Creek, "you could turn over any rock and find three companies" looking to locate in the U.S. market, he said.

Today, however, Hettinger said, "turn over any rock in Japan and you'll find three state agents" trying to lure Japanese firms to Kentucky or Tennessee or Indiana. "It's a whole lot more difficult," he said.

As part of Bridges' master plan, Fort Custer applied for and received federal sanction as a foreign trade zone, making it a port of entry, albeit a landlocked one. No duty is paid on imported materials and parts until those parts are installed elsewhere on American-built products.

The city has invested about $25 million in the park, including tax breaks for 25 of the 30 American, Japanese and European manufacturers there. About 60 businesses employ 5,500 people on 1,000 acres.

The first Japanese company, Hi-Lex Corp., opened a sales office in Fort Custer in 1976. Hi-Lex began making mechanical automotive cables at a 460-worker Fort Custer factory in 1978, the year Honda began building motorcycles in Ohio.

Compared to the hundreds of millions of dollars Detroit has spent securing land for two auto factories—GM's Poletown factory and Chrysler's North Jefferson plant for a total of about 6,000 jobs —Battle Creek's financial investment could be called minimal.

But the investment of time, patience and cultural understanding is another matter.

While the search for new tenants continues, Hettinger says the handful of people at his agency find that tending the blooming domestic and foreign businesses they already have attracted is a full-time job.

"Our emphasis is on after-care. We don't offer free land like everyone does," Hettinger said. The agency has arranged training for 3,000 local residents who have since been hired. A new skills facility under construction at the park will train workers for individual companies' needs. Battle Creek Unlimited helps foreign executives solve visa problems, find housing and cut through government red tape—as when it spent six weeks obtaining a customs reclassification for a special steel, not made in this country, that a German company needed to import. It finds trees for landscaping, obtains emergency loans and low-interest construction bonds and helps companies test-market new products.

One of its main tasks is helping foreign-owned companies feel welcome in the community and helping American workers make the adjustment to Japanese management.

At I I Stanley Co., a joint venture between two Japanese companies that make automotive lighting, David Bailey's title is personnel administrator. In addition to hiring employees, he is responsible for "making sure the associates are happy with the esthetics and the placement of machinery."

But his job also includes anything from making sure the grass is mowed and the ponds are clean to seeing that the parking lot at I I Stanley's new $40 million, 50-acre factory stays puddle-free.

After work, Bailey is one of 10 American employees who take free Japanese language and culture lessons from an interpreter at the plant, while Japanese colleagues study English in the next room.

Stanley production workers, 33 years old on average, start at $7.26 an hour and work up to an average $8.50 an hour, a pay rate little more than half that of a United Auto Workers member in Detroit but comparable to other medium-sized factories in Battle Creek, Bailey said.

By 1991, the factory that makes tail lights for Chrysler, Mitsubishi, Ford, GM, Mazda, Toyota and Suzuki will employ 500 workers.

For cities just entering the bidding for Japanese business, it's probably too late, Hettinger said. Japanese automakers and suppliers have nearly finished their North American production base.

But for Battle Creek, the task of helping its Japanese employers grow and assimilate will continue. For new business, Hettinger is turning his attention to Europe, where some suppliers are wakening to the need to produce in the United States.

October 22, 1989

The International Economic Environment 6

Sri Lanka's 'Model' Economy in Ruins

STEVE COLL

On many mornings, soon after the sun rises, steady traffic begins to flow both across and below the Ja-Ela Bridge. Vans and buses haul thousands of workers across the span to their jobs in a bustling free trade zone two miles north of here. But as they pass, the commuters often stop to look at the gruesome traffic in the Dunagama River below—the bodies of people killed in the night and dumped to float to the sea.

The two-way traffic here is emblematic of this island nation's tragedy. Just six years ago, sleepy and socialist Sri Lanka seemed on the verge of an economic miracle. Aggressive free market liberalization and a huge dose of foreign investment had pushed the country, previously ranked among the poorest in the world, into overdrive. "We were the model economy. People thought we would be the next Singapore or Hong Kong," said Ronnie De Mel, the country's finance minister from 1977 to 1988, now living in exile.

Today Sri Lanka more closely resembles Lebanon. Civil war has claimed more than 5,000 lives this year. An insurgency by radical youths in the south nearly overthrew the island's elected administration earlier this summer, until a killing spree by government death squads at least temporarily squashed the rebellion. And the "model economy," crippled by strikes and inflation, is a wreck.

How did so much go wrong so quickly?

At a time when aggressive free market liberalization programs are underway in countries as diverse as Poland and Pakistan, the Sri Lankan experience appears to offer some important cautionary lessons to nations seeking a quick economic turnaround.

Democratic Sri Lanka's problems are complex and its history of ethnic tension is in some aspects unique. And there no uniform agreement about what went wrong with the country's experiment with capitalism. Some conservatives believe Sri Lanka didn't move fast enough to encourage a free market economy. Others, mainly committed leftists, think it went too fast.

But in several key areas—education, worker training, technology and the distribution of resources—Sri Lankan analysts holding divergent ideological views agree that serious and avoidable mistakes were made during the country's dramatic liberalization, which began in the late 1970s. These mistakes, they said, have contributed directly to the island's present state of virtual political anarchy.

"We didn't realize that once you start off deregulating with an open economy, so many other changes have to take place," said Ranil Wickremasinghe, the minister of industry and a leading member of the governing United National Party.

Before its liberalization began, Sri Lanka represented a paradox among developing countries. Its literacy rate, more than 90 percent, was the highest in the Third World. Life expectancy on the island was 70 years, far greater than any other low-income developing country.

But despite its social health, Sri Lanka was poor. Per capital income lagged at less than $400 per year, only slightly above that of India and the poorer nations of sub-Saharan Africa. Socialistic, inward-looking, bureaucratic and moribund, the island's economy had stagnated by the mid-1970s. Unemployment ran at 26 percent in 1977, inflation more than 35 percent and the annual rate of economic growth was less than 2 percent.

That's when the experiment with free market capitalism began.

Elected with a comfortable majority in 1977, the UNP tried to tear down the protectionist and bureaucratic wall that held the economy in check. The government abolished exchange and many price controls. It set up free trade zones to create jobs and attract foreign capital. Billions of dollars poured in—from the International Monetary Fund, the World Bank and international banks such as Citicorp and Bank of America—to build dams and power stations and new businesses.

The island boomed. By 1983, unemployment had fallen to 12 percent. The annual economic growth rate more than trebled and the rates of savings and investments skyrocketed. Five hundred new businesses began with foreign capital, many in the garment industry, which quickly became the country's biggest exporter. Attracted by glistening beaches and new five-star hotels, tourists flocked to the island—half a million by 1983.

Then the island blew up. Riots erupted in the north and then the south, fueled by ancient enmity between Sri Lanka's ethnic Sinhalese majority and its Tamil minority. A numbing cycle of violent reprisals, carried out mainly by educated, unemployed and well-armed youths, began to escalate. Radical groups seeking independence for the Tamils in the north proliferated and gained strength. By last summer, killing sprees and strikes had undone most of the economic gains from liberalization.

"Another few years of this and we'll be back to square one," said former finance minister De Mel.

The government is widely accused of failing to address the expectations of a generation of young people at the same time it fanned their hopes with the promises of economic opportunity.

"With liberalization, you gave these rural Sinhalese and Tamil students the impression that they could gain not only an education, but could achieve upward mobility. This turned out to be not true," said Neelam Tiruchelvan, a Harvard-trained attorney and Tamil activist. "The close 1978 phase did not radicalize Sri Lankan society—it created middle-class aspirations that could not be fulfilled."

Tiruchelvan's assessment is widely shared in Sri Lanka today, although it is a thesis that is difficult to test scientifically. Still, it is supported in dozens of conversations with young Sri Lankans around the capital and in the south.

Typical was the bitter comment of an unemployed cook, N.M. De Silva, literate in English and with a high school education: "I know that I can do what they can do," he said, pointing from his perch on a rock above the ocean to the office towers of Colombo's new sky line. "I have done it already {in school}. But there are no jobs. It is very difficult."

Economists, sociologists, minority activists and a growing number of UNP politicians cite important failings in several areas as reasons for stagnant job growth:

Education: The economy changed during the 1980s but the school system didn't. Sri Lanka's highly regarded British-style schools were designed to churn out qualified civil servants for the colonial administration and, after independence, for the island's sprawling socialist bureaucracy. Classrooms emphasized literacy and the liberal arts, not science or vocational training, meaning that few graduates were prepared for the kinds of jobs available in a dynamic economy.

Less than a quarter of Sri Lanka's college students have concentrated on science courses during the 1980s, compared with 60 percent in Singapore and nearly 50 percent in South Korea and Hong Kong.

Said Nilam Goonatileke, assistant director of the Marga Institute, Sri Lanka's leading private think tank: "The problem is people coming out of the universities, saying, 'I'm ready,' and the country says, 'For what?' "

Planning: Tearing down protectionist barriers created more than 35,000 jobs in the garment industry on the island after 1977, but it also wiped out 40,000 cottage industry weavers in rural villages whose inefficient looms were protected by the old tariff—in effect, Sri Lanka's governments didn't even notice until 1984, when the riots led by rural unemployed were underway.

Nor did the government try to match new jobs with the unemployed. The biggest area of new job creation in the last decade has been in agriculture—where few university graduates with degrees in Sinhalese history are willing to work.

Technological growth: After throwing open its doors to foreign investment, Sri Lanka made little effort to attract technology—such as electronics, computers or even basic manufacturing—for future growth.

In the free trade zones where foreign companies receive big breaks on taxes, tariffs and work rules, most investors have concentrated on low technology, labor-intensive businesses such as textiles and basic assembly. That means few workers have acquired technological skills with which to start new businesses in competition with the foreign investors.

"We have not been able to attract companies with the high-tech inputs," said Niffanka Wijewardane, chairman of the government department that runs the zone. "That has been our biggest problem up until now."

UNP officials say these imbalances were inadvertent rather than deliberate, a product of administrative bumbling, not the perpetuation of a ruling elite. "Beyond the macroeconomic policies, we hadn't planned where all this {foreign} money was going," said Industry Minister Wickremasinghe. "Sometimes you just dug up a project because the money was just sitting there."

Plans are being made to develop trade zones and harbors in the south and north. And the government job bank effectively has been closed. President Ranasinghe Premadasa, elected amid widespread violence late last year, has even encouraged new companies investing on the island to "link up" with rural villages, providing employment directly to areas where the radical insurgents have flourished. The question for Sri Lanka now is whether the reforms have come too late. Although the pace of killing on the island has eased at least temporarily in recent weeks, political and economic stability seem a long way off.

Acknowledging that mistakes were made but arguing that smarter political management could have prevented Sri Lanka's anarchy, De Mel said that all things considered, he'd do it over again.

"With education and liberalization, rising expectations come," said De Mel, the principal architect of the liberalization. "It is very difficult for Third World countries to meet all of those expectations, particularly among the youth. But is that a reason to keep our people backward? I don't think so. You have to take that risk."

October 10, 1989

Rising Third World Energy Demand Imperils Economies, Environment:

Report Outlines Dilemma Of Poorest, Most Crowded Nations

THOMAS W. LIPPMAN

A rapid increase in energy demand in developing countries threatens to undermine their fragile economies and negate environmental gains in the industrialized nations, according to a new analysis by the congressional Office of Technology Assessment.

The report dramatizes the dilemma facing many of the world's poorest and most densely populated nations: the more their people gain access to motor vehicles, mechanized farm equipment and modern appliances, the more they have to spend on power plants and imported oil and the greater the risk of environmental degradation.

"Energy services are essential for economic growth {and} improved living standards," said the report, part of a study of Third World energy problems requested by several congressional committees.

But providing those services means buying oil and building power plants in countries already burdened by debt, damming rivers and inundating farmland for hydroelectric facilities and burning more coal.

Unrestrained use of coal, especially in China, along with increased urban bus fleets and the burning of wood for fuel in the poorest countries, contributes to the worldwide emissions of greenhouse gases believed to be responsible for global warming, according to the report.

The global warming debate has begun to focus international attention on energy and environmental problems in the developing countries. Delegates from more than 100 nations will gather in Chantilly, Va., on Feb. 4 to begin negotiations on an international agreement to limit greenhouse gas emissions.

"This will be one of the focuses of any global warming treaty," said Alden Meyer, director of the climate change and energy policy program at the Union of Concerned Scientists. "You can't ask these countries to forgo development, so you have to make it possible for them to develop in a more environmentally friendly way . . . . You don't want them to follow the fossil fuel model." "Concern about this was deader than dead when we were formed in 1984," said Deborah Blevis, executive director of the Washington-based international Institute for Energy Conservation. "All the arguments we have been making since '84 are coming out now."

Blevis said most projected growth in energy consumption "is disproportionately going to occur in the developing countries or Eastern Europe. They can least afford an out-of-whack energy system."

Jessica Mathews, vice president of the World Resources Institute, said the problem of Third World energy demand is "a deeply neglected area" because the World Bank has not made energy efficiency part of its development loan policy and because "American energy policy analysts have a little bit of a credibility problem. We ought not to be offering energy policy thinking when we don't have an energy policy of our own."

According to the OTA report, however, the issue of energy use in the Third World and its effect on the global environment can no longer be ignored. The increasing consumption helps to drive up oil prices, adds to air pollution and undermines the international banking system through energy loans that cannot be repaid.

Developing countries accounted for 17 percent of world commercial energy consumption in 1973, the report said. That figure is now 23 percent and is expected to rise to 40 percent by 2020. But among the countries classified as developing by the World Bank, the rate of consumption growth is vastly uneven.

The 50 countries of Africa consume less than 3 percent of world commercial energy. China, India and Brazil account for 45 percent. China alone will account for more than one third of the expected increase in the next 30 years, according to the report.

Meeting projected growth in electricity demand will require investment of 5125 billion a year, twice the current level, the report said, citing World Bank estimates. In countries that cannot provide enough electricity to meet demand for heat and light among their fast-growing populations, consumers will be forced to use more and more "biomass"—wood, crop wastes and animal dung—with potentially devastating environmental and social consequences, the report warned.

"Overuse of biomass already contributes to environmental degradation" through soil erosion and smoky emissions, the report said. "Moreover, gathering traditional supplies of fuel wood is time-consuming, exhausting work frequently undertaken by women and children, who are thus diverted from other activities (education and farming) that could eventually improve their productivity and living conditions."

A later OTA report will make recommendations about policy and technology for dealing with the Third World energy problem.

January 21, 1991

Latin America Told to Temper Market Economics

U.N. Regional Commission Cites Skewed Income Distribution as Challenge For Leaders

EUGENE ROBINSON

Latin America's young democratic governments should be cautious in their rush to sell unprofitable state-owned enterprises to the private sector, an influential United Nations organization recommended today. It said the new leaders must aim their development policies at bridging a widening gap between rich and poor if they hope to escape the economic doldrums of the 1980s.

In studies released to kick off a week-long conference that is to open here Thursday, the U.N. Economic Commission for Latin America and the Caribbean challenged the new conventional wisdom—espoused by Presidents Fernando Collor de Mello of Brazil and Carlos Menem of Argentina, among others—that top-heavy government sectors must be pared back and development left to a largely unregulated market.

"Privatization is fine in certain instances, but it is not something to put on a pedestal and venerate," said Gert Rosenthal, who heads the Santiago-based U.N. commission. "Making the state smaller does not resolve certain basic issues, like equity. Who is going to take care of the people who are left out?"

The commission also concludes that the U.S.-sponsored Brady Plan for debt reduction provides a framework for solving the region's $400 billion-plus foreign debt problem, but that it will succeed only if public funds committed to the project are tripled to at least $90 billion.

The commission helped define Latin America's development policies of the 1950s and 1960s—policies that now are under widespread attack as too state-oriented. Under the late Raul Prebisch, the commission advocated protected economies in which industrial development is planned by the state and carried out largely by government-owned enterprises, a system aimed at producing goods for internal markets. That strategy provided impressive gains for many countries—especially Brazil, now among the world's 10 largest economies—but it collapsed under the debt burden and the global economic shocks of the early 1980s.

The 1980s were a "lost decade" for the region, with real income levels stagnating or falling amid persistent inflation that last year reached nearly 1,000 percent for the region as a whole.

Leaders in the region have spent the last several years looking for a new set of principles to guide a recovery. Today's recommendations by the commission, which will be discussed here over the next week by economic planning and finance ministers, are an attempt to lay out a workable new philosophy.

The analysis represents a significant shift in the commission's thinking, in that it recognizes that deregulation and sale of state industries are in some cases useful, and it sees Latin America's economic future in becoming competitive internationally rather than focused narrowly on the home market.

But the studies advocate a continued large role for governments in fostering development, particularly in light of the growing social inequalities in Latin America.

"It is estimated . . . that in 1980 some 112 million people of Latin America and the Caribbean (35 percent of the households) were living below the poverty line," the commission said. "By 1986, this figure had increased to 164 million, representing approximately 38 percent of the households."

The disparities are perhaps greatest in Brazil, where some economists have estimated that the richest fifth of the population now has 28 times more wealth than the poorest fifth—one of the most skewed of income distributions.

The U.N. commission notes that drives to improve health care and education in many countries have stalled, a situation that "will have extremely adverse potential implications" for Latin America's prospects of joining a technology-based, post-industrial world economy.

A new generation of leaders has sought to attack the "stagflation" malaise by imposing severe economic adjustment plans and announcing efforts to sell off state enterprises, deregulate and let the free market manage.

Most of this has not yet taken place, and in many cases the leaders' praise for the free market has gone well beyond their willingness to take quick action on issues like protective tariffs and sweetheart subsidies for local businesses sectors. Still, the recent trend seems clear.

Last week, for example, bidders began rooting around inside Argentina's telephone monopoly Entel, with an eye toward deciding what parts of the huge business they might want to buy.

"Perhaps our main dispute with this orthodox approach is that it is too doctrinaire," Rosenthal said in an interview. "Why shove down every country's throat a preconceived notion of how to do things?"

What is not addressed, Rosenthal said, is the issue of social equity. "No matter how fast these economies grow," he said, "demographic trends mean that they are still going to have serious problems. To accommodate all the people trying to enter the work force would require unreasonable levels of growth."

The U.N. commission advocates that governments sell state industries and deregulate only selectively, that they adopt regulations and incentives to encourage industrial sectors they deem important and that they consider expenditures in such areas as education not simple altruism but necessary investments for the future. Likewise, Rosenthal said, the commission doubts that vital environmental issues—the fate of the Brazilian rain forest is a prime example—can be handled without firm government guidance.

The commission recommends emphasizing labor-intensive development projects that would thus have a strong impact on unemployment or others that seek to achieve competitiveness through boosts in productivity rather than suppression of wages.

The agency cites as exemplary the growth of Chilean agriculture, booming exports of fresh flowers from Colombia, poultry farming in Brazil and an aggressive Argentine computer maker.

May 3, 1990

7 The International Cultural Environment

Cheers, Jeers Greet Disney Debut in Europe

WILLIAM DROZDIAK

Five years in the making at a cost of more than $4 billion, Europe's first Disneyland opened its doors today to enthusiastic cheers from the young at heart and scornful snubs from French intellectuals who lament it as a "cultural Chernobyl."

Doves were released into the air, trumpets blared a fanfare and children sang a multilingual chorus of "It's a Small World," as Disney's chairman and chief executive officer, Michael D. Eisner, surveyed his new domain from the Chateau de la Belle au Bois Dormant (Sleeping Beauty's Castle) and declared that Disney's fourth theme park "represents a return to our roots." Disney's other foreign venture is in Japan.

Seeking to reassure those who abhor the vast playground—one-fifth the size of Paris—as a Trojan horse of American cultural invasion, Eisner sought to persuade the continental crowd that the Disney phenomenon was largely inspired by European fairy tales—including Germany's Snow White, England's Peter Pan, Italy's Pinocchio and France's Cinderella.

Even before today's opening, Europe's biggest construction project after the Channel Tunnel linking England and France had stirred heated controversy. Actors, writers, philosophers and essayists have warned that French youngsters could succumb to Disney's wholesome frivolities the way they have fallen for the Big Mac, which enjoys booming sales at McDonald's outlets in Paris.

Leading cultural arbiters, such as writer Marguerite Duras and critic Bernard Pivot, worry that teenagers will abandon their own rich heritage in favor of roaring down Euro Disney's Big Thunder Mountain railroad, flying aboard Dumbo the Elephant or ogling the 3-D spectacle of Michael Jackson's Captain EO.

People living near the site also have complained, but for different reasons. They loathe the prospect of noisy fireworks shows 120 nights a year, and they tell civic authorities that the horn-tooting by Euro Disney trains makes their dogs howl and their geese honk incessantly. Those concerns seemed overwhelmed, however, by today's turnout in spite of a suburban train strike that crippled public transport to the park site 20 miles east of Paris. Thousands of visitors from all over Europe jammed the entrances as early as dawn, prompting Disney executives to open the park an hour early to relieve congestion and avoid aggravating public sensibilities. Disney officials, citing company policy, would not announce the day's total attendance, but it was considerably less than the 200,000 that had been predicted by some French commentators.

When the communist-led transport union announced a strike to coincide with opening day, Disney executives tried to keep the trains going by offering operators and their families free tickets to the park.

The rank-and-file response was overwhelmingly positive, Disney officials said, but union leaders dismissed the offer, saying it did nothing to meet their demands for the state-owned transport system to install more modern equipment and hire more personnel.

George Sarre, France's secretary of state for transport, had appealed to the public "to show patience and wisdom" by postponing visiting the park until May, but many decided to come anyway.

Serge Gallier, 39, a clothing merchant from Villepinte, north of Paris, roused his wife Maissa and their son Gorka, 7, well before sunrise to drive the short distance to Euro Disney before 6 a.m. They were the first in line when ticket windows opened an hour later and were rewarded with free passes and a VIP tour as Disney's "First Family."

A bomb planted at the park toppled a power-line pylon last Saturday and caused brief electrical outages to the site's six hotels, but fears of a nightmarish traffic snarl failed to materialize, and California-style sunny weather glowed over the new Magic Kingdom on its inaugural weekend.

In launching Disney's biggest business gamble, Eisner lauded more than 1,700 European companies and 10,000 workers involved in building the park. Quoting Anatole France that "to know is nothing at all, to imagine is everything," Eisner said Euro Disney would become a living monument to the French axiom that "the most wasted day is that on which we don't laugh."

Roy Disney, the company vice chairman and nephew of the founder, said, "More than a few drops of French blood flowed through Uncle Walt's veins." He cited the family's origins in the little Norman town of Desinee-sur-Mer, which his ancestors left nearly a millenium ago during the Norman conquest of England. And he also contended that Walt Disney, who served in the ambulance corps here during World War I and was awarded the Legion of Honor, always said that "he got some of his best ideas from France."

The emphasis on Disney's European origins was aimed at countering the rise of chauvinistic resentment in recent weeks, as Left Bank intellectuals and "France first" right-wingers joined forces to challenge Euro Disney and its momentous impact on the French cultural landscape.

"A horror made of cardboard, plastic and appalling colors, a construction of hardened chewing gum and idiotic folklore straight out of comic books written for these obese Americans," complained conservative polemicist Jean Cau. The far-right National Front accused Euro Disney of trying "to impose the American language on France" and urged the nation to boycott the park until it collapses into bankruptcy.

Robert Fitzpatrick, a former professor of French literature who serves as president of Euro Disney, maintains that the support Disney has received, from France's Socialist government as well as the public at large, far outweighs the plaintive cries of cultural malcontents.

No French officials attended today's opening ceremony, but Fitzpatrick said "eight to 10 cabinet ministers" showed up discreetly at the park's preview party Saturday night. He said he would leave it up to the ministers to reveal their identities.

President Francois Mitterrand bestowed lukewarm praise on the Disney park in a television interview today for "boosting economic activity and bringing jobs to the region." But he said that in his personal view, "it's not really my cup of tea, culturally speaking."

The site east of Paris was chosen over 200 competing bids, largely because of its proximity to Europe's most affluent population centers and the attractive subsidies offered by French authorities. To woo the 12,000 jobs pledged by Disney, the French government financed a major extension of its high-speed rail network and new access roads to its highway grid to facilitate the flow of visitors from all over Europe.

Fitzpatrick said he is confident Euro Disney will draw the 11 million visitors needed to break even this year. But a vacation or a weekend stay will not be cheap—even for prosperous Europeans. Entrance tickets cost $40 for adults and $27 for children, while hotel rooms range from $100 a night at the austere Hotel Santa Fe to $360 at the luxury Disneyland Hotel.

After long deliberation, Disney executives decided to maintain their no-alcohol policy at the park despite the wine-drinking habits of the French and other Europeans. The prohibition has not provoked too much dismay.

One serious remaining concern is the chilly, rainy weather that can torment northern Europe at virtually any time of the year. Disney has tried to cope by building arcades to shield those standing in long lines for amusement rides, but executives say climate may turn out to be the key factor in determining profit or loss.

April 13, 1992

Old Black Stereotypes Find New Lives in Japan

Marketers Defend Sambo Toys, Black Mannequins, Insist Racism was not Intended

MARGARET SHAPIRO

Little Black Sambo, the racist caricature that most Americans thought had died a well-deserved death years ago, has been resurrected across the Pacific as the mascot of a hot-selling line of Japanese toys and beachwear.

Sambo and other stereotypical depictions of blacks—some with grotesquely fat lips and ethnic dialect—have become something of a fad here this summer in what appears to be an attempt at internationalization gone gravely awry.

The marketers of the products say that no affront to blacks is intended. "Nobody in Japan regards this as racist," said Kenichiro Ide, spokesman for Sanrio Co., which puts out the Sambo line. Instead, he said, it should be seen as "humorous" and "friendly." Japanese consumers, he said, "enjoy it with good will." Among the items put out by Sanrio is a beach cloth featuring Sambo and his sister, Hanna, both with very black faces and round, white eyes. Under Sambo is written: "When I'm hungry there's no stoppin' me. I'll be up a palm pickin' coconuts before you can count to three. (An' I can count way past three, too!)"

Despite the recent trend toward global travel and overseas investment, the Japanese remain a strongly insular people, with little understanding of or empathy for foreign cultures. As a result, many Japanese embrace timeworn, often offensive images of people who are not like them. For instance, anti-Semitic books continue to be bestsellers, and people here often explain the books' appeal by saying that Japanese are merely interested in the fact that Jews are good at making money.

In the case of blacks, many Japanese appear to assume they are all good athletes and dancers. They tend to agree with former prime minister Yasuhiro Nakasone, who once suggested that blacks were partly responsible for pulling down the intelligence level of the United States.

"Some of us who are ignorant still have a wrong idea" about blacks, said Mitsuya Goto, managing director of the Japan Center for International Exchange, which attempts to improve contacts between people in Japan and other countries.

He said that "the man on the street in Japan may still have certain prejudices" and pointed out that it is only recently that Japanese companies in the United States have started hiring blacks and begun advertising job openings in publications aimed at black readers.

Other Japanese said that blacks, so rare in Japan, seem exotic to many people and therefore very interesting.

Sanrio clearly thinks so: in addition to the Sambo line, the company markets a black character called Bibinba, with fat, pink lips and rings in its ears. Spokesman Ide said both lines are popular with children, who "enjoy it with good will. They will not grow up to become racists."

Sanrio is not the only Japanese company marketing a black caricature. Recently, black mannequins with grossly distorted lips and greased hair have appeared in department stores in Japan, modeling suits and other clothing.

At Sogo department store in Tokyo, two of those mannequins, clad in suits, are frozen in dance poses at the entrance to the men's clothing department. Nearby, clusters of white male mannequins pose sedately in business suits.

Masaaki Honjo, a spokesman for Sogo, said the department store has been using the black mannequins to model clothing in "high action. They wear a suit, but this suit is very good for action," he said, adding that no one at the store thought the mannequins might portray blacks in a less-than-flattering manner. "We never thought about this point. We have no intention of discriminating," he said.

Kauhiro Nakajima, an official with Yamato Mannequin Co., which makes the black models, said the company has 600 of them circulating around Japan for use in trendy displays. "They show strong personality, energy and charm." He said an employee once raised concerns that the mannequins might be racist depictions of blacks, but "our conclusion is it wasn't."

July 22, 1988

The Menu

Three-Ring Ribaldry—With Leisure Time to Spare, Germans Send in the Clowns

MARC FISHER

The typical German worker gets six weeks of paid vacation a year. He works fewer hours than his counterpart in any other industrialized nation, fully 341 fewer hours a year than the average American.

This presents Germans with a mind-boggling amount of leisure time to fill. American-style time-fillers don't work here—television is off the air much of the time and is heavily weighted toward droning talkfests and Sturm und Drang documentaries about the crimes of past generations. And shopping is out as a form of recreation—by law, all stores close evenings and weekends except for a few hours Saturday morning.

Enter Hans-Peter Wodarz and Bernhard Paul, masters, respectively, of one of Germany's finest restaurants and the country's most admired circus. They have taken affluent Germany by storm with a most contemporary and ancient entertainment, the boisterous, ribald, slightly decadent gourmet circus.

Named for ancient Rome's brilliant method of dampening dissent among the grubby masses, "Bread and Circuses" is playing to sold-out crowds night after night, offering a four-course menu served in a sumptuous turn-of-the-century, mahogany-and-beveled-glass big top.

While 280 diners are served a jellied turbot and salmon first course, 10 clowns dressed as waiters and cooks gallivant through the narrow aisles, tossing plates over customers' heads, picking pockets, smashing the occasional egg and doing anything possible to shock the well-dressed crowd.

A surly sommelier, who wears wine corks in his corn-rowed hair, cracks open a beer with a fork, samples it in the oversize saucepan hung around his neck, and promptly spits up. Spying two prim matrons, a couple of clowns wipe the plates and silverware off the table, begin smooching madly and end up mounting one another (still clothed) on the fresh linens.

Amid the slapstick, and before the tomato-carrot soup with roasted celery root is served, real circus acts squeeze onto the four-foot-wide stage at the center of the big top. A juggler spits ping-pong balls up toward the towering tent roof. A Soviet-Yugoslav trio plays classical favorites with spoons rapped against partially filled water bottles.

113

For $86 plus drinks (wines range from S50 to $180 per bottle), German yuppies, proper businessmen and their elegantly coiffed wives, and suburban yokels in for a big night on the town get to see what chef turned showman Wodarz calls "the perfect statement of Germany in the '90s."

"For the first time in history, the Germans want Lebensfreude, the joy of life," says Wodarz. "This is our Gay Nineties. There's been a shift in Germany. The people have their color TVs now. The auto is paid for. They want to spend their money on something live."

"Life is dreary enough," Marita Raiser, spokeswoman for the German Hotel and Restaurant Association, told Der Spiegel magazine. "People have so much money and they want to spend it." "Bread and Circuses" is not alone: A Hamburg hotel offers an evening of Mozart music accompanied by a "Mozart menu" served by waiters in period costume. A Cologne hotel built a sandy beach in its dining hall and staged a Mauritius Week featuring dancers, acrobats and a cook flown in from the tropical country.

But Germans looking for ways to consume are limited strictly to the western part of the country. "Bread and Circuses" started in Munich, and after its Cologne stint moves on to Hanover and Hamburg (the show will also hit Paris and Vienna, a European test run for the U.S. tour that Wodarz and other organizers crave). There is no stop in eastern Germany, where the collapse of the old communist economy has put nearly half the adult population out of work.

"The East?" Wodarz says. "That comes later. It would be impossible now."

Matthias Krahnert is a tall, gawky clown with magical eyes and a sneaky grin. He plays the maitre d' in "Bread and Circuses," a lumbering but lovable character who cannot understand a word of the haughty French chef's precious utterances.

Krahnert is from eastern Germany, a place where theater and the circus were not only an escape but an essential part of underground communication, a complex web of winks and wordplay by artists pushing the envelope of government censorship. His first job in the West is a world away from his hometown of Dresden, the city that was the only part of East Germany beyond the reach of West German television transmitters.

"In our Germany, especially in the Valley of the Clueless," the common East German name for the corner of the country deprived of TV's window on the West, "this would have been inconceivable," Krahnert says. "But here in the West, it's worth it to people to see something totally new, a whole evening of circus, theater, and a really good menu."

Wodarz says he has been flooded with interest from U.S. show biz types, including Disney executives and Broadway producers. But he's not sure if the four-hour production is quite ready to cross the Atlantic.

It's not that the show has too many local references—aside from a few obligatory East-West, commie-capitalist gags, the show is as language-free and international as can be—it's just that Wodarz isn't certain that the German '90s and the U.S. '90s are quite the same era.

Did Americans have their fill of excess in the deficit-ridden '80s, while Germany was still building up its surplus? Wodarz isn't sure.

Americans in his audience tell him not to worry. From the duck breast with cherries to the clowns' delightful slow-motion slugfest finale, "Bread and Circuses" is a "brilliant and unique production," said Philip Hardenberg, a Ritz-Carlton Hotels executive who came in from Houston to see the show this week. "It can't miss in the States."

While Wodarz ponders expansion, he is packing them in in Germany—25,000 in Munich last month, similar numbers now in Cologne.

In a Germany where rising taxes and mounting strife between the poor easterners and the affluent westerners have the population on edge, a little escapism may go a long way toward quieting the masses, Wodarz says.

Which is exactly how the Romans saw it.

In ancient Rome, the emperor ordered the staging of wild circuses for the unruly citizens, the idea being that a mass feed and show would tame any nascent move toward rebellion. For a time, it worked nicely. For a time. Then everything fell apart.

July 22, 1988

8 The International Political and Legal Environment

Cuba's Glimmer of Glitter:
Opulent Nightclub Brings in Tourist Dollars

LEE HOCKSTADER

The personification of capitalism's modest beachhead in socialist Cuba comes dressed in black tasseled loafers, cream linen pants and an Yves Saint-Laurent double-breasted blazer. His Spanish is delivered not in Havana's staccato blitz but in the aristocratic lisp of Barcelona.

But don't imagine for a minute that Spain's Jordi Escarra, manager of the impossibly glitzy Havana Club, feels out of place on this island of Creole communism. "The Spanish left two very good things here in Cuba," he confides with a twinkle. "Mulattas, like my wife, and rope sandals."

Escarra and a group of Spanish partners opened Havana's hottest night spot just four months ago in a joint venture with a Cuban government that is desperate for tourism dollars and outside investors. So far, it looks like a sweetheart deal for the simple reason that when it comes to nightlife in Havana, there is practically no competition.

Already, writer Gabriel Garcia Marquez has boogied on the dance floor, as have the Venezuelan national basketball team and more than 30,000 other tourists who shelled out $10 a head for a taste of a decidedly un-Cuban experience. The club, like many other tourism ventures in Cuba, requires dollars because the country can use them on the international market, where the Cuban peso is worthless.

Capitalism practically comes wafting out the doors of the Havana Club, borne like a seductive dream by the heady throb of salsa, the brilliant stab of strobe lights and the mingling scents of salt water and coconut suntan oil.

Set on the oceanfront on Havana's west side, the place is tailor-made for tourists, who are flocking to Cuba in record numbers from Canada, Spain, Germany and Mexico. But the club also has become tantalizingly popular with young Cubans, whose usual nighttime entertainment options range from hanging out on Havana's sea-splashed Malecon, the old boulevard atop the city's seawall, to standing in line for hours to eat ice cream of middling quality.

The hitch is that Cubans, who are legally barred from having dollars, can't get into the place on their own. So knots of young Cubans, dressed to the nines and ready to party, mill about on the sidewalk outside, putting the same suggestive question to every tourist who approaches the neon-bright entrance: "Would you like to be with us this evening?"

Evenings actually tend to begin in the small hours of the morning. In August, when Havana was flooded with some 17,000 visitors for the Pan American Games, the dancing went on till dawn.

"Cubans have the rhythm in their blood," said Escarra. "Look, everyone dances. In my country it's very difficult to get people to dance like this."

Cubans accustomed to relatively Spartan surroundings marvel at the flash and glitter. The walls are of rose-colored marble, the pillars are covered in glass, and four television screens pulse with the latest music videos. Streams of water cascade from practically every surface of the place at the rate of 1.2 million liters an hour. And the bar serves up imported liquor and soda, including American beers and soft drinks that circumvent the embargo by going through third countries. The lights, the sound system and the furniture are all Spanish imports, as are the disc jockey and his girlfriend, the ticket girl. "Most disc jockeys in Cuba just play cassettes," said Escarra. "They don't know how to mix music."

The club, built so close to the sea that Escarra installed windows of ballistic glass to protect the disco from high tides and storms, will soon contain a second club upstairs that features softer music and more romantic decor.

President Fidel Castro's revolution, 32 years old and growing long in the tooth, was a reaction to exactly this kind of Western-style decadence. But since the meltdown of communism in Eastern Europe and the Soviet Union, the Cuban leader has been forced to accelerate plans to expand Cuba's long-dormant tourism industry—while vowing never to revive the booze, broads and baccarat brand of tourism that lured thousands of Americans to the island in the 1940s and '50s.

Today's tourists, though generally not as well-heeled as those who visit other Caribbean islands, still bring greenbacks that help Cuba pay for foreign goods that were formerly available for barter from Cuba's communist allies.

The Maximum Leader's new policy meant an open field for Western entrepreneurs like Escarra, who arrived to find a country chockablock with investment opportunities and practically no competition. And with American business barred from the island by the 31-year-old U.S. trade embargo, the Cuban government has rolled out the red carpet for Europeans.

For Escarra, the absence of American competition is one of the delights of doing business in Cuba. But he fears the day that a thaw in U.S.-Cuban relations or a change in Cuba's government will bring Americans back to the island. "You've already kicked the Spanish out of Cuba once {in the Spanish-American War at the turn of the century}. I don't want to see it happen again.

"I'm a pioneer in tourism here," he added, "and Cuba is a marvelous country touristically. ... We'll make a profit much quicker here than we could in my country." He and his partners put down $1 million—a third of the cost of a similar venture in Spain—and expect to recoup their investment in three years.

Escarra, a 43-year-old veteran of Spain's disco and hotel scene, was invited to Cuba in 1988 for a week's visit by an associate who distributes Cuba's best-known rum, also called Havana Club, in Spain. He's stayed three years, meeting his 20-year-old-wife along the way.

While declining to describe the specifics of his deal with the Cubans, he said the government has a majority stake in the club but has left its management entirely up to him. "They don't interfere. I run it the way I see fit," he said.

His expansion plans call for a seafood restaurant on the patio by the crystalline waters of the Caribbean, and a yacht that will depart from the disco, cruise the length of Havana and deposit customers back at the Havana Club for a night of revelry. Escarra insists he is unfazed by Cuba's murky political future and the grim predictions of violent upheaval following Castro's death.

"I didn't think at all about that," he said. "I'm not going to lose everything . . . There are risks in opening a disco in the United States too, risks from competition, from the Mafia. In Cuba, at least, I don't have to worry about either of those."

September 24, 1991

Minnesota Defense Contractor Fined for Bribing Two Niger Officials

RUTH MARCUS

A Minnesota defense contractor pleaded guilty yesterday to paying more than $130,000 in bribes to officials of the Republic of Niger to obtain and keep an aircraft service contract funded by the U.S. government's foreign military sales program.

Napco International Inc. and its parent company, Venturian Corp. of Hopkins, Minn., agreed to pay $1 million in criminal fines, civil penalties, taxes and restitution. The companies agreed to plead guilty to conspiracy, to tax violations and to violating the 1977 Foreign Corrupt Practices Act, which prohibits U.S. companies from paying bribes to foreign officials.

The case is the first Foreign Corrupt Practices Act prosecution involving the foreign military sales program. Money from the program "is to be used for the military preparedness of certain governments. That, of course, is important to our national security," said Theodore S. Greenberg, deputy chief of the Justice Department's fraud section.

"Any diminution of the resources available to these foreign governments to buy military goods not only affects their national security but of course has an impact on ours," said Greenberg, who prosecuted the case along with senior litigation counsel Peter B. Clark. "The object of the program is to be getting the biggest bang for the buck—not to pay illegal bribes."

Napco, which sells spare parts, components and service for American-made military equipment to about 60 countries, could be barred by the Defense Department from receiving new U.S. government business and could lose its State Department export privileges.

The company paid the bribes to Tahirou Barke Doka, then the first counselor at Niger's embassy here, and Capt. Ali Tiemogo, then the chief of maintenance of the nation's air force, to use their influence to make certain that Napco obtained and retained the contracts to provide spare parts and maintenance service for C130 cargo aircraft.

The contracts were worth more than $3 million.

As outlined in the three-count criminal information filed in federal court in Minneapolis yesterday, the company engaged in an elaborate effort from 1983 through 1987 to set up and conceal the bribery scheme, opening a Minnesota bank account in the name of a fictitious commission agent named "E. Dave" and listing two relatives of Tiemogo as Napco's agents in Niger when in fact they merely served as intermediaries for the bribe payments.

The Defense Security Assistance Agency uncovered the fraud when it checked the name of one of the agents with the government of Niger. The Niger government cooperated with the investigation, Greenberg said.

Venturian president Gary B. Rappoport said in a statement yesterday that "the acts which were the subject of the investigation were isolated instances, and the person allegedly involved is no longer with the company."

In court yesterday, Greenberg identified a Napco vice president as a co-conspirator and said other officers and employees of the company also were involved.

Rappoport said "we strongly believe that we can demonstrate . . . that all necessary corrective action has been taken . . . and that accordingly the company should sustain its eligibility to contract and receive export licenses."

Under the terms of the plea agreement, the company will pay $685,000 for violating the Foreign Corrupt Practices Act, $100,000 for filing a false tax return and $75,000 to the Internal Revenue Service to settle its civil tax liabilities. It also will pay $140,000 in civil penalties, to be credited to the Republic of Niger's Foreign Military Sales account.

May 3, 1989

The Natural Environment 9

Disfigured Children, Distressed Parents
Suit Filed Against U.S. Firm Over Alleged Effects of Pollution in Mexican Border Region

EDWARD CODY

Francisco Zamala, 17, cocked his head to one side, hummed a tune recognizable only to himself and stared vacantly into space. On the other side of the little patio, Luis Reynua, 19, flapped his hands uncontrollably and shouted at his private demons.

The two youths, misshapen and irrecuperably retarded, are part of a group known in this industrial border town as the "Mallory children." The offspring of women who worked in an American-owned capacitor factory during pregnancy, they have grown up with deformed limbs, learning deficiencies and faces that make them look like victims of Down's syndrome.

For more than 15 years, the mothers of the Mallory boys and girls bore their pain in private, taking care of their children's special needs at home.

But on Sept. 23, the resignation ended. Forty-two families filed suit against the Mallory Capacitor Co., which was owner of the plant, now closed. They are demanding restitution from the current owners for what happened to the children and blaming daily exposure to a powerful solvent they say they were expected to handle without adequate protection or warning.

"We just didn't realize," said Paulina de la Cruz, 38, whose 16-year-old daughter, Elvia, was among a group of Mallory children gathered the other day on the family's modest terrace. "We had the children and we just took care of them. But little by little, in school, in the bus, we realized that we had a common problem."

Their lawsuit, lodged in a Cameron County, Tex., district court just across the U.S.-Mexican border, spotlights a down side of the new prosperity in Mexican frontier towns such as Matamoros—a particularly unwelcome glare as negotiations move forward on a U.S.-Mexican Free Trade Agreement designed to multiply industrial exchanges across the border.

Foreign companies, most of them U.S.-based, have opened nearly 2,000 cross-border assembly plants, called maquiladoras, to take advantage of cheap Mexican labor. Under the trade pact, they are expected to bring thousands more jobs. But the price in industrial pollution and untreated toxic waste—and, according to the suit, in human tragedy—has been high.

"If they could do in the United States what they're doing in Matamoros, they wouldn't have left," said Domingo Gonzalez, an antipollution activist in Brownsville, Tex., just across the border. "The wages, that's one huge incentive. But there's that other one too: getting away from regulation."

The U.S. and Mexican governments, preparing for the Free Trade Agreement, have started work on a binational border plan designed to expand on and update a 1983 antipollution convention and other accords that were supposed to prevent abuses by the maquiladora assembly industry. The goal is a single plan accepted by the Mexican Secretariat of Urban Development and Ecology (SEDUE) and the U.S. Environmental Protection Agency to discourage pollution on both sides of the border as the free-trade pact gets underway—projected to be sometime between 1992 and 1994. But the situation in Matamoros suggests the authorities have been late off the blocks. In the assessment of environmental activists on both sides of the border, SEDUE's ability to regulate foreign-owned factories has been sorely outstripped by the growth of border industries, particularly over the last decade. A SEDUE delegate, Abundio Gonzalez Gonzalez, told local reporters last week that the ministry's first complete study of maquiladoras in the Matamoros area showed that of 84 plants, only 11 register their waste discharges with Mexican authorities, and 19 treat them before releasing the flow into local sewers, canals and, ultimately, the Rio Grande and Gulf of Mexico.

About half of the plants acknowledge producing toxic wastes, the study showed, but nearly a third of these have failed to comply with regulations that require the toxic wastes to be cataloged and shipped back to the United States for treatment. Sergio Reyes Lujan, SEDUE's undersecretary for ecology, announced recently that 50 more inspectors have been taken on to increase enforcement among the border industries.

Chalky wastes were seen pouring directly into a canal from a U.S.-owned factory manufacturing auto bumpers and other parts in an industrial park dotted with maquiladora plants. In another part of town, a sharp stench hung over the Privada Uniones residential neighborhood, hard against a U.S.-owned insecticide factory.

"It's that way every day," said Ernestina Sanchez Martinez, 35, who has lived the last decade surrounded by the pungent odors wafting over the wall behind her house.

On the other side of her home, another U.S.-owned factory has buried wastes underground in a walled compound, giving the soil a gray color, she said. Juan Antonio Martinez, Ernestina's husband, said he and his neighbors recently met with the factory management to find out what lies in the ground. The effort failed.

The meeting did, however, persuade the factory management to stop dumping wastes directly into a canal running alongside nearby railroad tracks, Martinez said.

For Francisco Zamala's mother, Irma Duenez, the hard thing to put up with is the knowledge that her son will never be normal. He only began to walk five years ago, when he was 12, she said, and still has to be cared for like an infant.

Although no one suspected what would happen to their children, Duenez and her colleagues said they knew even back in the 1970s that they were affected by the chemical wash for the capacitors, which are used in television sets. Many among the several hundred women who worked there fainted regularly, she said, and some were euphoric from the fumes.

Doraelia Lerma, 36, said she spent a week in a Reynosa hospital on one occasion after being overcome—two months before getting pregnant with her daughter Maria, who at 18 still cannot speak. But no one complained, the women said, because they were afraid of losing their jobs.

De la Cruz, after seeing a newspaper advertisement, turned to Richard L. Palmer, a Brownsville lawyer. He and two other lawyers, Ernesto Gamez Jr., also of Brownsville, and Michael E. Shelton of Houston brought the suit against Mallory; the Emhart group, which acquired Mallory after it went out of business in 1977; Groendyke Transport, Inc., which carried chemical products across the border to the factory; and two local businessmen who were involved in managing the plant. Palmer said efforts were being made to determine actual responsibility, since the property has been involved in several corporate changes.

October 15, 1991

Japan is Set to Meet America on the Environmental Products Battleground

MICHAEL SCHRAGE

The Japan External Trade Organization, this nation's export trade promotion arm, typically loves to show off the latest in Japanese high-tech, high-value-added innovations. But the agency recently gave star treatment to the kind of product that would have been studiously ignored even a year ago: an adhesive tape that's totally recyclable.

Where Japan's Ministry of International Trade and Industry once preached the gospel of relentless industrial productivity, it now pledges to create a large-scale "eco factory" that stresses environmental harmony as much as production efficiency. The model plant would use high-speed robots to dismantle used cars, electrical products and other industrial waste into reusable steel, plastic and other raw materials. MITI's ostensible goal is to encourage Japanese industry to strike a better balance between economic growth and ecological soundness.

"Japanese companies are now becoming much more environmentally aware and innovative with the environment in mind," asserts Tomiaki Nagase, senior managing director at Kao Corp., Japan's household products giant.

To be sure, Japanese companies are giving a lot of lip service to environmental concerns. The Keidanren, Japan's Federation of Economic Organizations, last year adopted a global environment charter calling for its members to behave in ecologically desirable ways.

In reality, Japanese industry is about three years behind the United States and Europe in such areas as recycling, says Christopher W. Hirth, international coordinator for the Nippon Ecology Network, one of Japan's oldest recycling operations. "Most companies think recycling is too costly and they don't want to take the risk," he observes. "The government is just beginning to mandate recycling."

Nevertheless, many Japanese companies sense that the green movement is not a fad and are now preparing to invest in "ecology" with much the same verve that they invested in "quality" more than 30 years ago. Toray, Japan's leading textile company, recently put a household water purifier on the market based on its proprietary synthetic fiber technology. Fuji Photo Film Co. has introduced a system that makes its popular "throwaway" cameras recyclable. Less than two years ago, Mitsubishi Petrochemical Co. launched a plastics disposal initiative to develop clean-burning wrapping materials. Its new Yuka Wrap has subsequently done well both in Japan and abroad. Environmental innovation is gradually becoming linked to industrial competitiveness.

The biggest industrial stakes, of course, revolve around the "green automobile." The 1998 California deadline requiring that at least 2 percent of a carmaker's fleet consist of "zero emission vehicles" has set off a frenzy of research and development in electric vehicles. Sanyo Electric Co. introduced a prototype of a hybrid solar car that blends surface-mounted solar cells, rechargeable batteries and a small fuel cell. Toyota Motor Corp., Nissan Motor Co. and the other major Japanese auto manufacturers are all pushing to meet the deadline. They can't afford to lose their preeminent positions in America's most lucrative car market.

But if Japanese companies do a better job of manufacturing and marketing green automobiles in the United States, what happens to that $30 billion annual trade deficit in autos and auto parts between America and Japan? Much in the way fuel-efficient cars from Honda Motor Co. and Toyota gave the Japanese manufacturers a competitive edge in the U.S. market, environmentally superior automobiles could help carve out still greater market shares.

Indeed, if Japanese companies are as successful at creating green innovations and goods as they have been in so many other consumer and industrial markets, we face the real possibility that environmental competitiveness will ultimately exacerbate trade tensions. American policy makers would then be placed in the awkward political position of trying to discourage the domestic sale of environmentally sounder products even as they champion the virtues of clean air, clean water and reduced waste.

Of course, it's not yet clear if green innovations will play a vital role in establishing competitiveness. Or whether European, American or Asian companies will capture the high ground. What's certain, however, is that if Japanese industry can do in ecological engineering what they've done in quality engineering, then American industry is going to find itself in yet another bruising economic battle.

March 27, 1992

Green Giant

You Probably Think of It as a Zany Band of Whale-Watching, Seal-Saving Eco-Freaks. But Greenpeace is Now the Largest, Fastest Growing Environmental Organization in the World

CLARK NORTON

This is no ordinary sailing ship, this reincarnated Rainbow Warrior. It's sleek and shiny new, a North Sea trawler rebuilt for the high sea eco-exploits of Greenpeace International, the world's largest, most famous and most infamous environmental organization. But it's also a ship with a history. Right now, the Warrior is awaiting its official launch on a cool, overcast July morning in Hamburg, West Germany, and a number of notables are here to celebrate.

That's Peter Wilcox in the ponytail and Birkenstocks, the captain of the ship. The distinguished, white-haired gentleman is Lloyd Cutler, Washington superlawyer and former White House counsel during the Carter administration. There's Steve Sawyer over there, Greenpeace International's executive vice president, practicing his speech for the ceremony. It's Sawyer's birthday today. Probably the luckiest thing that ever happened to Steve Sawyer was being born on July 10. It saved his life—and the lives of 11 others. Because it was four years ago today, on Sawyer's birthday, that the first Rainbow Warrior met its untimely fate.

On July 10, 1985, just a few minutes before midnight, two underwater explosions ripped open the hull of the first Rainbow Warrior, sinking it in New Zealand's Auckland harbor. The ship was scheduled to lead a protest flotilla to the French underground nuclear test site on Mururoa Atoll in the South Pacific. Greenpeace photographer Fernando Pereira died when the ship sank; the rest of the crew was ashore celebrating Steve Sawyer's birthday. Sawyer, 29 and already a Greenpeace veteran, had started as a canvasser, soliciting money and members door to door. He'd worked his way up in the organization and had headed a number of missions. But this one, in ways no one could have predicted, changed not only the people involved but also Greenpeace itself, its influence and support.

When the facts surrounding what the French press called "Underwatergate" became clear, it was obvious the French government had to take responsibility for the bombing. (Two French intelligence agents arrested in New Zealand later pleaded guilty.) By the fall of '85, Greenpeace had filed suit, and Lloyd Cutler, a new-found friend in a high place, offered his services pro bono. At the head of an international team of attorneys, Cutler won $8 million in damages for Greenpeace from the French government. "It was an outrageous act," Cutler says now, "and they were entitled to the best legal representation they could get."

It would be unfair to accuse Greenpeace of welcoming the tragedy, but it would not be inaccurate to note that Greenpeace parlayed the incident into massive publicity, remuneration and public support. At the time, Greenpeace had about 1. 4 million members around the world and revenues of about $24 million. Four years later, it has more than 3.3 million members worldwide, 33 offices in 20 countries and more than four times the revenue, an estimated $100 million in 1989.

Certainly, not all of Greenpeace's phenomenal rise can be attributed to the disaster in Auckland harbor. Most environmental organizations have seen increases in membership and donations in the last decade as the federal government pulled back from its previous environmental commitment. But no other environmental organization has equaled Greenpeace's growth, achieved largely through contributions averaging $20 a pop. (Greenpeace accepts no corporate or government grants.) Greenpeace USA, for example, which is headquartered in Washington, is now twice the size of the National Audobon Society and the Sierra Club. (The National Wildlife Federation is still the largest in the United States, with about 3.2 million members.)

Though the image of Greenpeace may be that of a little band of zanies running primarily on guts and zeal, this is no longer an accurate picture. The organization has a fleet of eight ocean-going ships, including the new Rainbow Warrior, and a flotilla of Zodiacs (dinghies). Greenpeace boats are equipped with satellite communications equipment, and the group's offices can contact each other instantly through a sophisticated electronic network called "Greenlink." This spring, Greenpeace moved its international headquarters to a striking art deco building in Amsterdam.

Traditionally strongest in Western Europe—one of every 25 Dutch households contains a member—Greenpeace is trying to branch out; it recently opened two offices in Latin America and a base camp in Antarctica (which it wants to turn into a "world park" protected from development). The group even gained a foothold in the Soviet Union this spring, opening a Moscow office with money raised from sales of a Greenpeace record album featuring two dozen western rock stars. The album sold out 500,000 copies within hours to rock-hungry Soviets, raising $16 million worth of rubles. Greenpeace stuffed its fliers into every album—"creating hundreds of thousands of potential supporters there," Sawyer says, "if we can ever figure out how to communicate with them again." Back at the launching in Hamburg, a crush of European media has descended, with cameras rolling and flashbulbs popping. Lloyd Cutler has made a special detour to attend this ceremony, "which I would not have wanted to miss," he says. "I was generally sympathetic to Greenpeace's environmental goals, and as I started working with them, I came to admire them tremendously." Cutler suggests that Wilcox bring the

Warrior into the Potomac when the ship reaches the East Coast in late September en route to its final destination in the Pacific. Wilcox says he likes the idea: "Maybe we can get the Pentagon to cooperate with something." Then they toast the new ship with the traditional champagne. The bubbly? French, of course. A prime source of Greenpeace's growing appeal is its sheer brashness in confronting head-on those it views as despoilers of the environment. Whether its foes are small crews of Icelandic fishermen or superpower governments, Greenpeace pulls no punches.

In late July, four Greenpeace vessels halted the Navy's attempt to test-launch a Trident II missile from a submarine off Cape Canaveral. It was the first time a protest had halted a Cape Canaveral-based test in more than 30 years. Days later, several boats "escorted" the damaged Exxon Valdez, queen of the Alaskan oil spill, as it crept into San Diego harbor for repairs, one activist shouting that the tanker "represents a fossil fuel energy policy whose time is past."

In the past, Greenpeace members achieved acclaim (and in some quarters notoriety) for such actions as these:

Moving their Zodiacs directly into the line of fire of harpoons used by Japanese and Soviet whalers.

Throwing their bodies between seal hunters and seal pups on Canadian ice floes.

Landing on the coast of Siberia to protest an illegal Soviet whaling station. Five activists were arrested and temporarily detained while others eluded pursuit to bring home documentary film of the incident.

Handcuffing themselves to toxic waste drums about to be dumped at sea.

Scuba-diving to plug the underwater discharge pipes of chemical polluters and parachuting off industrial smokestacks.

Scaling Mount Rushmore and the cliffs surrounding Niagara Falls and dangling off the Golden Gate Bridge to protest various environmental and nuclear threats.

Dumping thousands of marbles in the office of then Interior Secretary James Watt. "We've always said Watt has lost his marbles," explained one activist. "We were just returning them."

Many of its actions are strictly guerrilla theater. The group announced, for example, that after preventing the Trident II test it had made its point and would not return to block another. But out of the antics have come some solid achievements:

The group's highly publicized campaigns against whaling and sealing—ignited by Greenpeace film of harpoons tearing into whale flesh and sealers clubbing defenseless pups to death—spurred worldwide outrage and led to regulations that drastically decreased whale and seal kills.

Its campaign against burning hazardous wastes at sea has led a variety of countries (including the United States) to restrict ocean incineration. Campaigns to expose industrial polluters have resulted in fines against several offenders and, in some cases, plant closures. The American Recovery Co. in Baltimore, which closed in 1984, and the Ciba-Geigy chemical waste pipeline in New Jersey, scheduled to close in 1992, are two polluters curtailed through Greenpeace efforts.

Founded in the early 1970s by a maverick ex-construction tycoon from Canada turned vagabond sailor, Greenpeace took its name and inspiration from a ragtag Canadian vessel that had sailed into a U.S. nuclear test site off Alaska, forcing postponement of the test. The ex-tycoon, David McTaggart (now chairman of the board of Greenpeace International), later used a similar strategy against the French at a nuclear test site in the South Pacific. After being severely beaten by French commandos, McTaggart told his story to the world. The outcry ultimately convinced France to retreat from atmospheric testing in the region. The Greenpeace formula was born: Start with brazen ideas for "direct actions," as Greenpeacers refer to their high-concept missions, find people brave or crazy enough to pull them off, produce some dramatic images, take pictures and publicize the hell out of them. McTaggart, a shoot-from-the-hip talker who one Greenpeace leader says "would have been Donald Trump in another life," insisted only that activists adhere to a credo of nonviolence and political nonpartisanship.

The early Greenpeace was notably unsophisticated. "When I first called the San Francisco office in 1977 to volunteer," recalls Dick Dillman, now head of Greenpeace special services and resident telecommunications genius, "I asked them who handled the radios on their boats. When they said, 'What radios?,' I told them, 'I'm coming right over.' "

Back then, Dillman says, "Greenpeace was literally a bunch of dope-smoking hippies who threw the *I Ching* to figure out what to do. We'd hire a hippie for a day, send him up to a hilltop in a truck with a radio and a sack of granola, and he'd be our transmitter." When the Washington office bought its first IBM computer in 1980, several staffers either refused to use it—or insisted on wearing lead aprons to block the radiation.

Dillman—a near legendary figure in Greenpeace who designed the organization's two-year-old Greenlink computer system—has revolutionized the way Greenpeace works. "All our boats have satellite communications," Dillman says with pride. "No other organization outside the government itself can match our technology." Then he adds: "Did you hear about my plans for a Greenpeace blimp?" With Dillman supplying the technical support and former mountain climbing guide Twilly Cannon coordinating the training and logistics, Greenpeace USA now has hundreds of volunteers (only a few are paid) available for direct actions. Each will follow the McTaggart formula for brazenness in the pursuit of publicity—now applied successfully thousands of times around the globe.

Other environmental groups may wield tremendous clout behind the scenes: The Natural Resources Defense Council, for instance, was instrumental in passage of such landmark legislation as the Clean Air Act and Clean Water Act. The National Audobon Society played a key role in securing last year's reauthorization of the Endangered Species Act. The Environmental Defense Fund spent years in court helping to ban DDT and reducing lead in gasoline. But Greenpeace has mastered the art of capturing the spotlight—and much of the glory in the process. There's even talk in Hollywood of producing a Greenpeace movie.

If you have trouble picturing a flick about any other environmental group— "High Sierra Club" or "Indiana Jones and the Environmental Defense Fund" probably wouldn't make boffo box office—that's exactly the way Greenpeace wants it. "We have our niche in the movement, and they have theirs," says Greenpeace USA Executive Director Peter Bahouth. But while Bahouth says there should be a moratorium on name-calling among environmentalists—the 'We've saved more whales than you' syndrome," as he dubs it—Greenpeacers sometimes display a smug contempt for their more button-down brethren.

"The traditional environmental groups are reluctant to join our types of battles," contends David Rapoport, Washington-based head of Greenpeace USA's toxics campaign. "They want to be seen as 'reasonable.' They treasure that. But the public is tired of analysis. They want action."

As if to underscore that point, Greenpeace's fund-raising mail for the toxics campaign trumpets: "While other organizations work mainly through courts and legislatures, we sail our boats—or hike, or drive, or scuba dive—directly to the scene to make a stand against the very companies that are poisoning our earth." The implication is that if you emerge from an environmental battle without your shoes soiled—or indeed, without a court date on the wrong side of the judge—you haven't fought the good fight. Greenpeacers wear their arrest records like badges of honor. "We had 104 arrests last year," Bahouth says proudly. Some activists have spent months in jail.

Such tactics don't sit well with more conservative environmentalists. "We're constantly bringing suits to get polluters to comply with the law," says Sierra Club Chairman Michael McCluskey. "You can't then go off and decide which laws you aren't going to obey. If that were the case, the polluters would be the first to follow."

George Reiger, national conservation writer for *Field & Stream,* calls Greenpeace an "environmental Ku Klux Klan. Just because they don't wear sheets doesn't mean they don't have a terrorist mentality." According to Reiger, Greenpeace's assaults on hunters are based on "simplistic thinking, in which the world is either black or green." He cites Greenpeace's role in stopping the Canadian seal hunts. "Now they've got hundreds of hunters on welfare up there— and the seal population is growing so fast it's threatening to wipe out the fisheries. They don't understand wildlife, that some animals die every day so that others can live." The Washington headquarters, occupying three floors of a high-security building on U Street NW, houses the guts of the national branch of Greenpeace. The rabbit warren of offices houses a six-person media department (featuring a library of 50,000 photographs and nearly 100 videos documenting Greenpeace actions), its direct-mail fund-raising operation and three of its four major issue-oriented campaigns—ocean ecology, toxics and nuclear, each with its own lobbyist. (The fourth, energy and atmosphere, is headquartered in San Francisco.) Mirroring the phenomenal growth of the rest of the organization, the Washington staff has ballooned in just a few years from a dozen people in an office over a drugstore near Dupont Circle to 85 employees today.

"Sure, we've made mistakes," acknowledges Peter Bahouth (though he doesn't number stopping the seal hunts among them). "But we think that's okay. In order to be creative, we have to be willing to fail sometimes." Bahouth, 35, succeeded Steve Sawyer as executive director of Greenpeace USA last fall.

An attorney, Bahouth first became involved with the organization eight years ago in Boston by volunteering his legal services —"representing the local board members there when they got arrested, that sort of thing." He was soon elected to the Boston board himself and, as the only lawyer in Greenpeace at the time, quickly worked his way up to national chairman, a job he held from 1984 till 1988, playing a key role in unifying Greenpeace USA into a cohesive organization. "There was a lot of rivalry," Bahouth says. "I had to convince people to put aside their parochial interests for the good of the group." Greenpeace USA —now comprising offices in Washington, San Francisco, Seattle, Boston, Chicago, Anchorage and Fort Lauderdale, Fla.—was formally united on January 1, 1987.

Most key staffers are young ("young but getting older," Bahouth quips. "When I turn 36 I'm out of here"), bright, hard-working, dedicated—and low-paid. Salaries range from $15,000 to $35,000. Bahouth points to a clipping taped to his door, listing Washington's 20 lowest paid heads of organizations, and says, "I don't even earn enough to make that list."

Staffers from Bahouth on down take pains to note that Greenpeace is not a "Washington organization" per se. "We don't want to lose touch with our membership by acquiring the Beltway mentality, where Washington is the center of the universe," Bahouth says. "Our support comes from frustration with the federal government."

In an era when the public is crying out for change—and a variety of world leaders from George Bush to Mikhail Gorbachev are jumping on the environmental bandwagon—it's fair to ask whether Greenpeace will be able to influence public policy to the same degree that it has influenced public consciousness.

"The tactics that work so well for them elsewhere—the direct actions, the unwillingness to compromise—are turnoffs inside the Beltway," says Robert SanGeorge, vice president of the National Audubon Society in New York. "The button-down types on the Hill perceive them as militant and zany. We've developed access, and people are more comfortable with our image."

Greenpeace has never been invited to participate in the so-called "Group of Ten," a loose coalition of the heads of 10 environmental organizations who have met periodically for the past decade to compare strategies and develop coalitions. Bahouth plays down this exclusion: "We do cooperate with individual groups on a variety of different issues—the National Day of Mourning over the Valdez spill, the reauthorization of the Marine Mammal Protection Act. We worked with 22 other groups on that one, and we all got along."

But for the most part, Greenpeace goes its own way. When the Oceanic Society and a number of other environmental groups organized a boycott of Exxon this spring, Greenpeace refused to join. "We had some mixed opinions on that," says Peter Dykstra, media director for Greenpeace USA. "But we don't want to endorse the idea that cutting up your Exxon credit card and buying Chevron will solve the problem—which is simply that we use too much oil, period. Exxon's no worse than any other company up there."

"Purple houses are a good sign. I don't know why. So are beat-up Volvos and VWs. Shingled houses are good too. Pink houses are a bad sign. So are Astroturf yards and new Volvos." The Greenpeace canvasser approaches a house with a whale door knocker. "Believe it or not, those aren't always good," he says.

If Hollywood ever makes a Greenpeace movie, this scene probably won't be in it—but it should be. It is played repeatedly all over America, and it is critical to understanding Greenpeace's robust financial health.

We are on a rolling, tree-lined street, this time in an affluent Northern California suburb. The Greenpeace canvasser has just started his nightly rounds, knocking on an average of 50 doors. One of approximately 1,400 canvassers operating across the country in every state except Arizona and New Mexico, he works for Greenpeace Action, a sister organization recently formed to enable Greenpeace to do grass-roots lobbying without jeopardizing its tax-exempt status. The canvasser is part of a local crew of five who meet each afternoon for lunch, Monday through Friday, to map out the territory. Each canvasser is assigned certain streets by the crew coordinator, who also hands them printed computer cards detailing which residents have contributed to Greenpeace in the past and exactly how much. The canvasser's job—and this is paid work—is to chat up neighborhood residents about Greenpeace, get them to sign some petitions and write their congressional representatives and, of course, make a contribution.

The canvasser is expected to fill a quota of $100 in contributions per night. It all adds up: 30 percent of Greenpeace's revenues are raised at the door.

"Hi. My name's Ray, and I work for Greenpeace. I expect you've heard of us?" Almost everyone he approaches nods yes. "Are you a fan of ours?" This question elicits a wide variety of responses, most commonly a shrug. Ray is undeterred. If he has not had the door slammed in his face already, he is almost to first base. He gives a short rap on Greenpeace's latest accomplishments: the $60 million boycott of imported Icelandic fish (to put political and economic pressure on the Icelandic whaling industry); the widely reported story that the United States lost a hydrogen bomb near Japan in 1965, uncovered by Greenpeace researchers; the fights against pesticides; the Trident II test; and offshore oil drilling.

Almost everyone, it seems, favors saving whales and stopping oil spills. Opinion tends to be much more negative on the subject of a comprehensive nuclear test ban. And eyes usually glaze over when pesticides are mentioned. Some people take the time to argue an issue. A few are hostile. "I don't like Greenpeace," says one elderly man. "It's constant agitation—one more thing I don't like."

Several say they aren't interested.

"What do you mean you're not interested?" Ray shouts to a closed door. "You're not interested in the future of the world?"

But at least as many reach into their pockets for cash or go for their checkbooks. "Anything you give is appreciated," Ray suggests, "but $20 will get you a membership and the Greenpeace Magazine. You can postdate a check up to three months if that'll help."

After knocking on doors and repeating his pitch dozens of times from 5 to 9 p.m., with a chill wind penetrating his open shirt, Ray announces that he has barely made his quota. "This is a tough job," he says, noting that a canvasser who lasts six months is considered a veteran. "Did I tell you I once had a gun pulled on me?" Then he adds: "But it's a good way to move up in the organization. This is how Steve Sawyer started out, you know."

In Hamburg, Steve Sawyer is also talking about beginnings. He calls the launching of the second Rainbow Warrior a "new beginning for Greenpeace and the end of a long and sad story that began four years ago."

The international crew is beaming as it prepares to set out for stops in Copenhagen, Stockholm and Leningrad before heading across the Atlantic to the United States, perhaps to Washington. Captain Wilcox, eager to get started, promises some unspecified direct actions along the way. "I needed some time off after New Zealand," he says. "But I never knew it would be four years."

Whatever awaits Wilcox and the Rainbow Warrior on the high seas, it's clear that this is where Greenpeace's heart will continue to lie, far from the coat-and-tie world of Washington's corridors. Greenpeace may be far richer and better equipped, but Sawyer bristles at the suggestion that it may be mellowing.

"We're still saying and doing the same things we were 10 years ago," he says. "But now they don't seem so radical. We've pulled the public debate in our direction."

September 3, 1989

Part 3

International Marketing Activities

The core of what international marketers do is reflected in this section. The topics begin with marketing research, then move to a number of aspects related to international marketing strategy. The section concludes with articles selected to cover the basic marketing decision making variables of product, price, place and promotion.

Topics covered in the pricing area, such as dumping, currency fluctuations and transfer pricing, give an indication of the challenges faced by marketers in an international environment. Likewise in distribution, the problems faced by companies such as UPS in Europe are the kinds of situations that make jobs in the field of international marketing exciting, interesting and creative.

Ideas found in this section, for example selling 900 number messages from the pope, are testament to the fact that international marketing is only as limited as the creativity and ingenuity of individual marketers. All products and promotions do not have universal appeal but many are adaptable to local culture. An excellent example of the requirements to change a U.K. ad to a U.S. ad are offered in the article titled: "Ads with Instant Intrigue: For Taster's Choice, the 45-Second Soap Opera." In sum, international marketing can be fun.

International Marketing Research *10*

Finding Opportunities Overseas Begins at Home for Exporters:
Consultant Market Research is Crucial to Success

JENNIFER CASPAR

When giving advice to small companies that are looking to expand into international markets, Kim Johnson, an international marketing consultant with Cassidy and Associates Inc., always starts with "don't be intimidated by the thought of doing business in a foreign country."

Though it sounds simple, such guidance is exactly what the majority of small companies trying to export need, she said. Many companies try to enter foreign markets after learning from news stories about opportunities there, but they are quickly discouraged by language and cultural differences that stand between domestic and foreign markets.

Market research—about local economies and the products in demand by their inhabitants—is the homework any business has to do before entering a new area. And many exporters can avoid failure by researching foreign markets the way they would any domestic market. Companies often neglect to use traditional sources of information—such as libraries and private companies—because of the difficulties many companies have tackling the concept of exporting.

If you look at a company on the East Coast trying to expand to the West Coast, Johnson said, "They do a lot of research, but they don't take the same steps when they look at foreign markets. You use your same business practices."

Tom Watson's accounting firm first discovered foreign markets when his firm was fulfilling a contract with the Agency for International Development in Egypt. Realizing the potential market in developing countries, the firm started looking for places to "export" its services.

Watson said identifying international clients entails gathering as much market data as possible. Foreign embassies and the U.S. and Foreign Commercial Service have information about countries' political systems, economies and basic business attitudes, as well as lists of accounting and consulting firms in the region. Watson said he also looked to professional trade groups for the same lists.

Finally, he contacted local government officials to evaluate opportunities in the market and to find a local accounting firm to work with. "It's fairly easy to find a local firm that needs help," he said.

Watson's ease at finding information about foreign markets is typical of companies that know where to look for it. The Commerce Department and foreign embassies readily provide information to potential exporters to promote international trade. This year, the Small Business Administration and the Commerce Department put together a free guide called "The World Is Your Market" that includes lists of state, federal and international programs set up to help exporters.

But Watson's experience also is different from that of a manufacturer, whose prime concern—sales—can be tackled by a local distributor.

Few entrepreneurs can afford to spend the time away from their companies that it takes to sell directly in foreign markets, Johnson said. But to find a good, trustworthy distributor, some research is needed. The relationship between distributor and small-business owner is crucial, requiring continuous follow-up. Many small-business owners find distributors at industry trade shows.

During its first 10 years in business, Darco Southern Inc. received a number of inquiries from foreign buyers but didn't know how to respond. Finally, the small gasket maker in Independence, Va., decided to explore opportunities abroad to expand its market share.

"We felt as though we had pretty much saturated the domestic market and we had a choice to make," said Jill Burcham, the family-owned company's marketing director. "Either we were going to stay at the same growth level or we were going to anticipate and we were going to grow.

For Darco, growth meant finding foreign buyers, and the Virginia Department of World Trade was able to help. A group of students from Virginia Tech analyzed the company's books and helped them to "smooth over the bumps" they were running into, in addition to identifying Australia as the best overseas market in which to begin exporting.

After ordering the telephone yellow pages from Australia, Burcham contacted some potential customers, made a few trips and lined up several distributors for the company's products.

Burcham is quick to point out the benefits of being a small exporter. "As a small company, we have an advantage because we have more flexibility," she said. "We're not locked into a particular production system." That flexibility allows the company to capitalize on opportunities a larger company might miss.

Marcus Griffith, however, thinks being too small can be a drawback when it comes to foreign markets. Marcus is president of Hairlocks Co. Inc., which makes hair care products for the black and Hispanic market. He said that competition is not as stiff in foreign markets as it is in this country, but that being a small company with little name recognition has complicated matters.

"As a relatively small company, we usually have to go with a distributor that is not as well established," he said. "And because of that, it will be more difficult to get paid." But in many instances, he added, he finds smaller distributors who are more aggressive because they have to prove themselves.

Still, getting past the initial fear of going overseas is a difficult step that confines many companies to domestic markets.

"A lot of people put up a brick wall and think it's overseas—I can't do it," Burcham said.

Overcoming Barriers to Overseas Trade

Learning about World Markets Can be
Difficult but Worth the Effort

MARIANNE KYRIAKOS

Joe Devermann thinks the world wants to buy his plastic trash can liners.

Last November, the Herndon resident was working as a handyman in California to support both his family and his dream of starting an export business.

"I was putting up a wall for a guy who makes household-type plastic bags," Devermann said. "I had been thinking about it {exporting} for a while, and I just kept my ears open, and here was this manufacturer. I asked him if he would consider a decent proposal. I figured he's either interested or he's not."

The manufacturer was interested, so Devermann joined the growing ranks of small-business owners who are hoping for a niche in the large and often confusing export market.

The international market is more than four times larger than the U.S. market, according to Department of Commerce statistics for 1991.

A spokesman in the Commerce Department's U.S. and Foreign Commercial Service office said the agency has been working "real hard" over the last couple of years to encourage U.S. businesses to enter the export market.

"It is not tied to size," the spokesman said. "The vast majority of the clients we deal with are small- and medium-size companies. A company with one or two employees can often become export-ready and going gangbusters much faster than a larger firm with 200 employees. It's more a function of export capability than the size of the company."

Small-business advisers said plugging into an accessible source of export information has long been a problem. Devermann found out just how frustrating the bureaucracy can be when he called the agency for help in learning about world markets, but he was bounced around. "I finally reached someone on the Mexico desk and asked her, 'How do I determine the price for plastic bags in Mexico City?' and she said 'Go there.' "

After a frustrating start, Devermann contacted a friend in Paris and a cousin in Mexico City and enlisted them to do some research.

"I said, 'Go to the grocery store and get the off-the-shelf prices for me.' Then I'll work backwards to try to determine the wholesaler's price and then I also need to know the shipping costs and the import duties, and tracking everything out I should end up with an amount, and then I'll take the manufacturer's price and see if there is any profit out there," Devermann said.

"Why small businesses don't export, when they should, is deserving of its own story because of the trade deficit," said Regina Tracy, executive director of the Small Business Foundation of America Inc. in Washington. "What is out there to help them?"

Tracy points to a 1986 White House conference on small businesses, where it was recommended that a single source of information be established on the subject. "Nothing officially ever happened with that," she said. "Let's face it, 85 percent of small businesses employ 25 people or less ... they perceive all these barriers."

Tracy's organization recently installed an Export Opportunity Hotline. "We give them an overview of the process; tell them how to find foreign agents. Answers are available for any question. We give them a road map, Tracy said.

"Because businesses are scared, they don't know how to do it," she said. "Export development can't be a one-shot deal. It has to be part of a company's overall strategy."

Once a company makes the commitment to seek international trade, the tools are out there, business advisers said.

"It's much easier than people think, if you do it right," said Ray J. McInerney II, operations manager for Cardio-Vascular Innovations Inc. in Chantilly. The company has been trying for two years to export surgical equipment. "We went about it just by beginning this network and starting very small."

In hopes of increasing its export base, the company is trying to get its name known overseas by way of promotional announcements through the Commerce Department. "We are also joining different associations and attending international meetings and trade shows," McInerney said.

David Phillips, owner of Magellan Trading Co. started an export business . He said the impetus came during a trip to Brazil with a local civic association. "I saw in general in Latin American countries ... that markets were opening up for used computer systems, both software and hardware."

Phillips said he too had trouble with what he called "a baffling array of government-sponsored export services that are available. Quite frankly, to wade through the various programs, for instance those within the Commerce Department or the Export-Import Bank, takes a substantial amount of effort."

The entrepreneur, who until recently practiced international trade law, said he finally decided to narrow his focus.

"I realized, as a smaller player, it's really important to define your mission and know one product and one location very well."

In addition to the following sources of trade information, most embassies will send free information on individual countries.

Export Opportunity Hotline, sponsored by the Small Business Foundation of America Inc., 202-223-1104. General information on doing business in more than 140 countries.

Trade Information Center Hotline, sponsored by the International Trade Administration, 1-800-872-8723. For information on federal export assistance programs.

Export Finance Hotline, sponsored by the Export-Import Bank, 1-800-424-5201.

Office of International Trade, Small Business Administration, 202-634-1500.

Overseas Private Investment Corp., 202-457-7010; general program information on financing for U.S. investors expanding into developing countries.

Export Virginia newsletter, published by the Virginia Department of Economic Development, Richmond, 804-371-8123; free calendar of events and seminars.

State of Maryland International Division, Baltimore, 410-333-8180.

February 3, 1992

International Marketing Strategy 11

Shock Market Strategies
Industry May Lack Inroads in Japan, but It Still Makes Tracks Around Globe

JOHN BURGESS AND WARREN BROWN

The humble shock absorber, which smooths the road for motorists around the world, has become another bump in the path of international trade.

During his visit to Japan last month, President Bush carried the flag for American-brand shock absorbers and the U.S. auto parts industry in general as part of a campaign he said was aimed at winning "jobs, jobs, jobs" for Americans.

His beef sounded like a replay of familiar American complaints against Japanese trade and economic practices.

Check under a car in Brazil, in India, in Mexico, South Africa, Australia or Britain and the shocks you find may well bear an American label. Do the same in Japan and you will almost certainly find a Japanese brand. There, American manufacturers remain bit players.

"The lowest-cost place in the world to build automotive components is the United States," said Jack Reilly, president of Tenneco Automotive, which owns Monroe Auto Equipment Co., one of the largest U.S. shock makers. "All we need is the opportunity to compete," said Reilly, who was in Bush's entourage in Japan.

Look more closely, however, and the stark black-and-white pattern of trade confrontation between the United States and Japan begins to dissolve into grayer shades.

American companies have prospered overseas—but generally by manufacturing there, rather than exporting from American factories. That's not an approach that generates a lot of jobs in the United States. Were American shocks to penetrate Japan by the industry's usual approach, it would probably mean Japanese factories employing Japanese citizens.

However, a deal that Bush struck with Japan to buy $10 billion more in U.S. parts each year requires that they be built in this country, which would create U.S. jobs. (Many of those parts may come from Japanese-owned plants in the United

States.) The tensions have arisen out of vastly different strategies pursued over the years by U.S. and Japanese auto industries. Japan's has stressed long-term close relationships between carmakers and suppliers, who are almost always Japanese. The United States has generally treated parts as commodity items, seeking the best deal from the low-cost bidder.

Although the leaders of the U.S. auto industry were the most vocal members of Bush's Tokyo delegation, American carmakers have often welcomed foreign shock makers into the S2 billion-a-year U.S. shock market, feeling that competition breeds low prices and quality. In Japan, the reverse has often held true: Automakers are loathe to dump loyal, long-term suppliers, even if the new ones are offering a better price and product.

Now, as they bang on Japan's door, U.S. companies are realizing that their past ways are obsolete, that to thrive they must mimic their foreign competitors. U.S. parts makers are courting automakers for long-term supply relationships and shouldering major design costs; in two cases, they have entered into joint ventures with foreign competitors.

In sum, few products are as thoroughly global as shocks are today. Consider this: One of the world's largest shock plants is located in Pamplona, Spain, the town where bulls run free in the streets at festival time each July. The factory used to be owned by British investors; now it is the joint property of an American and a Japanese company. Much of its output is exported to the United States.

U.S. shock makers weren't always so big. But in the 1980s, consolidation began. Ford Motor Co. and ITT Corp. got out of the business, leaving a "Big Three" in the shock trade—Monroe, Arvin Industries Inc. and General Motors Corp.'s Delco division.

One thing driving company size up was rising capital costs. Production floors on which shocks are shaped, sealed and tested were increasingly dominated by welding robots and automated conveyors, not people. "From coil of steel 'til it goes in the box, it's hardly touched by human hands," said Ben Parr, an auto parts specialist at State Farm Life Insurance Co.

Arvin and Monroe both say that their North American employment has declined in the past 10 years—due mainly to automation, not imports. Delco, however, estimates that its U.S. employment has risen during that period.

Protectionism also helped make the industry go global—European auto plants, wanting to maintain the local job base, would often buy only from companies that produced locally. "It's a global business," said Reilly. "You cannot be a regional producer and be successful, because of the economies of scale."

His company today manufactures shocks in 13 plants in seven countries. Keeping track of the trade is mind-boggling: Its plant in Brazil supplies foreign-owned auto factories there owned by GM, Volkswagen AG and a Ford-Fiat venture. Its plant in Australia supplies a Mazda Motor Corp. assembly line and the U.S. replacement market. Two Monroe plants in Spain ship to Europe and to the United States.

Delco operates plants in Spain, Mexico and France. Arvin has them in 11 countries and sells its product in about 100—including the former Soviet Union by way of an Arvin distributor in Finland. For the most part, said Byron Pond, chief operating officer at Arvin, borders are "not of any significant consequence."

The companies' U.S. plants have wracked up major surpluses in exports to Canada and Mexico.

But in their home market, these companies no longer have an iron grip. The U.S. imported $200 million worth of the older-style shock absorbers and the more sophisticated strut suspension assemblies in the first 11 months of 1991.

Japan led the way with exports of $65 million, but there were major exports from Spain, Germany, Brazil and Australia as well. In overall shock trade, the U.S. had a $30 million deficit, though that was down considerably from 1990's figures, as Japan's exports trailed off and sales to Canada expanded.

Perhaps bigger threats in the long term are the three Japanese and one German shock/strut makers that have set up "transplant" factories on the Americans' own home turf.

The Japanese firms moved here in part to serve Japanese auto companies that set up plants in the United States in the 1980s. Honda Motor Co.'s U.S. and Canadian plants, for instance, generate no business for U.S. shock makers—Honda gets all it needs from its Japanese "captive" supplier, Showa Manufacturing Co., which has established a factory in Sunbury, Ohio.

Other Japanese shock makers are focusing on business with Detroit. Ford and Chrysler Corp. do business with them, though GM gets almost all of its from its Delco unit.

Japanese-owned Tokiko (USA) Inc., feeling confident, has just doubled the size of a plant that it opened in Berea, Ky., in 1988. Its biggest business is building fancy systems for Ford's upscale Lincoln line. "Tokiko in Japan has run out of expansion room," said Bill Wildman, general affairs manager of Tokiko (USA), in explaining the decision to open an American plant.

A third Japanese strut plant opened in 1989 in Franklin, Ind. Owned by Kayaba Industry Co., it makes struts for Ford, Chrysler and Mazda.

Fichtel and Sachs of Germany, feeling there is still room for one more, has opened a strut plant in Florence, Ky.

Shifting rates of exchange were a big reason it came here, said Bob Chrysler, president of the company's U.S. operations. It once supplied suspension equipment from Germany for the Chrysler Minivan—but when the German mark rose in value against the dollar, German-made wares became too expensive for Chrysler.

Faced with these myriad challenges, U.S. shock companies are trying to modernize their equipment further and to find a larger role for themselves in the lengthy production food chain that eventually results in a finished automobile.

Delco points to a plant that it opened in 1989 near Dayton, Ohio, as a "transplant fighter." Employing about 270 people, it uses Japanese-style work rules that allow managers to shift workers from job to job on the plant floor as they are needed. Moreover, U.S. companies are moving to shoulder more of the huge cost and headache of designing the parts they make, rather than waiting for carmakers to do it. Japan's auto industry pioneered this approach, believing that over time it cuts costs, produces a better product and makes for a more secure financial relationship.

"We're in the process over the next three years of reducing our numbers of suppliers by one-third," said David Caplan, a spokesman for Ford's manufacturing operations. "The suppliers who survive will be the ones who are able to do research and development."

U.S. companies are also going into business with their foreign competitors. The plant in Pamplona, Spain, is a joint venture of Arvin and Kayaba. Monroe has a joint venture in South Carolina with German giant Robert Bosch GmbH, which has advanced skills in the electronics that run a new generation of suspension systems that adjust to different road conditions.

At the same time, U.S. companies are vying for business in Japan. They face few formal barriers such as tariffs. The hard part is breaking apart long-formed relationships between Japanese companies and convincing the automakers that their parts are as good as ones made by the local companies, where quality and cost-control are almost a religion.

Japan's replacement market is also hard to enter. One problem: It's against the rules there to install your own replacement shocks, as many Americans do. Certified mechanics must do it, and the shocks they provide are likely to flow from a long-standing pipeline to a Japanese manufacturer. This has crimped the development of a retail market, in which newcomers would probably have an easier time.

Arvin said it feels the Japanese market is already too "well served" to warrant the cost of trying for business with auto plants there. But Monroe and Delco are doing what the Japanese say must be done: They are taking the long view, trying to get involved from the first stage of a car's design. They both have operated engineering centers in Japan for the past three years. And they have won some business with Japanese plants, in both cases Toyota's—the product of a better strategy and more effective political pressure from Washington.

February 9, 1992

The Little Computer Company That Could

PETER MAASS

Nine years ago, a few computer whizzes from communist Hungary went to a trade fair in Western Europe and caught the eye of talent scouts from Apple Computer Inc.

With a wink at trade restrictions, Apple gave the promising Hungarians two computers, a couple thousand dollars and a challenge to develop world-class software.

Apple's investment behind the Iron Curtain led to the emergence of Graphisoft, a Hungarian software company that went on to create a popular software program for computer-aided design.

Graphisoft, whose sleek offices in a renovated Budapest mansion bear all the brash trademarks of Silicon Valley-style success, is an example of the commercialization of an unheralded asset in struggling Eastern Europe: brains.

Like its niche market, Graphisoft is small, with just $5 million in 1990 sales.

But the firm says its software, targeted at architects who use Apple's Macintosh computers, has gained a 50 percent market share in Western Europe and 10 percent in the United States.

Its success goes beyond numbers, marking one of the few instances in which an East European firm has bested Western rivals in a high-tech sector.

The company's founder, Gabor Bojar, has become an entrepreneurial hero in Hungary, and he met with President Bush during the latter's 1989 visit to Budapest.

The communist regimes in the Soviet Union and Eastern Europe may have ruined virtually everything they touched, but scientific and mathematical training was not among them, as demonstrated by the fears that Soviet nuclear experts might be lured away by countries trying to develop a bomb.

The former communist states rarely asked their engineers, scientists and mathematicians to perform work that would produce commercially viable products.

Their key tasks included designing new weapons and maintaining old machinery.

That is changing as the entire region seeks to reorient itself toward competition on open markets.

Many foreign investors believe the region's most important assets are the low-cost skills of its researchers, engineers and workers rather than the antiquated facilities they work in.

Hungary, whose flirtation with market economics over the past two decades gave it a head start on the rest of Eastern Europe, was the first to commercialize its brainpower, and its computer software industry is a prime example.

According to unofficial estimates, Hungary has several thousand software companies, although a minority of them are successful exporters.

Seeking export markets in the 1970s, Hungarian computer experts realized they could not keep pace with the West's advances in the hardware sector, according to Gyozo Rovacs, who helped plan Hungary's strategy. "The only area where Hungarians could compete was in software," he said.

In Hungary, as in the rest of the region, computer experts were obliged to work on outdated systems—and often used a printer from one Soviet Bloc country, a keyboard from another and a screen from a third.

But they thrived on adversity by developing complex software programs that squeezed as much as possible from their deficient hardware.

"The attitude of Hungarians was not to buy a better computer but to improve the software," said Reiner Schoning, head of the Hungarian unit of Siemens GmbH, the German electronics giant.

"They are sort of magicians sometimes. I have seen computer systems with parts from seven different countries . . . It was unbelievable."

Siemens was one of the first Western companies to exploit Eastern Europe's intellectual reserves.

More than 20 years ago, Siemens began selling computer hardware to Hungary and, instead of receiving cash payment, was "lent" some of the country's best computer programmers.

The little-known "body leasing" program was used by many West European firms that did business with Hungary.

Imre Pakozdi, a vice president of Graphisoft, believes Hungarian software developers now are as good as their Western competitors, thanks in part to their experience working in Western companies. But, he added, they suffer from a lack of marketing knowledge.

"Hungary is a superpower in mathematics, but we did not have any university that taught how to organize a company—we have to learn these things," Pakozdi said. He added that Hungarians are doubly handicapped because they do not live and work in their target markets.

Recognita Corp., a successful 50-employee software firm in Budapest, is trying to close the gap by relocating part of its staff to Sunnyvale, Calif.

A spokeswoman said the firm, which has developed an IBM-compatible software program that enables computers to read written text, decided that relocation is the best way to market its products and keep pace with advances in its field.

If firms such as Graphisoft and Recognita continue to succeed, they can expect some company from other once-communist nations, particularly the former Soviet Union.

Schoning of Siemens recalled being approached by a Russian businessman offering the services of 3,000 software developers.

The Russian promised to undercut anybody else's prices by 10 percent.

"He was ready to send them over to us," Schoning said. "It was meant seriously—but we didn't take it seriously."

February 20, 1992

High Definition Television Heads West

Mexico City to Get First Functioning
System Outside of Japan

JOHN BURGESS

North America's first high-definition television service for consumers could be on the way—not to Americans but to the wealthier residents of Mexico City.

The Mexican TV network Televisa S.A. de C.V. is pursuing a plan to transmit a single channel of newly released movies in the crisp images and sound of the new video technology as early as next year. They would be beamed to subscribers equipped with special HDTV sets that now are extremely costly. In addition, viewers would have to pay for each film they watch.

While the United States struggles to craft its own version of HDTV for introduction in the mid-1990s, Televisa is looking at moving ahead much sooner, using what is now the world's only functioning HDTV system, Japan's.

That would create the first significant foothold in the Western hemisphere for Japan's version of HDTV, which it has proposed as a world standard. The United States and Europe have insisted on developing their own standards in an attempt to foster local electronics companies and develop a more advanced HDTV than Japan's version.

The Japanese television network NHK, which coordinated development of the Japanese HDTV standard. sent a team to Mexico City last year to conduct six weeks of test transmissions.

HDTV sets start at about $30,000 in Japan. But Televisa is gambling that prices will come down and that significant numbers of the city's 18 million people will be willing to shell out generously to receive first-run foreign movies, which often are unavailable in local movie theaters.

Televisa has talked with an American company, Scientific Atlanta Inc., which makes transmission equipment based on HDTV standards developed in Europe. The sets and other gear would still come from Japan, which is the only country that makes them.

Many questions remain unanswered about the project, including whether it will go forward at all. "How many people are going to spend that kind of dough to watch a few movies?" asked one skeptical U.S. TV executive. ". . . But sometimes you trade off image for cash." Still, it is attracting attention here because it might provide information about how—or whether—to market HDTV in this country.

"One of the fundamental questions of high-definition is, would real people really want it?" said Tom Stanley, chief engineer at the Federal Communications Commission. The project would take "a little of the voodoo out of what high definition is."

Japan this fall plans to begin eight hours of daily broadcasts in HDTV, which has been widely heralded as the greatest advance since color television. It features a wide screen and sharper images. However, the sets' lofty prices have spawned talk in Japan that HDTV might flop and that TV makers would be better off focusing, for now at least, on upgrading conventional television.

Nonetheless, Televisa has pursued the project. The company has vast financial resources. Its network includes about 200 television stations in Mexico, as well as major production facilities that turn out Spanish-language newscasts and entertainment shown all over Latin America.

The project has attracted official interest as well. The Mexican government granted Televisa permission to conduct its test. And Mexican President Carlos Salinas de Gortari, during a recent visit to Japan, reportedly visited an NHK facility and received a demonstration of the Japanese HDTV system.

Televisa has talked with more than a dozen suppliers, in an apparent effort to negotiate large purchases of HDTV equipment at a discount. A Toshiba Corp. spokesman confirmed that his company is among them.

Drawing Televisa to the project is the fact that movie theaters in Mexico City often don't show Hollywood's hot new releases. Televisa proposes to "bring movies to people instead of people to movies," Jorge Kanahuati, Televisa vice president, recently told HDTV Report, a U.S. newsletter. The newsletter said the system could start in late 1992.

People familiar with the project say the idea is that members of the HDTV sets start at about $30,000 in Japan. city's elite would lease or buy the sets, then invite friends to watch films. Social clubs might do the same thing, perhaps informally charging members to watch. In addition, Mexico would get the prestige of pioneering a new technology.

Besides pent-up demand for first-run films, Mexico City has unusual topography well-suited to the plan.

Japan's HDTV systems was designed to allow satellites to broadcast directly from space to sets equipped with small dishes. Televisa would transmit HDTV pictures on the same frequency as ones for satellites, but using a transmitter located on a mountain peak at Pico Tres Padres, about 2,000 feet above the city. Dishes mounted on subscribers' homes would then pick up the signals.

A drawback is that homes located behind obstructions such as high-rise buildings or hills could not receive the pictures.

Last year, according to a technical paper prepared by Televisa and NHK personnel, Televisa tested reception at 148 locations around Mexico City and concluded that the picture would be acceptable at about half of all points located about 20 miles from the mountain-top transmitter. Due to their lack of such a high altitude transmission point, most cities could not use this type of transmission at all.

If a broadcast satellite is launched at a future date, subscribers might simply realign their dishes to receive its signal.

How the Televisa project would affect an international battle over HDTV standards remains unclear. The standards-setting process is often highly politicized, in the belief that adopting a foreign standard can undermine a country' s own electronics industry.

Mexico has said that the Televisa project does not mean it is opting for the Japanese standard, according to U.S. officials, and it has expressed keen interest in U.S. efforts to develop a standard. However,

If large numbers of people do subscribe and buy its equipment, Mexico might be pushed unofficially in the direction of that standard.

October 17, 1991

Bitterness at Benetton:

Store Owners Take Leagal Action against Italian Retailer over "European" Way of Doing Business

WARRNE BROWN

To Karle Falkenburg, the most alluring hue in the United Colors of Benetton was green.

She wanted to make money, lots of it. Benetton Group S.p.A., the famed Italian maker of pricey sweaters and fancy jeans, offered her the chance—or so it seemed.

That was in 1985, when Benetton stores were popping up across the country, pulling in millions of American shoppers eager to spend money on trendy European designs.

"I was a part of the 'Benetton family,' " said Falkenburg, who had held various modeling and community service jobs before opening her first Benetton shop in Alabama. "Benetton told me that all I had to do to make money was follow their system and work with them. They said I was going to do well. ..."

Today, the 39-year-old Falkenburg is angry, about $1 million in debt and embroiled in a multimillion-dollar lawsuit that alleges Benetton fraudulently misrepresented financial and other requirements for buying and operating its outlets.

Benetton officials say that they have violated no U.S. laws and that Falkenburg's lawsuit is simply an attempt on her part to evade payment of overdue bills to the company. But they admit that they have developed an unusual business strategy that greatly reduces the risk to Benetton and pushes the financial burden downstream to the individual store owners.

Falkenburg isn't the only Benetton store owner questioning the company's practices. In seven legal actions involving about 15 outlets, Benetton is accused of giving prospective store owners misleading information about their stores' earning potential; blocking the return of damaged goods and goods shipped too late to be sold as seasonal wear; and implying in oral agreements that store owners would have exclusive marketing areas but frequently setting up stores so close together that merchants were in direct competition with one another.

The charges have attracted the attention of the Federal Trade Commission, which is investigating the allegations and whether Benetton deliberately structured its operations in the United States to evade federal franchise laws.

Regulatory officials say the number of lawsuits pending against Benetton is not unusual for a company with 650 stores. What has drawn their attention is Benetton's widespread use of oral agreements, the lack of territorial rights for Benetton retailers and the unique business structure that mimics traditional franchise operations but requires store owners to assume nearly all the risk.

FTC officials declined to comment on the investigation by the agency's office in New York, the headquarters of Benetton's U.S. operations.

The lawsuits challenge the reputation of the clothes maker and the product-distribution system it has used to spin yarn into riches since its founding in 1965. Last year, Benetton reported a profit of $99.5 million on sales of $1.2 billion.

Also at issue is the adequacy of existing laws to protect the rights of franchisees—people who, either individually or as a group, buy the license and space to sell goods or services in the name of the company granting the license.

Aldo Palmeri, Benetton Group S.p.A.'s chief operating officer, said the lawsuits and FTC investigation stem from a misunderstanding of "a European way of doing business" upon which the Benetton system is modeled.

"We're trying to create a whole new generation of entrepreneurs, a new formula for doing business," Palmeri, a neatly dressed man of 42, said in an interview in New York.

The company's operation works like this: Benetton makes the clothes. It sells people the right to set up marketing regions, of which there are nine in the United States. Those regional representatives essentially work for themselves, using their own money to cover the expenses of recruiting potential store owners for their region.

Unlike most franchise operations, these representatives are free to set up as many stores in their territory as they can find buyers for, even if that means some are within blocks of each other. A store's startup costs typically run between $80,000 and $100,000, a sum that includes the leases and building construction costs. No licensing fee is paid to Benetton or the representative by the store owner, a point the company cites as evidence that it is not a franchise.

The store owners do, however, have to purchase all their merchandise through the representatives, who collect a 5.5 percent commission from the manufacturer of those goods, Benetton. Since the representative makes his or her money only on this commission, the incentive is to have as many retailers in a region as possible. In Washington, for example, there are 25 Benetton outlets, including two within the Tysons Corner shopping complex.

When buying merchandise, the store owners are responsible for all insurance, freight and other shipping costs. Until this year, the retailers were not allowed to send back clothes that were damaged or shipped late. Nor were they allowed to return erroneously filled orders, according to store owners and Benetton officials.

Benetton's "no-return" policy was an attempt to replicate European business practices in America, Palmeri said. "It is not common to return new merchandise in Europe," he said.

Benetton sells its products through 5,000 stores in 79 countries. Only in America is there a system in place to accept returned goods, Palmeri said. At any rate, problem shipments constitute a relatively insignificant part of Benetton's yearly sales, he said.

To keep Benetton from suffering any losses if a store owner doesn't pay for goods, the company demands that its representatives cover the delinquent payments for retailers in their region.

"Yes, we put the risks further down the line" from the parent company, Palmeri conceded. But by assuming those burdens, the representatives and retailers also stand to gain a greater share of the profits because there are less restrictions on their business, he said.

Palmeri also said the company prefers people with little or no business experience so that they aren't wedded to traditional American notions of how businesses ought to operate.

Benetton's insistence on oral agreements stems from its belief that all parties involved in the company's business should be independent entrepreneurs, allowed to run their businesses as they see fit, Palmeri said.

"We do not have written contracts because we find it difficult to have a contractual relationship between two entrepreneurs," Palmeri said. The glue that keeps the system together is composed of "trust" and the "Benetton spirit"—a gung-ho desire to sell, Palmeri said.

But behind the worthy sentiments he describes is a fiercely competitive operating policy that can be cutthroat in its execution. Lawyers for merchants suing Benetton say their clients were never told that they could be forced to compete with Benetton stores in close proximity to theirs.

"It's not illegal to go into business and to be hard and to say that we will put up a store across the street from yours," said Malcolm Hoffman, an attorney for two Oregon store owners who are suing Benetton. "But the problem is one of information. Benetton never told any of its franchisees that it would do those things."

Federico Minoli, general manager of Benetton U.S.A., denied that there has been any attempt to mislead prospective store owners. But he agreed that the company's approach could lead to a proliferation of Benetton stores in one community.

"We believe in letting the market regulate itself," Minoli said. "If you have two stores in the same neighborhood, and someone comes to us and says: 'I think there is room for a third store,' we're willing to let him go ahead and risk his money and do it."

If that means that an existing store in the same neighborhood is put out of business, so be it, Minoli said.

Falkenburg said she was shocked by Minoli's remarks and his comment about letting stores fail. In her suit, Falkenburg said she never received the support she was promised, such as Benetton's advice in selling products and the training needed to operate Benetton stores successfully.

Minoli counters that Benetton did work with Falkenburg and provide her support, but he said she simply proved incapable of running a business.

Falkenburg had never before worked as a manager, having spent most of her career as a fashion model and legal assistant.

"There is no way that I would have ever done business with Benetton if they had said the things Minoli said" about letting marginal Benetton stores fail, Falkenburg said.

Falkenburg lost two stores. Three remain in business. But they are being protected from creditors while Falkenburg reorganizes them under Chapter 11 of the U.S. Bankruptcy Code.

At the time she began negotiating for her first store in December 1984, Benetton had 4,000 stores around the world.

That year, she entered a "handshake" deal with Benetton representative Gilberto Casagrande to open a store the following year. "It was strictly a handshake agreement," Falkenburg said.

Her first store in Madison, Ala., costing about $125,000, was an instant success. Casagrande encouraged her to open more stores in Alabama, which she did.

Things started going wrong shortly thereafter, Falkenburg said. Benetton required that she hire Italian craftsmen—usually in teams of two—to put up her stores, she alleges in her suit. Falkenburg said she argued that she could get the job done more cheaply with local labor but said Benetton insisted that she use their workers. She yielded, paying all of the transportation, salary, feeding and housing expenses for the foreign craftsmen.

"Benetton said that only Italians could put an 'Italian decor package' in the stores the way Benetton wanted it," Falkenburg said.

Merchandise shipments started arriving late but she was forced to pay for them anyway, her suit alleges. To move the out-of-season wear, she had sales, which caused her to lose more money, according to the suit. Shipments also arrived damaged, her suit claims, and she was forced to pay for those, too. When she complained, she was told to work out the problems with Casagrande, her representative, the suit claims.

Benetton officials agreed that some shipments had arrived late at Falkenburg's stores as well as at the stores of other merchants. But company officials said that late shipments were infrequent and that, often, shipments arrived late because merchants were tardy in paying for orders.

"She didn't pay her bills," Minoli said. "We don't forgive debts." Falkenburg owes Benetton Group S.p.A. $1.2 million for shipped merchandise, Benetton officials say. Falkenburg admits owing the money but says the debt occurred because Benetton mishandled merchandise orders and created other business problems for her.

In retrospect, Falkenburg said she was foolish to ever sign up with Benetton, to be swept away by what she says were promises of wealth and independence. Certainly, she said, she was foolish to plop down hundreds of thousands of dollars on oral agreements.

Various other lawsuits filed against Benetton argue that the company tried to "obfuscate and disguise the nature of the Benetton Group's business operations" to avoid compliance with FTC franchise laws.

The FTC rule says a business must have three elements to he considered a franchise: It must license its retailers to use a common trademark it must charge a licensing fee of at least $500 during the first six months of a franchisee's operation; and it must exercise significant control over how the franchisee conducts its business.

Benetton requires its retailers to conduct all of their business under the Benetton trademark. The company also dictates the business format—store design and sales practices are examples—for what it calls its "independent stores."

But because Benetton charges no license or royalty fees, it does not consider itself a franchise, and it argues that it is exempt from requirements of the FTC rule.

Lawyers for Benetton's dissident retailers call the exemption a ruse.

Benetton extracts payments from its retailers through the sale of unsolicited catalogues and other unordered items to its stores, according to Hoffman, the attorney representing Oregon store owners Frances Robertson and her mother, Jesse Yarberry.

"The $500 fee does not have to be in money and it does not have to be a separate payment," Hoffman maintains.

Benetton is suing Hoffman's two clients on grounds that they have slandered and libeled the company with their charges.

"Our philosophy is that we are not a franchiser, and we feel pretty safe that we have not violated any rules," said Benetton's Minoli.

However, he said that if the FTC rules against Benetton on the franchise issue, "We will do whatever must be done to meet the law." Benetton already has made changes aimed at improving its relationship with its U.S. retailers, such as allowing the return of damaged goods and doing away with the requirement to use Italian craftsmen to build its stores, Minoli said.

What Benetton wants to do now is resolve its legal problems and embark on a new strategy that would discournge smaller stores in favor of "super stores"— similar to one at the Tysons II mall—which are four times the size of its traditional outlets and more capable of offering a wider variety of goods.

That strategy appears to be working. In the past year, the company has dropped from 750 to 650 stores, as smaller Benetton stores went out of business.

Will the change cause others to drop out? Palmeri seemed puzzled by the question. He started to answer in Italian, but then switched to English.

"The typical nature of the entrepreneur is to run the risk, to accept the risk," he said. "We want to establish competition within the system. The stores that do well will survive and grow. But some will fail."

July 30, 1989

Japanese Make Vintage Investments

Winery Takeovers in France Greeted with Blend of Dismay, Relief

WILLIAM DROZDIAK

The stunted, gnarled vines and ancient chateaux that dominate this peninsula between the Atlantic Ocean and the Gironde River are regarded as part of France's most hallowed patrimony. In a nation where wine is considered nectar from the gods, the Medoc is revered as a pantheon of sacred properties bearing such holy names as Latour, Lafite and Margaux.

Keiichi Fujimoto wants to join their ranks. Undaunted by France's notorious chauvinism and the Nippophobia exemplified by former prime minister Edith Cresson—who warned while still in office last year that Japan was bent on vanquishing the West with a fanatical labor force she described as "worker ants"— Fujimoto is seeking to transform the once struggling Chateau Citran into a world-class winery and beat the French at their own game.

Five years ago, the "Samurai of the Medoc," as he is known, spearheaded a round of quiet Japanese takeovers of important wine-producing properties in the Bordeaux region. Even though the Romans first planted the vines here and the British developed claret's global commerce, Japan's thrust at the heart of the French wine country has generated a variety of reactions—from spasms of xenophobic apoplexy to welcome sighs of relief that somebody is willing to invest huge sums of money to revive dilapidated estates.

For centuries, France's most venerated grape-growing parcels and supreme winemaking skills were passed like family jewels from generation to generation. But in recent years, soaring land values, high inheritance taxes and the temptations of urban life have induced some chateau owners to surrender their heritage to the highest bidder.

To the surprise of few and the consternation of many, Japanese investors have stepped into the breach. Flush with cash, disillusioned by rising hositility in the United States, yet still eager to buy prestigious properties abroad, Japanese entrepreneurs have been snapping up French estates.

Court actions and personal reluctance have stopped some of the nation's most treasured vineyards from passing into Japanese hands. A judge blocked the sale of Romanee Conti, one of the most valuable estates in Burgundy, to a Tokyo bidder because he said he could not tolerate "selling something like a cathedral." Corinne

Metzelopolous, a Greek-French heiress who is the principal owner of Chateau Margaux, turned down a Japanese offer of $700 million before agreeing to sell the estate for a much lower price to close friends—the Agnelli family of Italy.

But elsewhere in the Medoc, Japanese buyers have enjoyed better luck. Suntory, the world's fifth largest beer and spirits maker, now controls the St. Julien property of Chateau Lagrange. Sanraku, a wine and spirits importer, has taken over Chateau Reysson, and the farm machinery firm Otani owns Chateau Lagarosse near Bordeaux.

The financial strength behind Fujimoto's ambitions comes from his patron, Sukagiro Itani, the chief executive of Touko Haus, one of the biggest property firms in Japan. Itani has never visited the vineyard but has willingly poured tens of millions of dollars into upgrading the chateau because of what Fujimoto calls "a sentimental motive, like the purchase of fine art."

Fujimoto, a Tokyo-born architect who is married to a Frenchwoman and has lived in France for 22 years, said he scouted a dozen chateaux for nearly a year before informing Itani that he had discovered "a real jewel" in the 13th-century Chateau Citran, whose French owners could not sustain its huge maintenance costs.

His success in quickly reversing the vineyard's declining reputation while defusing French anxieties about his goals has turned Fujimoto into something of a guru for several Japanese tycoons eager to acquire French wine properties without arousing national sensitivities.

"I tell them they need to proceed slowly and carefully, because the French have a special character and there are lots of details that can trip you up," Fujimoto said during an interview at the elegant chateau. "Some French people still have a gnawing fear about a Japanese invasion, that their precious chateaux will be packed up and transplanted abroad. So we have to reassure them through these big capital investments that we just want to make the best possible wine."

Itani and his company also have acquired Le Relais de Margaux, the premier hotel in the Medoc region, to serve as a guest house for his clients and friends. Toshinari Hara, a Japanese chef who has studied French cuisine, has been placed in charge of the kitchen.

"Let's face it, the Japanese have the money to call the shots, so they can pretty much do what they want," said Frederic Storz, a Frenchman who is the hotel's assistant director. "These places cost a lot of money to maintain, as do the vineyards, and they are the only ones who seem to have it nowadays."

French winemakers are astounded at the scale of the Japanese investment in the Chateau Citran vineyard. "I can't think of anybody who would have thought of putting so much money into that rundown place," said Alain Meyre, who owns the respected Cap Leon Veyrin vineyard in nearby Listrac. "We'll just have to see if they have the staying power to make great wines."

With the advice of an innovative French winemaker, Jean-Michel Ferrandez, Fujimoto has torn up old vines and transformed the contours of the land to capture the best angle of the sun and improve irrigation. He has installed computerized fermentation vats, insists on buying only the best oak barrels and toasts the barrels at different temperatures to impart a more complex flavor to the wine.

Since the Japanese took over Citran in 1987, production has grown to nearly 600,000 bottles a year, making it the second largest producer in the Medoc region. Fujimoto claims the improvement in Citran's quality—which American wine critic Robert M. Parker Jr. described as "one of the bright shining stars" of the Haut-Medoc region—has tripled the value of the estate.

"We are creating a winery for the 21st century, and the beneficiaries will be our children," Fujimoto said. "But I try to reassure my French friends that this does not mean that the Japanese presence here will necessarily be eternal. Wine has been made here for more than 2,000 years, and many different nationalities have passed through already."

Fujimoto said his proudest achievement is persuading his French neighbors that a Japanese winemaker can excel at an art once considered to be a cherished French preserve, and he sees no reason why the French cannot succeed in sectors where Japanese manufacturers are considered invincible.

"The goal for everybody should be simply to make the best product for the best price, so why can't the French make cars as well as they make the Concorde or the Metro?" Fujimoto asked. "I guess the problem is because they tolerate mistakes that would be unthinkable, or unforgivable, in Japan."

After Cresson's harsh attacks last year on Japan's alleged economic imperialism, Fujimoto said he was heartened by his many neighbors in the Medoc who rushed to his support and apologized for her appeals to economic nationalism.

"Wine has the face and character of a human being," he said. "I believe you can understand the character of a man by the wine he makes, and that's why I am *happy* the French respect me for what I have done."

May 11, 1992

The Art of a Deal in East Europe—Poland

Town Sews, Reaps against the Odds

BLAINE HARDEN

Polish women began making Levi Strauss blue jeans here this month in a state-of-the-art garment factory with a sound system that bathes them in American soul music and video players that teach them how to negotiate awkward stitches.

The $20 million factory, in a refurbished warehouse in this down-at-the-heels industiral city on the banks of the Vistula River, was built for the Polish market, whose 38 million consumers are thought to have an exceptional appetite for stone-washed Levi's.

As it taps this market, Levi Strauss will create 1,000 jobs paying wages well above the Polish average and spin off work for local catering and construction firms, truckers and shop owners. For this city of 120,000, where several state-run factories are going bust and the jobless rate is 15 percent and rising, the pants plant could not have opened at a better time.

The San Francisco-based jeans maker was lured by cheap rent, a tax holiday and local people eager to please. Yet what is most arresting about the pleasantness that Levi Strauss encountered in Plock is that it is not part of a Polish trend.

The worrying news—news that raises doubts about the free-market future of this country—is that stories of painless foreign investment in Poland are anything but typical. What happened here, with so little bureaucratic niggling and with the boosterish backing of politicians, does not appear to be happening often in the rest of Poland.

To an extent that has disappointed and discouraged foreign companies and Western governments, investment in post-communist Poland is turning out to be maddeningly slow, complicated and, for some potential investors, not worth the bother.

"There is a lack of knowledge in Warsaw and in the provinces about the point of investment. Poles think, based on growing up in communist schools, that the point is to manufacture goods and create jobs—not to make a profit," said Andrzej Celinski, a legislator who helped lure champions of foreign investment.

Populist leaders and ultranationalist political parties have begun pandering to a growing xenophobia here as traditionally pro-capitalist sympathies evaporate. An authoritative public opinion survey here last week showed that Poles perceive foreign investors as a greater long-term economic threat than state involvement in industry.

Prime Minister Jan Olszewski, who has been in office for two months and who heads the third Polish government in less than three years, has made a series of statements that raise doubts about Poland's receptiveness to foreign capital, accusing his free-market predecessors of selling out cheaply to foreigners

Olszewski told shipyard workers in the port city of Szczecin last week that the sale of state industry in the past two years has been guided by the principle of "Any old way as long as it is fast, any old how, and any old way as long as foreigners are given as much as possible."

Poland was supposed to have been the mother lode for Western investors, particularly Americans, in Eastern Europe. This was the first country in the Soviet orbit to discard communism and root out communist subsidies; it won praise throughout the West for "courageous" free-market reforms.

Table 1 • Foreign Investment in Eastern Europe: Poland

Top Countries Investing In Poland

Country	No of Joint Ventures	Foreign Capital Invested
1. Germany	1483	$157 million
2. United States	406	$57 million
3. Sweden	345	$53 million
4. Austria	322	$38 million
5. France	254	$66 million

Source: Polish government

Joint Ventures:

According to Business International, a Vienna-based consulting company that specializes in Eastern Europe, the total number of joint ventures in Poland is about 6,000 and total capital invested is $1 billion. The following major foreign deals were initiated or signed since October.

Company	Product	Capital Invested
Gerber (USA) and Alima Food Co.	Baby food	$25 million
Fiat (Italy) and FSM	Compact cars	$800 million*
Ford (USA) and FSO	Cars	unavailable*
General Motors (USA) and FSO (under negotiation)	Cars	$400 million
Volvo (Sweden) and Jelcz	Buses	unavailable*
Volkswagen (Germany) and Polmo	Vehicles	unavailable*
Lucchini (Italy) and Warsaw Steel Works	Steel	$200 million*

*Letter of intent signed

But "shock therapy" economics have only half worked, allowing private shops to boom but failing to trigger significant management changes at state-owned enterprises, which still account for 65 percent of the economy. The reforms have put more than 2.1 million people out of work so far, and the rate of layoffs continues to accelerate.

"The people of Poland think that their country is a paradise that could be stolen by foreign investors. They demand too much; their style of negotiation is often improper. My opinion is that investors must be courted and helped," said Andrzej Dretkiewicz, the mayor of Plock and one of the few Polish politicians who acknowledge Western pessimism about investing in their country.

Poland has attracted only half the investment capital that has gone into Hungary, a post-communist country with just a quarter of Poland's population. Czechoslovakia, with less than half the population of Poland, also has soared past this country in winning commitments of foreign capital.

"The honest statement is that investment is not getting any easier in Poland, and in some ways it is getting harder. It seems to be getting easier in Hungary and Czechoslovakia," said a Western diplomat who specializes in trade.

"Most businessmen that I talk to tend to put Poland at the bottom of their list. For some, it is even dropping off the list," said John Balazs, a partner in charge of the tax and legal section at Price Waterhouse in Budapest. "It is a difficult market to operate in, with a high foreign debt and really a very unstable system of government.

Not everyone, of course, shares this bleak view of investing in Poland. An estimated 6,000 foreign joint ventures have been contracted here since 1989, attracting about $1 billion in foreign capital, according to Business International, a Vienna-based firm that specializes in Eastern Europe.

Despite its perceived liabilities, Poland has made astounding progress in just two years. It was an economic basket case until the end of 1989, with hyperinflation, bare shelves and food lines. Compared to either Hungary or Czechoslovakia, it had a shattered infrastructure, a decrepit industrial base and a dramatically lower standard of living.

Many of these disadvantages persist, but shortages are gone, almost the entire retail sector is in private hands, more than one-quarter of all Poles with jobs are working for private firms, and there are already foreign companies making handsome profits on multimillion-dollar investments.

"It does work here. Our ventures are profitable. Poland will pay off better in the medium term—that is, five years—than Czechoslovakia or Hungary. In the long-term it certainly is a better investment," said David R. Hunter, country manager for Asea Brown Boveri, a major Swedish-Swiss company that makes electrical equipment.

The company, which was one of the first to make sizable investments in Poland, has become this country's largest private employer, with 7,500 employees.

But Hunter acknowledged that there are growing worries for foreign investors in Poland.

"Poland moved much quicker than the other two reforming countries {Czechoslovakia and Hungary}, but now the government seems to have dug in its heels. It has been less consistent," said Hunter. He said his company, which bought into Poland before prices began to rise and regulations thicken, has been criticized "for coming in early and picking through the rubble to find a bargain deal."

The most successful foreign investors in Poland, as across Eastern Europe, have been the Germans. They have signed three times as many joint ventures in Poland as investors from the second-ranked country, the United States. This is a statistic that surprises few Poles.

Table 2 • Foreign Investment in Eastern Europe: Hungary

Top Countries Investing In Hungary

Country	No. of Joint Ventures in 1991	Amount
United States	300	$1 billion
Austria	unavailable	$380 million
Germany	3,000 to 4,000	$350 million

Source: U.S. Embassy and Business International

(U.S. Embassy says other investors, by order of deals, are: France, Britain and Japan.) Joint Ventures: Business International says there have been about 11,000 joint ventures in Hungary since 1989, and total capital invested is S2 billion. Here is a list of major deals in Hungary and amount of money committed, based on press reports and estimates. Investment capital does not necessarily come from the listed firm.

Company	Product	Capital Invested
Suzuki (Japan)	Building automobile factory	$265 million
General Motors (USA)	Building automobile, spare-parts factory	$220 million
General Electric (USA)	Purchased Tungsram light-bulb company	$150 million
Saofi. (France)	Purchased Chinoin (France) Pharmaceuticals firm	$150 million
Beacon Co. (USA)	Plans to build hotel-office complex	$150 million
Guardian Industries (USA)	Purchased Hungarian glass firm	$115 million
Electrolux (USA)	Purchased Lehel refrigerator company	$90 million
Ford Motor Co (USA)	Building car-parts factory	$83 million
Prinzhorn Group (Austria),	Purchased Hungarian paper firm	$82 million
Sara Lee(USA)	Purchased Hungary's Compack Food	$60 million

Table 3 • Foreign Investment in Eastern Europe: Czechoslovakia

Joint Ventures: In general, the Czechoslovak government believes there have been about 4,000 joint ventures since 1989. Seventy percent of foreign business ventures are small- and medium-sized deals involving an average of $30,000. Germany has more than a third of foreign investment, and together with Austria it accounts for 60 percent of foreign investment and 80 percent of total dollar value. This final number is skewed by huge Volkswagen deal with Skoda. Business International lists the following major foreign investments in Czechoslovakia:

Company	Product	Capital Invested
Volkswagen (Germany) and Skoda	Manufacture cars	$840 million
Mercedes Benz (Germany) and Liaz-Avia Praha	Manufacture trucks	$283 million
Siemens (Germany) and Skoda	Produce power plants	170 million
Ital Cementi (Italy) and Hranice	Cement factory	$135 million
Glaverbel (Belgium) and Sklofla	Glass work	$130 million
Linde (Germany) and Technoplyn	Industrial glass works	$106 million
Siemens (Germany) and Skoda Plzen	Build railroad	$105 million
BSN & Nestle (Switzerland) and Cokoladovny	Make chocolates	$95.5 million
Air France (France) and Czechoslovak National Airlines	Airline venture	$60 million
Dow Chemical (USA) and Chemicke Zavody Sokolor—Blaine Harden	Produce chemicals	$53 million

"The Germans are next door. They know the market and the character of our people. It is much easier for them to operate than the Americans or just about anyone else," said Ryszard Wojtowski, a former chief of staff in the Polish prime minister's office and now a public relations manager for Coca-Cola, which is building a $250 million plant in Poland.

Understanding the German advantage, however, doesn't keep it from being resented. Poland endured more killing per capita under German occupation in World War II than any other nation. Despite official statements welcoming German capital, the Polish government is clearly ambivalent about selling off industry to Germans. Defense Minister Jan Parys referred in a recent ministry meeting to the "disquieting economic expansion of united Germany."

Brick Wall of Bureaucracy

German or not, investment consultants say that all investors are running into the same brick wall of bureaucracy in Warsaw. As Levi Strauss learned in Plock, the only way around the brick wall is to have what Levi's executive Claude Flauraud calls "pullers."

"It is no secret that there are some people in this country that are very dubious about foreigners. You need to have a puller from the inside," said Flauraud, business development director for Levi Strauss in Euorpe, the Middle East and Africa.

The pullers in Plock were Celinski, the local legislator, and Dretkiewicz, the mayor. Dretkiewicz pressured the city council into buying suitable property to lease to Levi Strauss at below-market rates. He arranged for new telephone exchanges and rooms in guest houses, and he is working on a satellite linkup for banking transfers. When Levi's needed a gas line to power its big jeans dryers, the mayor immediately ordered the city to dig a trench.

"When Americans first come to Poland, they do not understand all the small details of Polish reality. We have decided to take care of everything for them," said the mayor. "Our motto is If you come to Plock, you will not leave."

In an office above the floor where Plock women were busily stitching jeans together, Levi's executive Flauraud said that the mayor "was probably the key" to the speedy opening of the factory.

"It would do a hell of a lot of good for the future of this country if it had a few hundred more politicians like him," Flauraud said.

February 10, 1992

12 International Product Development

Competing in a Diverse Market:
U.S. Firms Seek Unity on Product Standards in Europe

JOHN BURGESS

The flights to Europe are costly and the talk there is dry and technical, but Janet Schultz can't afford to be absent when members of Technical Committee 102, European Committee for Standardization, meet for business.

Schultz, a divisional vice president at Amsco International Inc. of Pittsburgh, is waist deep in a little-known but crucial process of Europe '92, the movement to merge the 12 European Community countries into one $5 trillion-a-year market with common tariffs and uniform technical standards for products.

For Amsco, which hopes to export to Europe its equipment for sterilizing medical equipement, millions of dollars in sales are at stake at these meetings, where representatives from rival European industries draft the fine print of standards for equipment of this type sold in Europe.

If requirements are set in ways that would force Amsco into a costly retooling of plants in Pennsylvania and North Carolina, where it makes sterilizers ranging in price from $2,500 to nearly $750,000, the company may decide Europe isn't worth the effort and stay home.

Across Europe, industry groups like Technical Committee 102 are huddling to devise standards for products as diverse as toys, beer, computers and earthmovers. The deliberations will help determine who can and who cannot compete effectively in the huge, affluent European market.

Standards ensure a product functions safely. The standards also serve as a crucial underpinning of the industrial revolution by ensuring a part built at one factory will fit a product built at another plant.

But behind rulings on calibration and product design may be fears that new standards would expose national industries, long protected by national standards, to the uncertainties of competition. "In the end it's not a technical problem," said Patrizio Sanchioni, a meeting participant who is engineering director at Italian sterilizer manufacturer Omasa SRL. "It's a problem of economics."

In addition to a voice in devising European standards, the United States also is pressing for an end to rules that European inspectors must test U.S. export products for standards compliance. European inspectors, for instance, fly to the U.S. plants of Caterpillar Inc., a manufacturer of earth-moving equipment, to determine if production methods meet Europe's standards.

Europeans, for their part, say the American standards system can impede their exports to the United States. While Europe's system is centralized, European manufacturers say the United States is a tangle of confusing, often poorly coordinated rules devised by a wide range of trade associations, and individual states also may enact conflicting product requirements.

But American standards experts said their system has nothing to match the chaos of Europe's: In Britain, steam sterilizers must include sensors to detect air leaks. France requires tests to ensure that models work on rubber products. Germany requires special-size holes in the walls of the instruments for the insertion of test devices.

Thus, a product that meets the requirements of one nation might not necessarily meet those in another country. Even if Amsco designed a sterilizer that somehow met the conflicting standards of the Western European countries, "it would be so costly as to not be competitive in the marketplace," Scholtz said. Euopean manufacturers face the same problem. To cope with the rules, many manufacturers find it easier to sell only to buyers in their own country.

The architects of Europe '92 want to replace this muddle with harmonized standards. Applied to each industry, the approach is intended to eliminate trade barriers and generate economies of scale by allowing manufacturers to produce uniform products for sale across Europe.

Reaching an agreement, however, is easier said than done: The talks Schultz attends have been underway for about a decade. Jack van Asten, a Dutch health and environment official who is a longtime participant in the talks, said the United States and Soviet Union spent less time working out major disarmament pacts.

Disputes between countries over standards have been around for more than a century. In the mid-1800s, the United States considered adopting a standard that Britain had proposed for the common screw. U.S. manufacturers decided to keep their own standard and the result decades later frustrated American owners of British cars, who found that screws from local hardware stores wouldn't fit their vehicles.

Even now nations remain divided over such basic requirements as clothing sizes, electrical plugs and units of measurement.

When world trade exploded in the 1980s, foreign standards gained new importance for U.S. businesses because they can serve as a barrier to markets. To open these markets, many U.S. companies have favored pushing for creation of standards the whole world could adopt.

"Unless we understand and adopt international standards, we cannot compete effectively," said John Hinds, a senior executive at AT&T. This year, Hinds became the first American since the early 1970s to be elected president of the International Standards Organization, a Geneva-based group that determines the world standards countries adopt voluntarily. U.S. companies "could be frozen out" if they don't recognize this aspect, he said.

U.S. trade officials, meanwhile, believe they must pay close attention to regional standards, like those Europe is developing. In meetings, the trade officials have proposed giving U.S. manufacturers a louder voice in the European standards-setting debate.

The European subsidiaries of U.S. companies generally get full rights in the process while U.S. companies that lack European units don't receive a vote but get a voice through industry emissaries like Schultz.

Amsco, with sales in 1990 of $350 million, dominates the $70 million-a-year U.S. market for with of its products—steam sterilizers. The company also has major sales in Canada, Saudi Arabia, Singapore and Taiwan, nations were standards for sterilizers are similar to U.S. standards. But Amsco does not have significant business in western Europe, Schultz said, in large part because the company could not justify the cost of building many different models to satisfy the standards of many countries.

Reports in the 1980s that Europe would harmonize medical equipment standards was of deep interest to the U.S. medical equipment industry, which has been a competitive success story for the United States. In 1990, the industry had foreign sales of $5.8 billion, giving the United States a $2.1 billion surplus in the medical equipment trade. Almost half of the exports went to Europe.

Through telephone calls and meetings of domestic trade associations and standards groups, the U.S. medical equipment industry mapped out a response to Europe's move on setting standards.

One part was to send executives to Europe's own standards-setting meetings and try to soften rules that might penalize American firms.

Schultz went to her first meeting in 1989, representing the U.S. steam-sterilizer industry. Amsco foots the bill for her travel as an industry representative, she said, adding, "It is an investment in our future."

Most recently, she flew to Berlin in July for a day-and-a-half meeting with about 15 European officials and medical company executives.

On the agenda: final language governing certain aspects of large steam sterilizers. A major concern at that session was how to ensure that steam in the sterilizer is not too dry.

Talks drag on in part because technicians from rival engineering factions come armed with reams of experimental data to prove their way is best. A typical retort across the table, van Asten said, might be: "We've been doing it this way for 20 years. Do you mean to say that we've been doing it wrong for 20 years?"

Schultz has no vote but believes she can still make a difference. At the meetings, which are conducted in English, and at breaks around the coffee urn she is there to propose alternatives.

Schultz believes the partial consensus that has emerged would require some significant changes in how Amsco builds sterilizers. Control systems, for instance, would have to be redesigned to change how they regulate temperature and pressure.

Technical Committee 102 "has written its standards around the equipment that it's familiar with—which happens to be European equipment," Schultz said. "And therefore some companies in Europe may have an advantage." She suggested that pride in existing ways was the reason for the committee's actions, not some secret "Fortress Europe" agenda to keep out foreign products.

Whether the rewards of entering the market will outweigh the costs of converting Amsco production lines to a new standard is unclear, Schultz said. "We haven't decided whether the market is attractive enough," she said. "Standards will drive what our cost factor will be.

There is a fallback for U.S. medical companies: The industry has initiated an effort to organize a global sterilization standard through the International Standards Organization. Once officially in place, Europe could be prodded to adopt the standard.

At the request of the American National Standards Institute, the International Standards Organization in 1990 convened Technical Committee 198 to draft rules for sterilization equipment that could be adopted worldwide. The Europeans also are involved, but in these talks the United States can vote and, as an initiator, has a strong voice.

In October last year, 50 sterilization specialists, including Schultz, from around the world met in Arlington. This summer in Bilthoven, the Netherlands, there was a second meeting. "We're in a race with the Europeans to see who gets there first," said Michael Miller, executive director of the Association for the Advancement of Medical Instrumentation.

December 2, 1991

Hot Line to Heaven:

On 900 Number, a Daily Message from the Pope

MARJORIE WILLIAMS

Feeling blue? Inspiration is at hand, courtesy of the Vatican's hunger for outreach and old-fashioned American marketing know-how: Pick up your phone, dial a 900 number, and you can get a daily spiritual pick-me-up from Pope John Paul II.

It is worldwide, multilingual and duly authorized by the Holy See. It is officially titled "Christian Messaging From the Vatican."

But when the National Conference of Catholic Bishops was respectfully telephoned for comment on this outreach program, it was stumped. On what? asked the Rev. Ken Doyle, director of media relations

Um, you know, the Vatican-authorized 900 number that plays daily recorded messages from Pope John Paul II.

"Oh, you mean the Dial-a-Pope thing," he said.

The Vatican began authorizing the Dial-a-Pope thing worldwide a year ago "to service the increasing demand to hear Pope John Paul's inspirational words," according to a Vatican press release issued at the time. World rights are sold by a London-based company called Global Telecom Ltd.

But to the folks marketing the pope's message in the United States, he's just one more potential revenue source in the booming telemarketing industry, an infant science that is expected to generate more than $1 billion in calls to 900 numbers this year.

Audio Communications Inc. (ACI), the Las Vegas-based firm that markets and actually services the calls, also markets taped messages from the likes of Paula Abdul and M.C. Hammer. And Tribune Media Services (TMS), the Florida syndication company that is trying to interest newspapers in running ads for the pope line in return for a cut of the fee, touts "Christian Messaging" in a brochure that also offers "Soap Opera Reviews," "Lottery Hot Line," "Joyce Jillson Personalized Horoscope" and "Used Car Appraisal Line."

However, Barbara Abramson, TMS Audiotext products and services manager, believes her firm is on to something special: "There are other syndicates that have horoscopes and crosswords and sports," she said, "but there's only one pope."

If you dial the pope, you will first hear some religious choral music. ("Didn't the music blow you away?" asked Abramson. "Like angels descending, or something.") Next comes a sonorous, Don Pardoesque voice—the voice of a Las Vegas actor hired to introduce each tape:

"Welcome to 'Christian Messaging From the Vatican,' bringing you daily inspirational messages spoken by Pope John Paul II. His Holiness hopes these words are of benefit to you, and that you are able to listen to his messages daily. Part of the cost of these calls is used to support the apostolic mission of the Holy Father, and by listening to his words, you are contributing toward his work."

The voice goes on to introduce the day's papal message ("Today . . . His Holiness Pope John Paul II talks to us about the divine activity of the Holy Spirit in the incarnation of Jesus Christ," for example). And now the message itself, snipped from tapes of recent sermons that the Vatican periodically sends to Las Vegas. "Those sermons are basically recorded, they're not done specifically for the 900 number," says Charlie DeNatale, western sales manager for ACI. "Our people, my company, listens to the messages, and we might get a batch of messages that cover about two or three weeks. And each day we'll put a different message on. It's a very simple process."

Fortunately, the pope is multilingual, so callers have a choice among sermons he has given in English, Spanish and Italian.

Unfortunately, the pope's English is thickly accented. So after the announcer has introduced the message, the tape is virtually unintelligible, full of a sound like Henry Kissinger after Novocain.

"I've called the line," DeNatale admits, "and sometimes it is hard to understand what he's saying." But he sees this as only a minor problem. "People have called and said, 'What did he say?' that kind of thing. But it hasn't prevented us from getting people's interest, or making money or anything like that . . . I tell them, 'That's the pope.' It's like listening to Lucy and Desi. I never understood what Desi Arnaz was saying either."

Several men and women prominent in Catholic life were asked whether there is a disturbing element of hucksterism to the enterprise—especially the line in the tape that says, "His holiness hopes these words are of benefit to you, and that you are able to listen to his messages daily."

Does this imply that the pope has personally assigned these calls as the daily duty of a good Catholic?

"That seems to me a questionable use of the pope's words," said Michael Novak, author of several books on Catholicism. "I don't know that the pope said anything like that. To make it available is one thing; to encourage people to call it without saying 'depending on their means' is another."

Just how costly is it? If you call the number featured in a newspaper ad, it will cost $1.95 a minute, for a message somewhere between 2 1/2 and five minutes. (Ads being test-marketed in other media offer a different number for a slightly lower fee. And yes, one of them ends P-O-P-E, or, for the Spanish-language version, P-A-P-A.) "We do try to keep {the length} down," said Abramson. "Because our theory of 900 numbers is that you want them to call frequently, and not get hit with a bill so high they won't call again. You want it to be something of value for the call."

But assuming you dial for the minimum duration of three minutes a day, inspiration would cost you $40.95 a week.

"I think anyone using that would of course, as with any expenditure, have to evaluate the merit of that in proportion to the other responsibilities that person had for his or her finances, particularly family responsibilities," said Doyle at the bishops conference. "I think what's said on there is meant in that context."

"My own feeling, initially, is that the $40 could probably be spent some more profitable way," said James Finn, former editor of the Catholic journal Commonweal. "You could probably buy a lot of the pope's {printed} words for $40. Or make some contributions to soup kitchens."

Advertisements for Dial-a-Pope do promise that some of the call's cost will go to "the apostolic mission of the Holy Father." But no one interviewed for this article could explain quite what that means in practice. According to a spokeswoman for the Vatican Embassy here, "It's just a general term to mean all the expenses of the pope. All the—how do you say it?—all the money the pope needs for his mission. Partly for his travels, partly for the expenses of the Roman curia. It's just a general term."

Abramson of Tribune Media Services said, "How do I explain what that is? It's sort of the—I believe it's the charitable organization of the Vatican."

How much of the money goes to the Vatican? "I believe it might be 25 percent, but I don't know if that's gross or net," said Abramson. "Or it might be 25 cents." She pondered a moment, and continued, with an air of inspired improvisation: "This is like the world's first electronic collection plate. You don't want to go to church today? Just call the line, you've made your donation for the day."

Dinesh D'Souza, editor of the Catholic monthly Crisis, said he thinks Dial-a-Pope is a symptom of the Vatican's wish "to imitate some of the high-tech strategies of Protestant evangelists . . . I think there's a sense that 'we've got to enter the 20th century, technologically speaking.' That's a recurrent theme at these bishops conferences."

But he doubts that anyone will spend his life's savings dialing the pope. "I think there's a great deal of personal affection for the pope, but I don't think it's likely that even devout Catholics are going to be making daily phone calls, any more than they would—let's say—make a daily phone call to hear Ronald Reagan comment on America."

August 13, 1991

A Hidden U.S. Export

Higher Education—American University Degree is a Highly Prized Commodity among Foreign Students, Especially Asians

PAUL BLUSTEIN

Mathura Khemnak, a 22-year-old Thai student, is planning a major purchase—and she intends to buy American.

On a recent rainy afternoon, Khemnak went to a government office in downtown Bangkok to fill out an application. She knew it was an American product she wanted; asked if she was considering a Japanese alternative, she responded with a grimace and an emphatic "No."

Khemnak was not shopping for the sort of thing that the Japanese excel at making, like a video camera or an automobile. She was in the market for a university degree—specifically, a graduate degree in international relations. She chose to study in the United States partly because she speaks English, partly because the curriculum offers some freedom and partly because she simply feels in her bones that "it's better. I'm not sure why."

Asian students like Khemnak are flocking to American universities in huge and rapidly growing numbers. Nearly 230,000 of them were studying on U.S. campuses in the 1990-91 academic year; 10 years ago, the figure was a bit less than 95,000, according to the New York-based Institute of International Education.

The Asian contingent, especially those from China, Japan and Taiwan, has risen sharply even as the number of students from the Middle East and other parts of the world has declined, so Asians now comprise 56 percent of the foreigners studying in the United States, up from 30 percent a decade ago.

The result is that a university degree has become a major U.S. "export" in this part of the world—a phenomenon that shows the flip side of the much-lamented decline in American manufacturing, educational standards and international influence.

While Asian companies making various high-tech gadgets and low-tech widgets have been clobbering American firms, and Asian schoolchildren have been surpassing their American counterparts in math tests, young Asian adults are concluding in record numbers that the United States is the No. 1 competitor at providing university-level study.

"It's the best American product," said Caroline Matano Yang, the Tokyo-based director of the Japan-U.S. Educational Commission, better known as the Fulbright program, which promotes and funds international educational exchange.

The Commerce Department estimates that foreign students brought $5 billion into the United States in 1990 in the form of tuition, room and board fees and other payments; Asians accounted for roughly half of the amount.

Moreover, the intangible benefits for the United States are considerable. In a region of the world where Washington is often said to be losing influence to Tokyo, the fact that Asia's elite students are being educated in such large numbers on American campuses helps to maintain U.S. superpower status.

For every foreigner attending classes at a Japanese university, there are more the five Asians studying at an American one.

Indeed, Japanese universities are widely regarded as second-rate by international standards; Japanese students work terribly hard to gain admission to the most prestigious schools, but once there they often loaf before settling down to the grind of a corporate job.

By contrast, American universities are generally regarded as the superior link in the U.S. education system.

"It is clear that the trend in Asian students coming here is strong and continuing, and that is good news both for our educational institutions and for America's political and economic relations with Asia." said Peggy Blumenthal, vice president of the Institute of International Education (IIE).

"Many of these students are self-funded, so they bring revenues to the schools they come to," Blumenthal said. "But equally important, they bring enormous talent; they are used by those institutions as teaching assistants and research assistants. And they go home with a very profound understanding of the American economy and American educational system."

The consequences of this are mixed.

At many U.S. universities, foreign students—preponderantly Asian—have come to dominate graduate programs in science, engineering and mathematics, because American students generally find they can get good jobs after receiving bachelor's degrees in those fields without pursuing their studies at the master's or doctorate levels.

According to IIE figures, almost 50 percent of all foreign graduate students in the United States in the 1990-91 academic year were in the fields of science, engineering and mathematics, although a substantial 13.5 percent were in business management, more than the social sciences, the humanities or education.

Universities often end up heavily subsidizing foreign graduate students in technical fields in order to have sufficient numbers of students to keep their programs alive.

Many academics have become concerned about the dearth of Americans in such advanced programs, warning that the United States risks losing its supply of experts in cutting-edge technologies as foreigners often return to their home countries after receiving their master's degrees and doctorates.

On the other hand, the United States also is getting an infusion of foreign talent, since as many as half of those students end up staying here after graduation, according to some surveys.

Also, without the flood of Asian graduate students, it would be difficult for universities to educate American undergraduates in these fields because of the lack of teaching assistants. So there is more "boon" than "bane" to the presence of foreign graduates, according to an IIE study in the late 1980s of U.S. engineering programs.

Seen from the Asian vantage point, the broad benefits to the United States seem obvious. "Education is very highly prized among people here, yet there is a lack of sufficiently top-notch universities," said Peter Everington, a Hong Kong-based expert on East Asian economies.

So what is effectively happening, he said, is a trade of Asian-made goods for a valued American service.

Politicians tend to focus on the decline of the industrial competitiveness of their countries, but they don't realize that the service sector tends to compensate," Everington said.

"Everyone likes to protect their industry, but the reality is, if you can get someone else to produce the same TV set cheaper than you can, why not do that? If you manage your economy properly, then the person who was making those TVs can take on a service job that may provide better pay and better conditions."

Not that educating foreigners is going to provide the cure for America's economic problems. After all, few unemployed factory workers can expect to find work as college professors, and the service sector could hardly thrive without a reasonably healthy manufacturing base.

Moreover, the $5 billion that the United States received in 1990 from foreign students, while an appreciable sum, took only a modest slice off the $92 billion current-account deficit the nation recorded that year.

But the influx of Asian students has come at a good time for the nation's universities as they struggle with falling domestic enrollments. The foreign student influx helps to sustain employment in the face of financial pressures and budget squeezes.

"In the past couple of years, we have seen recruiters come here from institutions that would never have recruited students in the past—I'm talking elite institutions, said Yang of the Tokyo Fulbright office. "They need students."

Yang won't name names, but Linda Heaney, who runs a Bethesda-based service bringing college recruiters to Asia, said that this year for the first time she brought a group from Amherst, Chicago, Carleton, Wesleyan and Pomona for visits to Tokyo, Seoul, Hong Kong and Singapore.

Then there is the political aspect. The fact that the cream of Asia's youth tends to favor American schooling is a classic example of what Joseph S. Nye, a Harvard professor of international affairs, calls America's "soft power"—the nation's ability to exert influence by dint of its pervasive culture, language and values.

In Taiwan, 12 out of 20 cabinet members hold degrees from U.S. institutions of higher learning, including the country's president, its premier, the minister of finance, the minister of education and the director-general of the department of health.

Asia's powerful government bureaucracies are loaded with U.S.-educated talent.

In South Korea, for example, U.S. universities are the overwhelming choice among the 140 or so elite young bureaucrats who are selected each year by examination to go abroad for study. In 1990, 84 chose American schools, compared with 21 for Japan and 20 for Great Britain.

When members of this group return to Korea, they are put on a fast track for promotion, and they occupy about 70 percent of the key director-level jobs in the nation's ministries.

"This is one of the great sources of power for American diplomacy and politics," said Hiromi Yano, a fast-rising bureaucrat at Japan's Ministry of International Trade and Industry.

Yaho himself is a graduate of Harvard's Kennedy School of Government, and he said the experience gave him insight into the rationale for many of Washington's trade complaints with Tokyo. "Some of the things I had thought were unreasonable really were not, from the American perspective," he said.

Measuring such effects is impossible, of course, but one IIE study of Brazilian students who attended U.S. universities concluded that they "left America well aware of its problems, mistakes and contradictions, but remain enthusiastic advocates all the same of its free society, economic vitality, open and vigorous public debate, and demonstrated generosity."

The Brazilian students should not be expected to embrace all aspects of U.S. foreign policy, the study added, "But by dint of their American training there is a high likelihood that {they} will be far more positively than negatively predisposed toward the United States."

Perhaps best of all, they consider themselves likely to use American computers and other equipment that they became familiar with in the United States, the study said.

Japan is starting to catch up. As part of its effort to shoulder more international responsibilities, Tokyo has embarked on an ambitious program to welcome more foreign students, especially Asians. Japan's goal is to educate 100,000 foreign students annually by the end of the decade. The 1991 figure stood at 45,066, according to the Education Ministry, up 9 percent over 1990.

But Japan faces some formidable barriers, particularly the language problem. Thais, for example, require two full years to learn Japanese properly, but most Thai students learn English in primary school and high school.

Moreover, "the cost of living in Japan is unbelievable," said Kanda Vajrabhaya, head of the Bangkok government office that handles student applications for overseas study.

Many Asian students attending Japanese universities are forced to live in squalid, small quarters without a shower or bathtub because landlords are often loath to rent to them.

Even countries such as South Korea, China and Taiwan, whose people generally find it much easier to learn to speak and read Japanese than English, send many more students to the United States than to Japan.

"Learning English is very difficult for us," said a Korean diplomat. "But a degree from Japan is not as prestigious as a degree from the United States."

February 16, 1992

Latest Import Wave—House Components:

Foreign Firms Snaring Bigger Share of Appliance, Parts Market

H. JANE LEHMAN

U.S. home builders began worrying about a Japanese invasion of their market five years ago when a delegation of Japanese construction officials showed up at the industry's annual convention. The Japanese did not disappoint them. The assault, however, has not taken the form that most industry insiders expected.

Back then, home builders thought they would have to contend with foreign factory-produced homes shipped en masse and assembled here on vacant lots. Instead, foreign competitors have tackled the U.S. construction industry on a piecemeal basis by producing a growing number of the components used to construct homes, in much the same way that foreign car manufacturers now produce engines and other parts that power "domestic" automobiles.

The Department of Housing and Urban Development looks upon the increased domestic use of foreign appliances, building components and other building products as a "far more immediate threat" than the import of whole houses.

"Unlike factory-built housing systems, these specific products can easily be absorbed into the existing methods and processes of domestic residential development and product distribution," HUD warned in a recent white paper on the subject.

But the growing pervasiveness of foreign building products represents little cause for concern for individual American home buyers and may actually confer some benefits, according to industry experts.

"This will eventually force the American equivalent product to become competitive" whenever the foreign version is higher in quality, more innovative, better designed or cheaper, said Deane Evans, a principal with Steven Winter Association, a New York-based building systems consulting firm.

In the wider scheme of things, though, the foreign invasion of yet another U.S. industry threatens to further exacerbate the country's negative trade balance, leading to a weaker economy, the loss of more American jobs, and higher interest rates and home financing costs due to the country's dependency on foreign capital.

Although a self-described advocate of free trade, Kenneth J. Beirne, HUD assistant secretary for policy and development, warned that if measures aren't taken now to stem the flood of foreign building products "in 10 to 15 years the calls to restrict trade and close down our borders will become more intense."

While foreigners have yet to exert much influence over the assembly of homes, they have prompted "quite a change" in the fundamental building supplies industry over the past several years, according to a Commerce Department analyst.

In 1981, the United States enjoyed a $700 million trade surplus in building products, said C.B. Pitcher, director of the Commerce Department's building materials and construction division. By 1987, however, the U.S. was importing $2.3 billion more in building supplies than it was exporting. In fact, the trade balance in building products, including plumbing fixtures, bricks, kitchen cabinets, building hardware and gypsum, comes up negative in every area but raw logs.

Within specific building product categories, the foreign influence is even more pronounced. For example, the United States not only imports more ceramic tile than it sells abroad, but those imports account for 55 percent of total U.S. consumption of tile.

Certain parts of the United States also rely more heavily on particular imported building goods. Florida counts on foreign manufacturers for 60 percent of the cement used in construction there, while total U.S. consumption of imported cement is closer to 20 percent, Pitcher said

The eastern ports also use relatively more foreign-produced cement, while U.S. suppliers take care of most of the inland demand, he added.

Mexico has supplanted Canada as the largest outside supplier of cement. Other foreign suppliers, according to the Commerce Department, include Colombia, Venezuela, Japan, South Korea, Spain, Greece and France.

Relatively speaking, imports still constitute a relatively small percentage of all building material products used in this country, although no precise figure exists to document the total. Nonetheless, the federal government is concerned about where this trend could eventually lead, said David Engel, an official with HUD's building technology division.

"It's remarkable we've seen this much activity at a time the dollar is weak because this is when our competitive advantage should be greatest. When we get a stronger dollar, then we could really see an expansion," he said.

Japan in particular remains a formidable contender. Engel said he believes the Japanese are using their acumen in the consumer electronics field to break into the building products market.

Apparently, the gambit is working. For example, one local builder—CPL in Reston—is already sold on Mitsubishi's security systems, which it installs in the $450,000-plus Northern Virginia homes it builds.

One way to compete, according to many industry officials, lies in the product research and development area where foreign countries already hold a decided advantage. Many industrialized nations subsidize and coordinate industry research programs. Sweden spends $150 million or $17 per capita annually on housing research, Engel said. At most, HUD has spent $100,000 a year over the last five for research and development of building technologies.

Foreign companies also sink millions on dollars into housing research in any given year, while the comparable U.S. effort is puny. According to David J. MacFadyen, president of the research arm of the National Association of Home Builders, "the American research system has been emasculated over the last few years from leveraged buyouts and the emphasis on short-term profits."

What's more, other countries are quick to usurp what innovations this country does produce. "We've discovered that most American building product companies, which are relatively small, don't get access to foreign research whereas foreign companies tend to extensively scavenge the U.S. for what we are doing," Beirne said.

As a result, foreigners are positioned to introduce a host of new products to the United States. Michael Joroff, head of the architecture and planning laboratory at Massachusetts Institute of Technology, believes the "smart toilet" under development in Japan is the wave of the future. The toilet, outfitted with water jets and hot air dryers, eliminates the need for toilet paper, warms up the toilet seat and automatically flushes, Joroff said.

In an effort to fight back, HUD is setting up a clearinghouse to track and disseminate information about technological advances made in Japan and Western European countries with immediate applicability to the United States.

February 4, 1989

Fast Food in a Russian City Leads to Red Ink

FRED HIATT

When this city's first fast-food, all-American restaurant opened 10 weeks ago, manager Rashed F. Zorba discovered that, after living under communism for 75 years, Russian consumers had a lot to learn.

"People here are not like Americans," the manager of the Gardinia Restaurant complained. "If they have chicken today, they don't want chicken tomorrow."

From its plastic banquettes to its unvarying crispy fried chicken to its Houston-based owner, the Gardinia is as American as a fast-food oasis on the Volga River can be. With red-white-and-blue bunting and a no-smoking rule that strikes Russians as odder than tea in a cup instead of a glass, the Gardinia is bringing the best of capitalism—hot coffee and chocolate-glazed doughnuts served all day—to this long-benighted land.

So far, however, the land is not returning what any capitalist expects for his doughnuts—a reasonable profit. In fact, Zorba said, he loses money with every doughnut he sells. Which leads to a central, if impolite, question:

Why would an American entrepreneur build a fried-chicken emporium 250 miles east of Moscow on the road to Siberia, in a city where no one has heard of fried chicken or doughnuts and where, until recently, foreigners were barred from visiting, let alone investing?

Zorba, a Palestinian with years of experience working for international airlines and hotel chains, had a ready answer: "It was a mistake."

Financier Victor Khoury, who said he has spent $512,000 on the project, was less gloomy, expressing confidence that the restaurant will pay off in the long run.

In the meantime, the Texas-based businessman said he views the restaurant, and a supermarket he plans to open next month, as "a humanitarian cause."

"When we first visited this place, they had nothing," he said. "These people—they need food, and they love to have what America is eating." In the heady days of incipient democracy and capitalism, Zorba recalled, the reform leaders of Russia's third-largest city—formerly known as Gorki—had promised that an all-American restaurant couldn't miss. "Everything will be easy, we were told," the manager said. "What you need, you can have, we were told."

There was pain in Zorba's eyes as he stared out at the wide, ice-choked river, recalling his nine months in Nizhny Novgorod since those promises were made, and the 10 weeks since the restaurant opened. Ever the professional in his white tunic and neatly combed, wavy hair, Zorba needed little prompting to recount the troubles he had faced: workers who don't work, suppliers who won't supply, farms that smell so bad you can't stay there more than two minutes.

There are mice in his hotel room. When he complained, he was told, don't worry, there are mice in every hotel room. And when a reporter sought to cheer Zorba by complimenting him on the stylish coffee cup in his hand, he merely sighed some more.

"We started with 280 of these, and all but 10 have been stolen," he said. 'In Africa, the people are more modern than here."

In fact, the people have taken to Gardinia's fare with gusto. Of course, that may owe something to the competition, which offers—when it offers anything—fetid salami beaded with pork lard on stale white bread, and don't expect a smile from the cashier.

Still, the chocolate-glazed doughnuts are the talk of the town, and the sparkling-clean dining area is rarely empty, despite relatively high prices—about a dollar for a full lunch, well over an average day's pay—and the bizarre no-smoking rule.

And therein lies another of Zorba's problems. Like the apocryphal businessman who lost a nickel on every sale but planned to make up the difference in volume, Zorba said, "The more we sell, the more we lose."

The reason isn't difficult to grasp. The business buys its chickens, onions and potatoes locally, but the Kool-Aid, the chicken batter, the doughnut mix, the coffee and virtually all the equipment and furniture are imported from the United States. As the Russian economy has collapsed, the value of the ruble has plummeted too, from 6 to the dollar to more than 100. So the Gardinia is purchasing in dollars, selling in rubles and winding up short.

"Believe me, it will take 200 years to recoup the investment," said Zorba.

"He's optimistic," laughed Khoury when he heard his manager's estimate, but then said he thinks two years is more realistic. "I believe Russia will be a very good market in the future," Khoury said.

Still, Khoury agreed that his seven months living in Nizhny Novgorod have been "not enjoyable, because you keep losing your temper." The Jordan-born financier first came here at the invitation of the mayor, whom he met while pursuing a now-abandoned project involving the financing of a moscow hospital.

Construction fell behind two months, costing Khoury considerable lost revenue, he said. "The contractor would send 30 guys," Zorba explained. "Two or three would be working, and the rest would be sitting around drinking tea."

The restaurant has had trouble finding suppliers, and still hasn't been able to rent storage space, Zorba said. "Everybody you go to has troubles of their own," he said. "They want you to invest to rebuild their farm."

Still, neither Khoury nor Zorba is giving up. "I know it's going to pay off in the long run," Khoury said.

Indeed, if private business takes root in Russia, Khoury may be right. Gennadi Berezovski, a typical new-age entrepreneur involved in everything from timber to textbook publishing, was visiting Nizhny Novgorod on a business trip from his home in Irkutsk.

"This is the only place in town you can eat well," Berezovski said, tucking into a plate of wings, fried potatoes and slaw. "I just come for a good lunch. I don't care whether it's American or not."

Neither, at this point, does Zorba. The manager of the Gardinia eats his own fried chicken every day, two meals a day, but he appears willing to adapt. Now the Gardinia offers beet salad too.

March 28, 1992

13 International Pricing Issues

U.S. Says Asian Firms Dumping Cheap Phones

Commerce Ruling Affirms AT&T Complaint

STUART AUERBACH

The Commerce Department yesterday confirmed what American Telephone & Telegraph Co. had charged—that many of its competitors in Japan, South Korea and Taiwan are illegally dumping small-business telephone systems in this country far below their cost of production.

The preliminary ruling found that Japanese companies were dumping telephone systems in the United States at prices that were as much 179 percent below cost, Taiwanese companies at 130 percent below cost, and Korean companies at 9 percent below cost.

AT&T filed the trade complaint in December, saying that it was losing market share to foreign competitors because of the artificially low prices the rivals were charging.

Comdial Corp. joined AT&T in the complaint on behalf of the U.S. industry.

If the preliminary Commerce Department findings are upheld and the International Trade Commission rules that AT&T suffered economic injury because of the dumping, the foreign competitors face penalty tariffs that could more than double the price in this country of their products.

The trade commission already has issued a preliminary ruling saying that AT&T suffered injury.

The phone-dumping case is being closely watched here and abroad because of fears that foreign competitors will dominate the $44 billion-a-year U.S. market as they have in consumer electronics.

When AT&T filed its complaints, the communications company claimed that foreign competitors already had made substantial inroads into the American market. AT&T General Business Systems division, the largest U.S. supplier, has suffered reduced profit and has laid off thousands of workers, company officials said.

"Making the decision to file the case was not an easy one for AT&T, but we had no choice," a company spokesman said yesterday.

"We are committed to being a profitable competitor in the small-business communications marketplace, and once this pervasive underpricing ends we intend to be very successful," the spokesman said.

Toshiba Corp. and Matsushita Corp., both of Japan, refused to supply data for the investigation, sources said, so Commerce officials used the best information they could get, which was supplied by AT&T. Toshiba was found to be selling telephone systems at 136.77 percent below cost while Matsushita was selling at 178.93 percent blow cost.

The Commerce Department has until October to make its determination in the case. After that, the International Trade Commission will have a chance to review its preliminary finding of financial injury. A final ruling on the complaint is expected to be issued in December.

Imports of Japanese small-business phone systems totaled $775.7 million last year.

The imports from Taiwan were $342 million while imports from South Korea amounted to $227 million.

July 7, 1989

A Little Guy's Fight to Regain a U.S. Edge

Computer Screen Firms Seek Trade Relief

EVELYN RICHARDS

For much of the last five years, Israeli-born entrepreneur Zvi Yaniv has waged a tireless crusade to convince rich financiers and large U.S. computer makers that his struggling firm in the Detroit suburbs is a good alternative to the Japanese companies that supply flat-panel displays for laptop computers.

It is a missionary cause, to which he has given weeks of nearly sleepless nights and untold hours in his cramped office just down the block from a bus repair depot.

But Yaniv has had little success, and now some of the same customers that he wooed have turned against him. Several of the nation's largest computer companies are fighting an effort by Yaniv and six other small U.S. firms to get the government to slap "dumping" duties on imported Japanese flat computer screens.

Yaniv believes that unfairly low Japanese prices are depriving him of customers. Without import duties, he contends, his OIS Optical Imaging Systems Inc. will have little hope of putting the United States back in the race in a key technology for the 1990s.

But firms such as Apple Computer Inc., International Business Machines Corp. and Compaq Computer Corp. say that the little U.S. display companies can't produce big volumes of the kind of screens they want.

"The people who have lobbied Washington for protection have really misled the government people into believing they are a credible alternative," said Apple Chairman John Sculley last week.

Computer makers warn that they will move manufacturing overseas if they cannot be guaranteed large quantities of inexpensive, high-quality flat screens from Japan. And they have forged an unusual alliance with Japanese manufacturers in opposing the dumping duties being considered by the U.S. International Trade Commission. A ruling is expected this month.

Color "active-matrix" flat screens like those OIS makes are seen by many as a key to sustaining a healthy domestic electronics industry. Such screens are sharper and brighter than the "passive matrix" displays that are common in today's laptop computers. In the future, they are destined to be crucial not only in laptops, but also in aircraft cockpits, automobile dashboards, wall-sized "high-definition" televisions and potentially almost anywhere that information is electronically displayed.

186

"We have to do something," said Lewis Branscomb, director of the Harvard University technology policy program and the former chief scientist of IBM. "From a future trend point of view, [the technology] is very important."

A U.S. company, RCA Corp., invented the thin screen in the 1960s, using liquid crystals as an alternative to the bulky cathode ray tubes found in conventional displays. But firms in the Far East honed the technologies and invested the large sums needed to mass produce the screens. Sharp Corp., Hitachi Ltd. and Hosiden Corp. have led the Japanese effort to refine technology pioneered at Westinghouse Electric Corp. to make "active-matrix" screens, the latest generation of the technology and the one that may dominate for much of the rest of the decade.

Meanwhile, since 1984, 14 U.S. companies have dropped out of the flat-panel business, from tiny start-up firms to giants such as Exxon Corp., American Telephone & Telegraph Co. and General Electric Co. Now, the U.S. industry consists of about 20 small companies, many of them supported by Pentagon contracts and producing only small lots of screens that are too specialized and expensive to appeal to computer makers.

The combined sales of these companies total roughly $100 million, or just 3 percent of a $3.3 billion, Japanese-dominated global industry that is expected to swell to $7.3 billion by 1995.

OIS is the nation's only manufacturer of active-matrix displays. At times barely hanging on, its yearly losses have ranged from $2 million to $9 million on annual sales that peaked at $6.5 million.

Since 1986, when OIS broke off from nearby Energy Conversion Devices Inc., Yaniv and his team have knocked on the doors of 50 companies and institutions in the United States and Europe in search of financing. At times they sought a few million dollars to improve OIS's small production line. Other times they hoped for $100 million—no more than Hollywood spent to produce "Terminator 2"—to build a high-volume factory.

But Yaniv says his pleas have been dismissed nearly everywhere. OIS's image, he says, was tarnished by its association with Energy Conversion Devices, a company with promising technologies but poor financial performance. Another problem was that investors feared backing a company going head to head against tough Japanese manufacturers that seemed always to promise technological breakthroughs and cutthroat prices.

"American investors . . . are petrified of competing with the Japanese," said Lionel Robbins, a recently retired OIS vice president.

In the early stages, Yaniv pinned his hopes on winning business from Apple. In fact, an Apple technical manager wrote in an internal report that OIS's active-matrix technology was "superior" to any other.

Apple officials visited OIS at least three times between 1986 and 1988, but despite their apparent interest in OIS's technology, they were put off by its financial instability and lack of proven manufacturing ability, according to Apple attorney James Burger.

OIS, Burger said, wanted $5 million from Apple to design prototype screens, as well as guidance in manufacturing large quantities of displays. And OIS had no "credible" plan for raising the $100 million or more to build a factory that could turn out the 8,000 screens a month Apple thought it might need for its upcoming portable Macintosh computer, Burger said.

While the computer company was willing to help OIS defray some engineering costs, "we had a concern it was like taking a pack of money and dumping it into a well," Burger said.

OIS told Apple that it would not be able to turn out even 1,000 screens a month, according to Burger. OIS's top monthly production now is about 300 display screens.

Yaniv denied he asked for $5 million, but says he did seek a firm commitment from Apple to purchase screens. Without an order, he said, he couldn't hope to find financing for a factory. But "the commitment was so weak that I couldn't buy ice cream for that," Yaniv said.

Instead, Apple turned to Japan and to a company called Hosiden, a somewhat obscure maker of electromechanical parts. It had begun research in active-matrix displays in 1980 and had completed prototypes by 1985.

Apple officials, according to Burger, were encouraged by Hosiden's skill in mass manufacturing and by its plans for an active-matrix screen factory. Hosiden, in contrast to OIS, could get bank loans and use its own funds generated from other businesses.

After reimbursing Hosiden for routine engineering costs to tailor its prototype to Apple's needs, Apple signed up.

Yaniv sees things differently. He is convinced that Apple picked Hosiden because of price. A Hosiden attorney said the company set no firm price until 1989. Yaniv said he believes Hosiden promised earlier to meet Apple's target of $500 for black-and-white active-matrix screens. At the time, OIS was selling screens for $3,500. A large-volume commitment from Apple might have brought the price down to $1,000, Yaniv figured.

The Japanese pricing puzzled Yaniv: Hosiden didn't have a factory at the time, yet it seemed to be making optimistic assumptions about potential manufacturing efficiencies. Producing active-matrix screens is so tricky that frequently only 10 percent or so of the screens produced in new plants are acceptable, raising the price of the usable screens.

At that moment, Yaniv said, he suspected dumping. He concluded that OIS could survive only by avoiding direct competition with Japanese firms, as a military subcontractor supplying screens for aircraft cockpits. So far OIS has supplied only prototypes, but Yaniv expects to win several contracts, including one to upgrade portions of display panels in F-15 fighters.

OIS has been able to stay alive by borrowing money and selling stock. William Manning, a Rochester, N.Y., money manager who says he isn't scared by Japanese competition, has invested $16 million. Yaniv has found investors in Italy and Britain, including customer Smiths Industries PLC, a British defense contractor that bought an equity stake for $2.5 million. Another customer, South Korea's Samsung Electron Devices Co., paid $1 million for equipment OIS could use to develop flat screens intended for portable Samsung televisions.

In a recent deal, Guardian Industries Corp., a Michigan-based supplier of automotive glass, said it would invest $10.5 million and possibly as much as $21 million in OIS over three years.

Yaniv sees the Guardian investment, coupled with the potential dumping duties, as marking a turning point for OIS. The "deep pockets" of Guardian will assuage potential customers' concerns about the company's viability, he said. The Commerce Department last month recommended a stiff new duty on imports of active-matrix screens. That would wipe out the Japanese price advantage and create a level playing field, Yaniv said. Since the Commerce Department issued its recommendation, numerous potential customers have called OIS.

"I feel very upbeat," Yaniv said.

An ebullient man with a heavy accent, Yaniv, 45, earned a doctorate at Kent State University in the field of liquid crystals and is so enraptured with the technology that he can gush for hours about the beauties of active-matrix screens. Nowhere is he more at home than in OIS's cramped, ultra-sanitary "clean rooms," where delicate chemical and photographic techniques are used to produce the displays.

To Yaniv, saving OIS, with its 85 employees, and the U.S. display industry is not so much a job as a cause.

What the fledgling U.S. firms lack in financial muscle, they have made up with hard work and a missionary zeal.

At Standish Industries Inc. in Lake Mills, Wis., one executive has a personalized license plate on his car that reads "LCD MFG," for "liquid-crystal display manufacturing." The company makes "passive-matrix" screens.

At Photonics Imaging Inc., an Ohio firm that makes another type of flat panel called a "plasma" display, founder Donald Wedding mortgaged his house to start the company in 1978.

OIS and Photonics both hope to make the difficult transition from selling to military customers to the commercial market. But military orders are usually small—50 screens constitute a big purchase—and prices are high. OIS's screens range in price from $3,500 to $20,000, far more than any computer maker would be willing to pay. In a sense, experts say, OIS screens are over-engineered for the commercial market, crafted with precision beyond what computer makers would need.

"The idea is fundamentally flawed that you can take a military contractor making military products and turn it into a commercial contractor with commercial products," said Paul DiSenso, a display market specialist at SRI International, a California think tank.

In addition to the handful of small U.S. manufacturers, an assortment of U.S. universities and large corporations are researching technologies that they hope will get the country back into the flat-screen game.

Xerox Corp. and the David Sarnoff Research Center have been working separately for more than a year to interest other firms in financing new factories to manufacture displays developed in their labs. Ronald Roach, chief of Sarnoff's advanced displays technology research group, said he hopes to raise $20 million for a pilot production line by year's end.

IBM has formed a partnership with Toshiba Corp. to develop and make advanced displays, so far just in Japan. The microelectronics and Computer Tecknology Corp., an Austin, Tex.-based consortium of U.S. companies, is researching a new display technology that some say could supersede active matrix.

The Pentagon's Defense Advanced Research Projects Agency has been sprinkling $110 million among more than two dozen firms and universities to promote work on "high-resolution" displays. The Air Force and Army fund some research, as does the National Institute of Standards and Technology.

Meanwhile, however, eight major Japanese companies expect to spend about $2 billion over the next few years, in addition to participating in a cooperative research project that involves the Japanese government and 18 companies.

Despite the overwhelming Japanese lead, the market for high-quality flat displays is still new enough to provide hope for a U.S. rebound, some experts say. Recent production problems encountered by some Japanese firms suggest that they are having more difficulty than expected honing the technology and filling demand.

To spark a U.S. revival, however, "there's got to be investment by either the government or industry or both," said Roach of Sarnoff. "It's got to be a long-term commitment."

July 28, 1989

Multinationals Find Ways to Make the Most of Taxing Situations

DANIEL B. MOSKOWITZ

One of the big economic pluses a multinational company can take advantage of is allocating to its subsidiaries in each country the jobs which can be done most efficiently there.

Complex key components may be produced in carefully controlled environments in the United States, for instance, and than assembled by low-cost labor in a Third World country before the final product is shipped to Europe and sold by another subsidiary there. Obviously the way a company sets prices on these dealings has a lot to do with the bottom line of the individual subsidiaries.

Give the assemblers a bargain price on the component, and the subsidiary there will show a healthy profit; double the price of the component and it will produce red ink in the Third World and gains in the United States. Varying national tax rates and tax incentives provide motives for shifting the profit from one jurisdiction to another.

Year after year, foreign-controlled U.S. companies in the aggregate report lower profits as a percentage of assets than do similar-sized U.S. businesses.

A recent study by U.S. Treasury economist Harry Grubert and colleagues from Florida International University and Duke University statistically eliminates a lot of the possible explanations for the differences—such as the fact that the U.S. companies have been in this market longer or that the overseas companies may suffer a loss on varying exchange rates.

That suggests that foreign parents really are playing with the prices they charge U.S. subsidiaries. And there's no reason to believe that U.S. corporations play differently when setting prices for their overseas affiliates.

Tax authorities are not complacent about taxable profits being shifted out of their reach by a simple intra-company pricing change, and may step in and redo a company's books if they think the figures are phony.

The Internal Revenue Service has been particularly aggressive in this area, and cases challenging their reinterpretation of fair pricing are piling up at the Tax Court. It is not unusual for a case about the correct transfer price to drag on for a decade or more.

To avoid the clog at the Tax Court, more corporations are trying to work things out with the authorities ahead of time.

Speakers at a meeting of the National Tax Association urged more company officials to follow this route. It means negotiation with the IRS for something called an Advance Pricing Agreement (APA). Two dozen are close to final approval.

In many cases, governments of both countries are brought into the talks, so a corporation won't be squeezed by the United States assessing a tax based on a high price for an exported component and the receiving company figuring the tax as though the component was cheap. "The real issue for me with these APAs," Washington lawyer James Mogle told the conference, "is the problem of double taxation. An APA can help you avoid that."

It's not an easy chore. Negotiations can take as long as a year, and the burden is on the company to prove that the method it uses to set prices on sales from one affiliate to another are reasonable.

That often first requires some rethinking at the top levels of the corporation itself, since prices to subsidiaries frequently follow some dimly remembered decisions made years before and now without any apparent reasonable explanation.

"The information in APAs is so confidential that the threat of publication would prevent companies from seeking them," said Washington lawyer John S. Nolan. But it is not clear that under the Freedom of Information Act (FOIA) the IRS can turn down bids to get the figures.

In fact, the Treasury is working on a request to Congress to amend the FOIA to specifically exempt the data it collects in working out a pricing agreement. Not everyone will back such a move.

Some tax lawyers complain that if the details of APAs remain under wraps, they amount to secret law, an anathema in the U.S. system.

Cautions Cleveland lawyer Charles Kerester: "Vague policies only invite the very litigation that APAs were supposedly designed to avoid."

December 23, 1991

Putting Money on EC Currency

U.S. Firms See Both Sides of Coin in Unified Monetary System

PATRICK OSTER

The European Community's decision to adopt a single currency within the next seven years is good news for International Business Machines Corp., AT&T, General Motors Corp. and U.S. multinational firms that pay bills or receive payments in German marks, pounds, francs or the EC's other nine currencies.

But companies involved in European money changing, such as American Express Co. and Citibank, stand to lose substantial revenue.

"A single currency should certainly simplify our operations," said Ali Bahaj, manager of Caterpillar Inc.'s finance services division in Europe. "When you deal with multitudes of currencies, you have cross-currency risks. And it complicates collections and payables, so we see [a single currency] as a positive development."

"The single currency probably won't have as much effect on us as some other firms because most of our transactions are between Europe and the United States," said a finance official for AT&T, who requested anonymity. "But it would reduce some risk and provide better assurance of return on income because we won't have so many currencies to worry about."

Businesses such as AT&T and Caterpillar spend $13 billion a year exchanging one EC currency for another and another $2 billion buying insurance to hedge against unexpected fluctuations of one EC currency against another.

Business executives and tourists spend another $3 billion a year in using one EC currency to buy travelers checks denominated in another currency, according to a 1990 study by the EC's executive branch, the European Commission.

"People who do those jobs [foreign exchange and hedging] will have to be retrained or let go," said Peter Praet, chief economist of Belgium's largest financial institution, Generale Bank, which stands to lose as much as 4 percent of gross revenue from such activities. In 1990 that would have cost Generale $74 million.

Citibank also expects to lose such revenue, said Thomas Huertas, a vice president based in London. "But other opportunities in ecu [the name of the new EC currency] should take up the slack," he said.

For example, many European firms are likely to switch from borrowing needed funds from local banks to financing operations through ecu-denominated bonds or commercial paper, said Julian Oliver, a spokesman for American Express, which earns most of its foreign exchange revenue in Europe through trading one EC currency for another.

"We're looking at a whole range of things to offset the loss of foreign exchange and hedging business," he said. "Many consumers who keep their savings to their own currency might be interested in a much wider range" of ecu products, said Oliver, who predicted there eventually would be pan-European advertising about ecu bonds and other financial instruments.

Using a weighted value of the 12 EC currencies, there already is a fledgling market in ecu bonds, which is growing at nearly 50 percent a year. And analysts estimate that just the conversion of EC government debt from current currencies to the ecu would create a new capital market equal to $3.5 trillion, surpassing the $2.5 billion Japanese yen bond market, the world's second largest after the $6 billion market for U.S. treasuries.

That's good news for U.S. financial rating services, such as Standard & Poor's Corp., that now do only a tenth of the business in Europe that they do in the United States, even though the EC alone has a larger economy and population.

The potential for growth is there, said George Dallas, S&P's senior vice president in charge of the London office. "We could see a scenario in which the single currency would enhance the logic to go to the public capital market instead of bank financing. And with more companies in the market, the demand for ratings is promising."

Even better is the absence of any European rivals with the sort of global resources and experience that S&P and its rival Moody's Investors Service Inc. have. "We have 70 analysts here alone," he said. "It's hard to compete with that."

The rise of ecu bonds could hurt the Eurodollar market, which was partly a response to the absence of any large, single-currency capital market in Europe, said Generale's Praet. But looser issue regulations "could still make Eurodollars interesting."

The single currency, part of an overall monetary union that will include a new European central bank, should mean lower inflation and interest rates for business.

To qualify to join the monetary union, approved at an EC summit Dec. 11, members must get their inflation rates to within 1.5 percent of the average of the three lowest rates in the EC.

Those lower rates are expected to boost productivity by 5 percent as well as increase the EC's annual gross domestic product by 0.3 percent. Last year the EC's GDP was $6.4 trillion, just a shade larger than that of the United States.

Prices across Europe, which in one EC country can be double what they are in another for everything from cars to computers, also should fall as it becomes more apparent to consumers what firms are charging just across the border.

Initially, however, it may be more expensive to do business in some EC countries because not all may be eligible to join right away. Members must have a budget deficit of no more than 3 percent of GDP and a government debt of no more than 60 percent of GDP. Italy, Greece and Belgium, with debts in excess of their GDPs, are doubtful starters.

If Italy, for example, initially doesn't make the monetary union, which will be created no later than Jan. 1, 1999, Italian firms and banks are expected to have to charge interest rates one percentage point higher than those in the monetary union.

"The market will be worried about the [currency fluctuation] risk between the lira and the ecu," said Daniel Gros, a researcher at Brussels's Center for European Policy Studies. "And they'll make Italy pay a price for it."

"If Italy is out," said Arjen Ronner, a top corporate finance official of the Dutch electronics giant Philips Electronics NV, "it will be less attractive" as a prospective site of any new operation. "We'll still look at Italy to see if consumers have enough money to buy our product, but with capital costs higher, profits would be lower. And we'd have to think about that."

December 26, 1991

High Canadian Dollar Hurts Paper, Pulp Mills

Producers Urge Ottawa Government to Lower Currency's Value

WILLIAM CLAIBORNE

Canada's ailing pulp and paper industry has issued a desperate New Year's appeal to the federal government to lower the value of the Canadian dollar in an effort to stem a tide of mill closings and reverse a dramatic decline in spending on plant modernization and expansion here.

Beset by recession, an inflated Canadian dollar and increased competition in the United States, Canada's forest products industry estimates it lost $1.3 billion in U.S. dollars last year, a nearly sixfold rise in annual losses over the last decade.

The forest products association is the most recent export industry group to urge Finance Minister Don Mazankowski and Prime Minister Brian Mulroney to soften the government's monetary policy. The Canadian Exporters Association has said that because of the high value of the Canadian dollar, many of its members have not even bothered to try to take advantage of the 1989 U.S.-Canada free-trade agreement and step up their exports.

"In our view, no policy measure would have a more immediate effect on this country's export sector than a lower Canadian dollar, one that is more in line with economic fundamentals," Robert T. Stewart, chairman, and Howard Hart, president, of the Canadian Pulp and Paper Association, said in a letter to Mazankowski.

The Canadian dollar, currently pegged at 86.2 cents, remained consistently high through 1991, reaching nearly 90 cents under a tight monetary policy implemented by Ottawa in an attempt to curtail inflation.

The association maintained that the monetary policy has already achieved its objectives and that the high dollar value is only hurting exports of forest products, which in past years have contributed nearly $20 billion to Canada's balance of trade—more than the combined exports of the energy, mining, fishing and agriculture sectors.

Kevin McElhatton, the association's chief economist, said in a telephone interview from Montreal that a 1 cent change in the value of the Canadian dollar against the U.S. dollar has an industry-wide impact of $100 million.

"The dollar is the major factor. We believe with inflation under control, the time has come to shift the emphasis to growth," McElhatton said.

The forestry sector also has been under pressure from the combined effects of the worldwide economic slowdown and a steady rise in the capacity of U.S. producers at a time when demand has been declining, making Canadian paper products less competitive, industry officials said.

Of particular importance, they said, is newsprint, which accounts for about 35 percent of all of the pulp and paper produced in Canada. The United States is Canada's biggest newsprint customer, McElhatton said, but a downturn of consumption there has coincided with an excess of supply.

The effects have been particularly sharp in Quebec, Ontario and the Atlantic provinces, where many of the large pulp and paper mills date back to the turn of the century and need to be expanded and modernized.

However, the association said that spending on plant improvements, which totaled over $3.5 billion in 1989, slipped to $1.1 billion last year and is expected to drop to $600 million by 1994.

Stewart and Hart said five Canadian pulp and paper mills closed last year, and that virtually every other mill, including the newest ones, are "financially stressed" because of the dollar's value and the increased competition by U.S. producers.

January 3, 1992

14 International Distribution and Logistics

Firms Find Vienna a Door to the East

Access to Former Communist Bloc Brings Business to Austria

MICHAEL Z. WISE

Coca-Cola Co. and McDonald's Corp. have become the latest American companies to choose this former capital of the Austro-Hungarian empire as a regional base for operations in the former communist bloc.

The U.S. Embassy estimates that some 220 American companies are doing business in Eastern Europe from offices in Austria. Many firms have added East European divisions to existing operations formerly aimed at the Austrian market.

Others, including Mobil Corp., Hewlett-Packard Co. and Honeywell Inc., are expanding already well-established East European headquarters here.

Total U.S. exports to Czechoslovakia, Hungary and Poland, the countries in which the Vienna-based firms are most active, rose by $183 million to $758.8 million between January 1990 and November 1991, according to Commerce Department figures.

Austrian officials had initially feared that American companies would respond to the political transformation of Eastern Europe by trimming their Vienna offices in favor of new branches in Hungary, Czechoslovakia and Poland, as well as what was the Soviet Union.

While dozens of Vienna-based U.S. firms have recently opened joint ventures or subsidiary operations in these countries, Vienna's central location, infrastructure and communications links have helped it attract managers overseeing business throughout Eastern and Central Europe.

"The company understands that the living conditions in all these countries are low and, as a motivation tool and productivity factor, it's worth it to them to pull me out to Vienna to recover," said Tom Bergmann, a Vienna-based finance manager for Honeywell who spends half of his time away on business in Russia, Czechoslovakia and Hungary.

Office rents have also skyrocketed in central Prague and Budapest over the past two years, with well-located properties often costing twice as much as those in Vienna, according to real estate brokers. Continuing uncertainty about the viability of East European markets has led dozens of firms to concentrate their operations in Austria for the time being, now that the initial gold rush atmosphere that followed communism's demise has faded.

General Motors Corp. enlarged its 10-year-old engine and transmission plant on Vienna's outskirts while also setting up sales companies in Czechoslovakia and Poland, but business has been slow. "I'm disappointed that the economies don't recover faster," said GM Austria managing director Edwin Kiefer.

GM still has high hopes for a joint venture to assemble Opel Astra cars at a plant in neighboring Hungary. The first vehicle is due off the assembly line this spring.

Austria's traditional ties with Eastern Europe, dating from its imperial heyday, were never entirely severed during the Cold War, as Austria maintained political neutrality.

Now, those ties are considered a boon to Vienna-based businesses. "I am recommending that whoever tries working in the Eastern countries should use the historical knowledge and expertise of Austrian people who know how to deal with the East," said Kiefer, who also heads Vienna's chapter of the American Chamber of Commerce.

Coca-Cola, which transferred its East European business to Vienna from Essen, Germany, in 1990, is opening a new headquarters building next month. Gillette Co. is considering a similar move from London.

Among the many others who have expanded Vienna-managed East European sales are Eli Lilly & Co., International Business Machines Corp., Eastman Kodak Co., Polaroid Corp., PepsiCo Inc. and Wang Laboratories Inc. The U.S. advertising firm Young and Rubicam as well as Ogilvy and Mather also have experienced a boom in the region, using Vienna as their base from which to introduce one of capitalism's essentials.

Executives from most of these companies say their Vienna offices are likely to retain an essential oversight function for several years until East Europeans are sufficiently trained to manage separate offices on their own.

"Vienna has a bridge function," said Josef Antos, Young and Rubicam's regional director for Eastern Europe. "In the mid- or long-term there is no doubt that markets in individual countries will become more and more self-sufficient. But at the moment they need a lot of supervision. We function as an interpreter between the common Western market language and the language there, because there is no such sophistication in marketing."

East European capitals are still a long way from matching Vienna's relatively clean and safe environment, cultural offerings and established English-language schools, all major-factors in encouraging U.S. firms to set up here.

"It's not so depressing in the East as it was once but Western standards they don't yet have," said Peter Hana of the Vienna Business Promotion Fund, a municipally backed agency. "Here the environment is more or less in order . . . On a day like today you can hardly breathe in Prague."

"I fly in and out to Prague, spend four days there, but my house is in Vienna," said Andreas Hacker, managing director for McDonald's Central Europe, which opened its Vienna headquarters last September.

"I appreciate doing business in this part of the world, but personally I feel no desire to live there."

March 5, 1992

In Europe, UPS Tackles a Rail Chore
Transport Problems Slow Shipper's Expansion Bid

DON PHILLIPS

When United Parcel Service speaks, the U.S. railroad industry listens.

UPS is the country's largest shipper of rail-and-truck freight, giving railroads $500 million in business every year. And UPS is not the least shy about demanding high service levels.

But in the European Community, it does UPS no good to demand anything from the railroads. No one is listening.

"No preeminent rail authority exists in Europe," UPS Vice President William M. Gorecki said last week at Intermodal Expo '92, an international conference on shipping. "Each country operates its own rail system with all the inherent bureaucratic problems. Most railroads are state-owned. They have little incentive to meet service schedules at economical rates. A lack of customer orientation is pervasive."

This will come as a surprise to most Americans, who hear only of the vast European passenger train network and the growing high-speed system that will link most of Europe within the next decade. But while Europe spreads the gospel of passenger rail, it has all but ignored its freight trains—or "goods trains," in continental parlance.

Gorecki said that only 4 percent of all EC freight now moves by rail. Trucks have virtually taken over freight service throughout Europe, where population is denser and hauls are shorter than in the United States. UPS's dealings with European railroads have brought about "a sobering dash of reality," he said.

That is not the only sobering shock to hit U.S. package express companies as they strive to serve the unifying European market. For some, the problems have been too much.

On March 16, Federal Express Corp. announced it would discontinue delivery between European countries, maintaining its intercontinental service but turning local European delivery over to European partners.

Federal Express faced growing losses, reaching $125.5 million in its third quarter ended Feb. 29. And the company said the promise of a "borderless" Europe was coming too slowly.

UPS, however, is determined to succeed big in Europe. For one thing, it has been there longer than Federal Express, growing slowly from modest beginnings in

Germany in 1976. Unlike Federal Express, its European operations are profitable. Today it delivers 500,000 packages a day within Europe, and Gorecki said that volume could triple over the next decade despite intense competition.

UPS is now serving European customers the way its competitors do, by airplane and truck. So why worry about rail at all?

For one thing, the success of UPS's low-cost, reliable service in the United States has ridden on the rails. The UPS concept is based on moving packages between major hubs by rail, then putting the trailers on the highway for local and regional delivery. "We benefit from the railroad handling the longer-distance volume as the most efficient and flexible way to move our packages between hubs," Gorecki said.

With rail for the long haul, UPS drivers can concentrate on pickup and delivery in local areas. Keeping up with shipments and coordinating schedules is easier. On top of that, rail movement of truck trailers or containers is cheaper, and in many markets faster, than movement by truck.

As UPS looks toward expansion in Europe, it sees some of the same conditions developing that made rail movement necessary in the United States. "We're managing it now by air and road," said UPS spokesman Robert G. Kenney. "But as you expand the service, you can see down the road that rail should become more of a partner in the transfer of freight."

The European Commission is beginning to see the same thing, and is making moves to encourage more rail movement, spurred by environmental considerations. "If you go by road, you've got congestion, you've got a problem with pollution," Kenney said.

The trouble is that European railroads aren't ready. Some systems have different gauges—the width between rails—forcing the transfer of freight at borders. Electric power supply is not standard, and rail equipment is not compatible between countries.

In the 19th century, U.S. railroads standardized gauges and equipment, and became a force that helped weld the states and territories into one country. Not so in Europe. "The 19th-century American railroad brought the revolutionary concept of a common carrier oblivious to previous restraints of distance and state boundaries," Gorecki said. "The railroad became an invention that required us to think and act nationally.

"In Europe, by contrast, national politics driven by protectionist sentiments have contributed to the technical, financial and physical barriers created in the Europe of the past. These manifestations of protectionism still abound in the rail system infrastructure."

Gorecki said railroads still can play an important part in the commerce that he expects to be unleashed in Europe. "But are they ready to play that part?" he said. "The answer, unfortunately, is . . . maybe next decade."

May 12, 1992

International Promotion 15

Tobacco Firms' Sales Efforts in Asia Draw Fire

FRED HIATT

U.S. tobacco companies, dismayed by a shrinking market at home, are rapidly recruiting new smokers in Asia and the developing world, often with the aid of the U.S. government, delegates to an antismoking conference here said today.

The percentage of people who smoke in the industrialized world has decreased steadily in recent years, health experts here said, but the proportion of smokers in developing countries is rising. Tobacco companies have particularly targeted young people and women, who traditionally have not smoked in many Asian countries, they said.

"The industry plan is to create demand among Oriental females," said Gregory N. Connolly, an adviser to the World Health Organization. "If you have one billion Oriental females who don't smoke as a market, that would more than replace the quitters in western Europe and North America . . . And death and disease will follow."

Only 14 percent of Japanese women smoke. But more young women are smoking since U.S. pressure forced Japan to import U.S. brands, triggering a television advertising war between U.S. and Japanese manufacturers, according to Tadao Shimao, former director of the Japan Anti-Tuberculosis Foundation and an organizer of the conference.

After the conference, Donald Harris, a spokesman for Philip Morris International, denied that his company has targeted nonsmokers in the Third World. "We're trying to increase our business every place, whether it's Washington, D.C., or Tokyo or any place we do business," Donald Harris said.

Asked about the health consequences of increasing sales, Harris said, "That's not at issue. The science, we've been through that before, and we're comfortable about that . . . It's a statistical matter, not a direct causal connection."

But Roberto Masironi of the World Health Organization said the rise in smoking in the developing world will lead to "a real epidemic of lung cancer." Worldwide, 600,000 new cases of lung cancer are reported each year, he said; by the year 2000, the number will rise to two million, nearly half of them in China.

Several delegates said that U.S. officials, in their zeal to open Asian markets to U.S. tobacco firms, also have interfered with local government efforts to implement health measures. Among the cases they cited:

Last year, Hong Kong announced that it would become the first Asian country to ban "smokeless tobacco," meaning snuff and chewing tobacco. Elaine L. Chung, deputy secretary for health and welfare, said that the U.S. Tobacco Co., maker of Skol and other chewing tobaccos, lobbied hard against the ban and that a trade official of the U.S. consulate called her to complain.

"My reply was that it was a health issue, not a trade issue," Chung recalled today. "We are very proud of having lowered our infant mortality rate, and we would not want all that effort to bring up our precious children wasted when they become teen-agers, to die some horrible death from oral cancer."

In Taiwan, when the U.S. government pressured Taipei to allow imports of U.S. cigarettes, officials also wanted Taiwan to end its ban on cigarette advertising, arguing that new entries in the market need to advertise. David D. Yen, businessman and chairman of a health foundation, said Taiwan held firm on television advertising but agreed to allow magazine ads.

"Now you go to our dance halls, you can see young girls smoking cigarettes," Yen said.

In South Korea and Japan, U.S. officials lobbied hard for lower duties and taxes on imported cigarettes. When the Japanese health ministry formed a committee to study possible measures to reduce smoking here, the U.S. embassy said in a message to the State Department that the committee "poses the danger that, intentionally or not, action which might discriminate against foreign cigarettes might be recommended and subsequently adopted. The embassy will monitor ..."

"The one thing I've come away with is how much our State Department is an agent for spreading disease," Michael Pertschuk, former chairman of the Federal Trade Commission, said here today. "They're an adjunct of the tobacco industry."

Industry officials said they are seeking to persuade smokers to switch to their brand, not to entice new smokers.

But delegates from dozens of nations said that new smokers, particularly young girls, are being lured by western advertising.

They also said that lung cancer, heart disease and other smoking-related "advanced" illnesses are rapidly catching up to the more traditional causes of death in Third World nations such as infectious disease.

Halfdan Mahler, director general of the World Health organization, said that tobacco consumption is declining in industrialized nations by 1.1 percent each year and increasing in developing nations by 2.1 percent. "The tobacco promoters seem determined to turn developing countries into their biggest market," he said.

Mahler spoke on the first day of the four-day conference, which was sponsored by the American Cancer Society, the Japan Cancer Society and several other health organizations.

November 13, 1987

Ads with Instant Intrigue

For Taster's Choice, the 45-Second Soap Opera

PAULA SPAN

In the first episode, she's run out of coffee mid-dinner party and borrows a jar from her attractive male neighbor. They exchange half-smiles, provocative glances and more eyebrow activity than has been seen on television since Groucho Marx, but nothing much happens except that they discuss the merits of Taster's Choice.

The encounter might have gone largely unremarked upon amid the clutter of commercials—another nicely produced attempt to convince skeptical Americans that instant coffee is worth drinking and that one brand transcends another—except that now there's a second episode. She returns the jar, prompting another volley of teasing looks and quirked brows; he's entertaining another woman, but the prospect of a subsequent and more intimate rendezvous is left open.

Well. This isn't just an ad campaign; it's a narrative, a soap, one of the few instances ad people can recall of serialized commercial-making on network television. "We're writing a movie," says Matt Lester, the campaign's art director, "and we're going to cut it up in 45-second pieces." The third spot in the series will be shot this summer and debut in the fall.

The caffeinated romance is a direct steal from a British campaign launched in 1987 to sell Nescafe Gold Blend, which, like Taster's Choice, is a freeze-dried instant coffee made by Nestle Beverage Co. The U.K. version, dreamed up and produced by McCann-Erickson in London, has been a smash, extending to seven episodes and turning its actors into celebrities; it's credited with boosting sales of the brand 20 to 30 percent.

McCann-Erickson in New York, the ad agency for Taster's Choice, was impressed. Those upscale dinner party scenes and "Masterpiece Theatre" accents might work equally well here for a "premium" brand that costs 10 to 20 percent more than its competitors, the ad team figured. The U.S. version, accordingly, features the same flirty actors (Tony Head and Sharon Maughan by name), the same director and virtually the same scripts.

But not quite. In Britain the man working at home when his knockout neighbor rings his doorbell is wearing a tie. A tie? At home? In the more casual American spot, written by Irwin Warren, Tony Head goes tieless. In the second commercial, in which he has company, he apologetically says, "I'm busy right now." A slight revision: In the U.K. he said he was "in the middle of something," a line that would have sounded odd to American ears.

In fact, Head largely neutralized his British accent for the American commercials. In Britain, where people are more attuned to such nuance, viewers could tell from the pair's speech that she was an upper-class swell and that he was a regular Joe. "It adds to the intrigue; there's a difference between them," Lester explains. Here, the same effect is achieved by letting Maughan keep her rounded British vowels.

(A mildly insulting notion, that American speech denotes inferior social status. But consider this: Those Brits who use coffee—a minority in a tea-drinking nation—buy instant 80 to 90 percent of the time. That's high class? Less than 30 percent of the coffee sold in the United States, by contrast, is instant.)

Anyway, Nestle is betting more than $20 million—last year's advertising expenditures for Taster's Choice, according to the researchers at Leading National Advertisers—that Americans will become as caught up in the liaison as the British, and as willing to buy more of its instant coffee. Taster's Choice, being more expensive, is already the "dollar leader" in the $900 million U.S. instant coffee business, but it generally runs third in market share behind leader Maxwell House and runner-up Folger's.

Few national advertisers have tried to keep American viewers hooked on a continuing story line. The four-parter that Pepsi unveiled in 1988, in which Michael Jackson was pursued by rabid fans, was something of a gimmick, the commercials shown only once, on the Grammy Awards broadcast. Backer Spielvogel Bates has made a few "to be continued" commercials for Miller Lite, but they have been tied to promotions like sweepstakes and have run for only two or three months.

McCann-Erickson, however, is hoping to sustain the Taster's Choice chronicle for several years. "This campaign will go on as long as everybody stays interested," says account supervisor Stuart Klein.

So far the public is. Nestle's headquarters in San Francisco has received hundreds of letters about the campaign, an uncommon response. A few correspondents picked the usual nits (the other woman in the second episode ended her sentence with a preposition, someone felt compelled to point out), but most thought the campaign reeked of class. Three lifestyle writers at the Detroit Free Press suggested that in subsequent commercials, the couple should honeymoon in Colombia and that, post-divorce, she could take up with Juan Valdez. The Baltimore Sun has announced a write-in contest to solicit readers' recommendations for the campaign's conclusion.

In the British saga, Maughan and Head meet by chance in Episode 3 and go out for dinner in Episode 4. There follows "some subsequent conflict" caused by "a misunderstanding about another man," Lester relates. "Their relationship hits sort of a snag that's resolved in the following spot. They make up"—with a decorous kiss—"in the latest spot."

It is giving away nothing to recount this, since the American commercials, which "broke" late last year, will henceforth depart from the British prototype. The ad folks are naturally tight-lipped about the plot, except to say that the romance will unfold as unpredictably as in real life, sort of. Real-life lovers generally seem less likely to natter on so about coffee.

April 10, 1991

In Japan, a Cultural Filter on Trade News:

Press in Tokyo Often Uses War Language in Reporting on Commerce Issues Involving U.S.

ELEANOR RANDOLPH AND STUART AUERBACH

By American standards, it was a routine story. U.S. officials last week released an annual report of global trade barriers, including those in Japan.

The *Washington Post* didn't use it. The *New York Times* ran it on Page 31. Even the *Wall Street Journal* tucked it at the bottom of a story on Page 3 about U.S.-Japanese trade issues.

But the report made big headlines in Japan, where news about trade negotiations with the United States often sound as though the two countries are close to a rerun of Pearl Harbor, this time in reverse.

One major newspaper, Mainichi Shimbun, ran the story under the headline: "35 Items of Barriers Pointed Out. Dissatisfaction Against Japan in Almost Every Area." Yomiuri Shimbun, another major daily, blared: "America's Severe Trade Impediments Report. New Pressure on Structural Talks. 34 Items in 8 Areas Against Japan."

To be sure, these trade issues are important for both countries, not only for businesses but also for consumers.

On the surface, the ongoing talks between the two countries are designed to try to lower the massive U.S. trade deficit with Japan, but some analysts say they have the potential of lowering prices on some goods for the Japanese consumer and increasing the costs for the U.S. consumer.

The results could also change the way U.S. and Japanese industries compete around the world.

But to read U.S. and Japanese press coverage of these and other trade talks is to view the relationship through two different cultural filters. U.S. reporters use the jargon of commerce and trade; Japanese often prefer the language of war.

"I rarely hear 'trade' mentioned without the accompanying 'friction,' " U.S. Ambassador to Japan Michael H. Armacost told the Japanese media last fall.

"There is no nichibei sensoh [Japan-U.S. war], but we have read a lot about the grapefruit 'war,' the beef and citrus 'war' and the like.

"A foreign reader is thus encouraged to see Japan as an armed fort. I urge you to search for some new metaphors."

Said Yoshi Komori, Washington Bureau Chief of Sankei Shimbun, "Sometimes, it fits—those war-related terms can best describe the atmosphere."

Officials from both countries complain that the Japanese media tend to translate U.S. requests into demands. An invitation by President Bush to Prime Minister Toshiki Kaifu becomes a presidential "summons."

In a press briefing Tuesday, a Japanese reporter asked about U.S. "demands." The trade official scolded that the United States doesn't "demand," it "requests" or "suggests."

Mikio Haruna, staff correspondent for Kyodo News service, said that there is some "sensationalism" involved in coverage of U.S.-Japanese relations. But he explained: "The U.S. is our biggest market and the U.S. is our former enemy. We have the closest interdependence with the United States, and we don't have this kind of relationship with other countries."

Moreover, specialists on Japan note that the U.S. media seldom can resist the language of war to describe any conflict between the world's two largest economies—the United States and Japan. *Fortune* had a cover story that bore the headline: "Where Japan Will Strike Next." *Newsweek* wrote a cover story last October that ran with the headline, "Japan Invades Hollywood."

But such stories in the U.S. media are occasional, not constant as they are in Japan.

The Japanese media don't see trade matters as business news reserved for economists and business executives. It is national policy, earning big, front-page headlines and leads for the television news.

The issue also is a highly sensitive one for Kaifu and his government, which is viewed as one of the reasons that the amount of Japanese coverage of these talks has been about 30 times that of the U.S. media, one expert estimated.

"They give it massive treatment. It's big-time stuff over there," said Nathaniel Thayer, professor of Japanese studies at Johns Hopkins School of Advanced International Studies in Washington.

"But they write it in such a way that they make it interesting. They personalize it; it's not just economic forces and such."

Like some of the U.S. media—especially on political campaigns or pursuing a troubled public figure like Mayor Marion Barry or Ivana Trump—Japanese reporters tend to move in swarms. The difference, according to analysts of the Japanese press corps, is that Japanese reporters are more likely to share information with each other. They often determine in advance the most important questions that need to be answered for all of them.

"It would be as if at a White House press conference, everybody came to Helen Thomas [of UPI] and agreed what are the three most important questions, and she would ask all three," said one State Department official.

"In Japan, they function as a club, as a group . . . It leads to a little bit of group think, but they are also aggressive in a different way, persistent."

The Japanese press corps also tends to transmit official information more than challenge it. "If you tell them something, it's almost like stenographic journalism," one U.S. government source said.

Japanese officials often like this practice, although like their American counterparts, they tend to like it less when other voices have the center stage.

"My personal feeling is that the Japanese press tends to overemphasize everything and try to make big news out of some small incident," Makoto Yamanaka, director of the international press division of the Japanese Foreign Ministry, said of the coverage of the trade talks. "They tend to prefer this."

For critics of the media, microscopic coverage of what seems like a minor event is a favored complaint in the United States as well. Seldom, however, are critics talking about coverage of trade talks.

When Bush gets the date wrong for Pearl Harbor, or Sen. Joseph Biden (D-Del.) forgets attribution for part of a political speech, such gaffes are meat and potatoes for huge armies of hungry political journalists who amass each campaign season.

The Japanese media also don't like to see a good story fade.

In Japan, for example, Rep. Helen Delich Bentley (R-Md.) is a national figure. To illustrate how strongly some U.S. citizens feel about Japan's trading policies, the Japanese media still use pictures of a Bentley event that was staged in 1987. The congresswoman from Baltimore County is shown smashing a Toshiba radio with a sledgehammer.

Bentley aide Pat Wait said that Japanese media consider Bentley a spokesperson for American attitudes, even though she seldom hears from the national media in this country.

Wait said that after a trip to Japan, House Speaker Tom Foley saw Bentley on an elevator and spoke to her for the first time. "He said, 'Helen, you're the most famous American in Japan since Admiral Perry.'"

April 6, 1990

For U.S. Firms, A Burgeoning Business in Ex-Republic Relations

GARY LEE

Russian President Boris Yeltsin's visit to New York and Washington last week cast a spotlight on the cottage industry of American power brokers scrambling for position on the bridge that has opened between the United States and Russia.

Until recently, the list of middlemen representing clients from the former Soviet Union or Americans doing business with the former republics was limited to a stalwart few. But with the fall of Soviet communism, the list has burgeoned to include a vast array of lawyers, image-makers, lobbyists and consultants.

The firms involved are diverse, their range of interests wide. For example, Allan Weinstein, head of the Washington-based think tank Center for Democracy, has emerged as a Mister Fixit for everyone from Russians anxious to rewrite their constitution to American dairy companies wishing to help keep milk on the tables of Moscow. O. Roy Chalk, Washington lawyer and entrepreneur, is just completing the first of a two-year bid to drum up American business investment in Russia.

Under the "just-say-nyet" communist system, Russians had little opportunity to hone the art of power-brokering. "We don't know how to put the best face on a situation or how to haggle or to finesse a difficult situation," said Alexander Borisov, head of a fledgling public relations organization in Moscow. "We have just not been trained in these techniques."

Russians' public relations skills, too, are roughly hewn. The most striking instance was evidenced by their handling of the 1986 Chernobyl nuclear crisis. "The problem," one Russian source said, "is that we have no public and no relations."

Last month Borisov appeared before the board of the Public Relations Society of America to ask for help in developing relations with the United States. The society responded with a program to train Russian interns at American firms and promised to participate in a seminar in Moscow later this year.

Some of the biggest public relations challenges are not in Russia but in the other former Soviet republics. Reports circulating in the Ukrainian capital of Kiev that all of the government ministers of Ukraine soon will be replaced is "not exactly the thing to instill confidence in potential investors in the region," said Mark Cowan of the Jefferson Group, which maintains affiliates in Moscow and Kiev. Nonetheless, a number of Washington public relations firms, including Hill and

Knowlton and Robinson, Lake, Lehrer and Montgomery, are bidding to represent the newly independent nations.

In the past, Soviet officials who did business in the United States received their instructions from Moscow and were not allowed negotiating flexibility. While an American might arrive at talks with a half-dozen options, his Soviet counterpart usually had only one. Deals often fell apart at the drawing board.

Today, with the old Moscow structure gone, a void exists at the Russian-American negotiating tables that U.S. business people are trying to fill. "Particularly in business, there is no shortage of people on both sides who want to explore the options, to see what is possible," said Cowan.

Last month Cowan handled a call from a Moscow businessman who wanted to buy 85,000 pairs of tennis sneakers. "We're here to see that the rules and regulations on both sides get followed," Cowan said, "to clear away the red tape, to remove the hassles for the client."

Since very few Russian lawyers are trained in international affairs, American firms have been quick to offer their expertise to Moscow officials. Among others, Philadelphia's Wolf, Block, Schorr and Solis-Cohen, New York's Skadden Arps and Washington's Arnold and Porter have made deals with various officials from Moscow. Public relations giant Burson-Marsteller has opened an office in Moscow. Fleishman-Hilliard spent five months last year training Russian clients on media and client relations.

The firms are discovering there are economic and cultural gaps to bridge. "We always need a guarantee that the products we order will be there on a certain date," said Cowan. "Russians sometimes don't seem to understand that. They have plenty of interesting products to sell but they seem to think as long as the products get there someday that it's all right."

John Adams Associates represents the former Soviet republic of Georgia in Washington. Staff there found themselves counseling deposed Georgian leader Zviad Gamsakhurdia on how to project a "positive" image in the West. "We had to get him to moderate his language at every turn," said Adams. "One of the major battles was to try to convince him that it was not in the Western style to call your political opponents 'hooligans' and 'criminals.' "

Like most others working on behalf of the former Soviet republics, Adams's group is not being paid, at least for the time being. Most clients in the region cannot pay in U.S. dollars. "We thought about it," Adams said, "and decided that Georgia has no one else to speak up for it at the moment. So we agreed to work pro bono. But we're hoping something else will work out." For Adams, representing Georgia is proving to be difficult. For the past couple of months, the small country, located in the Caucasus region to the south of Russia, has been embroiled in a bloody civil war that recently led to Gamsakhurdia's ouster.

Hired by the Georgian Foreign Ministry, the American firm's mission is to prove that the area is nonetheless stable and deserves diplomatic recognition. During the last few weeks, the firm has kept close contacts with the Tblisi government and served as the key conduit of information between Georgian and State Department officials. In the next few weeks, the firm will be organizing a tour of Georgian officials to Washington and European capitals. "Georgia," said John Adams spokesman Dan Priest, "is as deserving as any of the republics in the region to be recognized as free and independent."

So far, the United States is not buying the pitch. The State Department has singled Georgia out as one former Soviet republic unlikely to get aid until substantive changes are made in the way the country is managed. "In this case," said a U.S. official, "cosmetic changes and PR are just not enough."

February 3, 1992

Part 4

The Future and
International Marketing

This final section covers activities, ideas, and trends that will be important to the future of international marketing. One topic of importance in international (and some domestic) business negotiations is the activity of bartering, where one good is traded for another. There is every indication that barter arrangements will play an increasing role in the future of international business. Likewise on the increase is worldwide counterfeiting. Rampant in some nations, counterfeiting has become a serious problem for certain industries such as footwear, computer software, and publishing.

Other topics in this section include regional integration and competitiveness issues as well as education and consumer issues. Many of these topics, such as the development of trade blocs, have been hotly debated and will continue to grow in world importance in the years ahead. The article titled: "Schools Learn to Go Global: MBAs Take on Curricula with International Flavor" may be of special personal interest to those seeking a future as an international marketer.

Grey Markets and Barter 16

Black Times for Gray Market?

Supreme Court Holds Key to the Future of Bargains in the Land of Discount Stores

KAREN MILLER

The Christmas shopping season of 1987 is well underway. The shelves of discount houses are stocked with a full range of products at bargain prices. But at this time next year, those shelves could be bare.

Could this be the last Christmas to find bargains on genuine trademarked merchandise?

The Supreme Court's decision in Coalition to Preserve the Integrity of *American Trademarks (COPIAT) v. United States et al.,* scheduled as early as this month, could mean the end of many types of discounted merchandise imported under current laws. Name-brand products ranging from Colgate toothpaste and Johnson & Johnson baby shampoo to top-of-the-line luxury items like Seiko and Cartier watches, Waterford crystal, Godiva chocolates and even Mercedes-Benz and Porsche automobiles, may be affected by the high court's decision.

Known as "gray market" goods, or "parallel imports," these are genuine trademarked foreign manufactured products that are imported without the consent of the U.S. trademark owner. The goods are typically purchased from a third party or the trademark owner's authorized distributor overseas and sold in competition with the trademark owner's authorized distributor in the United States.

Often, the authorized distributors are wholly owned subsidiaries of the foreign manufacturer, who refuse to sell to U.S. retailers that will not sell the product at the manufacturer's suggested retail price. Independent American importers can purchase genuine products overseas at prices so far below those set for the U.S. market that even after paying shipping costs and Customs duties, they can offer the same article for 20 to 40 percent less than the authorized distributor.

The high court's decision could stop what one report has estimated as a $7 billion business touching almost every industry. According to Toby Collado, executive director of COPIAT, as many as one of four watches purchased by consumers are gray market, depending on the watch brand. Brands currently in demand on the gray market include Seiko, Pulsar, Cartier, Citizen, Bulova, Piaget and Movado. Gray-market sales of Gucci products also have increased dramatically in the past year.

In the Washington area, luxury products—particularly perfumes and fragrances—make up a high percentage of gray goods. One reason for this is that such goods generally have a high markup, thereby allowing for greater price maneuvering. Another reason is that local discounters cannot obtain them any other way but on the gray market.

"Authorized distributors are less likely to distribute their luxury products to anyone but the most exclusive store. They want to maintain that elitist image," explains Hank Hankla, a lawyer with a lobbying firm representing the American Consumer Trade Council, an association of importers and distributors, and also representing Cosmetic Centers, the discount health and beauty chain. Prestige cosmetics, perfumes, and fragrances obtained on the gray market make up a large part of Cosmetic Centers' sales.

"In stores like ours," says Hankla, "luxury perfumes such as Opium and L'Air de Temps are more likely to be obtained through the gray market than something like Max Factor, which can be purchased through normal channels of distribution."

Prestige cosmetics and perfumes, along with certain name-brand watches, also make up a large portion of K mart's parallel imports. And the savings to consumers are substantial—30 percent to 50 percent below suggested retail price. A Seiko watch retailing for $195 at an authorized dealer could cost a K mart shopper $100 to $120 and a Citizen brand watch with a suggested retail price of $110 could sell for as low as $50.

Other products, such as cameras, have nearly dropped out of the gray market. Single lens reflex cameras, the biggest category of parallel imports four or five years ago, have "basically dried up," says Hankla. "Today you just can't buy cameras cheaper overseas than you can here."

It is the availability of such bargain merchandise that is at stake in the COPIAT case. The Supreme Court will decide whether the Customs Service's regulations permitting the importation of gray-market goods are consistent with section 526 of the Tariff Act of 1930. Enacted in 1922, this provision prohibits the importation of any foreign manufactured goods bearing a U.S. trademark without the trademark owner's consent. Customs has interpreted the statute to allow the importation of trademarked merchandise if the domestic and foreign trademark owners are under common ownership or control, or if the goods have been trademarked abroad with the authorization of the trademark owner.

COPIAT members—manufacturers and distributors of trademarked goods such as tires, crystal, perfumes, photographic equipment and electronics—argue that this interpretation goes against the intent of Congress. They argue that the influx of gray-market goods leads to consumer confusion, damage to reputation, injury to business, lack of quality control in the marketplace, and allows gray marketeers to "free ride" on the reputation that trademark owners have built for their products.

In a recent Customs gray-market survey, numerous companies such as Jos. E. Seagrams & Sons, Godiva Chocolatier, Colgate Palmolive, Ford Motor, Minolta, Duracell and others, cited problems such as no factory-authorized warranties, no instructions, improperly labeled products and health and safety defects associated with gray-market goods.

"The overall problem is that gray goods are not made and designed for sale in this country," says COPIAT's Toby Collado. Some of the problems associated with the sale of gray-market goods in this country could be serious: Richardson-Vicks reported a case of several gray-market imports of Oil of Olay cosmetic products that were found to contain Red Dye No. 2, a color additive deemed by the Food and Drug Administration unsafe and thus not approved in the United States, but still allowed in Canada and the United Kingdom. The American Automobile Dealers Association reported that as many as 99 percent of gray-market cars do not fully comply with U.S. emission and/or safety standards. "The question is whether consumers truly get a savings under these circumstances," says Collado.

Those in favor of continued gray-market imports argue that the Customs regulations allowing parallel imports are consistent with the intent of Congress, as expressed in the legislative history of section 526 and by congressional inaction over years of Customs interpretation and practice.

They claim that, more importantly, parallel imports benefit the consumer by saving then billions of dollars a year through lower prices. And they provide greater availability of popular products to a wider range of consumers, many of whom may not live in the large cities or near retail centers where exclusive authorized distributors are typically located.

Gray goods are not counterfeits, proponents emphasize, but rather genuine products bearing legitimate trademarks. "We don't buy from back alleys. These are reputable and legitimate products," says A. Robert Stevenson, a K mart vice president.

If the Supreme Court finds present Customs regulations illegal, what then?

"K mart would survive," assures Stevenson, noting that gray-market imports make up less than 1 percent of K mart's total sales.

But even those discount stores with only a small percentage of gray goods may experience some heavy losses if importation restrictions are enacted. In some cases, the appeal of a particular discount article may be the very thing that attracts a consumer to a store. One may go to K mart or W. Bell for the purpose of buying a Seiko watch and stay to purchase $50 more in products that may not be gray market. Even if only 20 percent of a store's total inventory is gray market, it could account for far more than 20 percent of its business.

Those stores whose gray-market goods do account for only a small percentage of its total merchandise cannot afford to do without them: with profits of more than $26 billion, even a 1 percent drop in gray-market sales for K mart would mean a loss of $260 million.

Jay Freedman, whose law firm Freedman, Levy, Kroll and Simonds represents W. Bell, explains that some authorized distributors refuse to sell to discount houses, forcing discount stores like W. Bell to import thorough the gray market "just to have access to popular products." Without the gray market, some stores may have to drop more popular items from their inventory altogether.

Gene Rowan, an attorney with Patton, Boggs and Blow, which represents Revco drugstores, says that stopping the importation of gray-market goods will place extreme limitations on the "availability of certain products and accessibility of its present variety of products to large selections of the population."

Others say consumers will be hit right where it hurts the most—in their pocketbooks—and it may be a double-whammy as they encounter both the absence of bargain goods and the presence of higher prices for authorized articles. Some retailers now drop their prices for authorized merchandise to compete with gray-market goods. Without such competition, authorized dealers may raise their prices again.

COPIAT's Collado disagrees. "Inter-brand competition, i.e., Seiko versus Citizen brand watches, often results in just as much savings to consumers as intra-brand, i.e., authorized Seikos versus unauthorized Seikos."

He notes that even with the presence of gray-market goods, many of the so-called discount houses do not really offer prices that are lower than those offered by authorized retailers. And in many instances, such as in the case of a shampoo or toothpaste, both authorized and unauthorized versions of the product are sold out of the same bin.

Until the Supreme Court decision, however, holiday shoppers may want to purchase enough bargain goods to last a few Christmases, just in case.

December 14, 1987

Supreme Court Ruling Favors "Gray Market"

5-to-4 Decision Backs Brand Name Discounters

AL KAMEN AND CAROLINE E. MAYER

The Supreme Court, in a major victory for discount retailers, yesterday upheld the controversial practice of importing so-called "gray-market" goods—brand-name cameras, luggage, perfumes and other items purchased abroad through unauthorized channels and sold here at steep discounts.

The court, in a 5 to 4 decision written by Justice Anthony M. Kennedy, ruled that the Tariff Act of 1930 does not require the U.S. Customs Service to bar importation of most of those goods—valued at up to $10 billion annually.

The law was "ambiguous" enough, Kennedy said, to justify Customs' interpretation that such goods could be legally imported without the express approval of the U.S. manufacturer or authorized distributor.

The discount retailing industry immediately hailed the decision. "It is an important victory for consumers who will probably be paying hundreds of millions of dollars less each year for these products," said Richard B. Kelly, general counsel for the National Association of Catalog Showroom Merchandisers, such as W. Bell & Co. and Best Products Inc.

But the Coalition to Preserve the Integrity of American Trademarks, an ad hoc association of 80 U.S. companies and trade organizations, said it would continue to fight against the gray market, either by seeking legislation or by initiating further court battles.

"We feel the gray market is a disservice to consumers, to U.S. labor" and to others, said Eugene A. Ludwig, an attorney for the group, called COPIAT. The group has argued that while prices on the gray market are often lower, consumers are not always getting genuine goods or full warranties or services.

"They differ in almost every case from U.S. goods," Ludwig said. "The gray market is a disaster."

The gray market began expanding rapidly several years ago as a result of the increase in the value of the dollar against other currencies. Independent retailers could easily purchase goods abroad, bypassing authorized distributors, and then sell the items—Nikon cameras, Waterford crystal, Seiko watches and the like—at discounts as much as 40 percent below the retail prices suggested by the authorized dealers.

With the devaluation of the dollar, the gray market has shrunk somewhat, but discounters say it still remains an important channel to obtain goods at a discount.

Two years ago, a federal appeals court panel here sided with COPIAT and overturned the Customs Service's 50-year policy of allowing the importation of such goods. Lawyers for the discounters, headed by K mart Corp. and 47th Street Photo, appealed, arguing that Customs' regulations were faithful to the intent of the 1930 Congress. They were joined by the Customs Service.

The high court agreed for the most part with the discounters, ruling that the Tariff Act did not protect foreign manufacturers from competition by unauthorized distributors.

Justice William J. Brennan Jr. said in a concurring opinion, "The most blatant hint that Congress did not intend to extend [the law's] protection to affiliates of foreign manufacturers is the provision's protectionist, almost jingoist, flavor. Its structure bespeaks an intent, characteristic of the times, to protect only domestic interests."

As a result of the court's interpretation, manufacturers such as Seiko, Nikon or Cartier cannot set up American companies to be the sole distributors here of their products. Discounters continue to be free to buy these products from other channels, including dealers in other countries.

However, the court, in another 5 to 4 vote involving the same case, ruled that not all gray-market goods can be imported into the United States. The decision exempted goods made by an independent foreign company that has a licensing agreement with a U.S. company but is not owned or controlled by the American firm.

Thus a U.S. cosmetics company that authorized the production of a shampoo for distribution abroad by an independent foreign company could ask Customs to block importation of that product by another dealer.

Importers of gray-market goods yesterday predicted that more stores would begin selling the items.

"Some people who were afraid to change their pattern of distribution as long as the Supreme Court case was pending are now going to do so," predicted Don Larsen, president of Osaka Trading Co., one of the largest importers of gray-market Seiko watches into the United States, with sales of $25 million a year.

"Now that they don't have that stick over their head, there could literally be hundreds who want to make the switch" from getting their goods from authorized dealers to importing gray-market goods, Larsen said.

June 1, 1988

A Brisk Barter Business in Contraband

Honduran Market Offers Scarce Items to Nicaraguans Who Brave Border Crossing

WILSON RING

Standing on a path just inside Honduras, Marta was busy stuffing bottles of shampoo and packs of cigarettes into her underwear as she prepared to recross the Guasaule River into Nicaragua.

All around her the ritual was being repeated. On both the Nicaraguan and Honduran side, dozens of women struggled to put on as many layers of new clothing as possible while hiding other goods in the folds.

They were coming from a clandestine Honduran market tucked into the edge of the valley about a quarter mile from the river. The market sells exclusively to Nicaraguans crossing into Honduras, and the medium of exchange is either barter or Nicaraguan Cordobas.

The women had to hide their purchases before returning to Nicaragua, they said, because they were afraid of being searched by Sandinista border guards who would confiscate their contraband.

Marta made the trip from Managua to buy things to resell there at an enormous markup. She said she needed the money to buy medicine for an ailing child. Most came with a simpler motive: profit. They came to buy shampoo, deodorant, clothing and dozens of other consumer items that have been unavailable in Nicaragua for years.

"If we didn't bring them, there wouldn't be any of these things in Nicaragua," Marta said.

Every day at dawn, hundreds of Nicaraguans, the vast majority women, wade across the Guasaule to visit the market at Palo Verde and three similar sites along the river. Most come with beans, clothing or agricultural products to sell.

"You can't even buy a good pair of underwear in Nicaragua, so they have to come here to buy," said Maria de Jesus Rivera, a Nicaraguan refugee living in Honduras who sells to her countrymen at Palo Verde.

While most of the 300 or so people a day come to do business, others come to visit exiled relatives or to try to enter Honduras illegally and begin new lives.

The market is set up inside a small barbed-wire compound. Dozens of crude stalls made of sticks cut from scrub brush are covered with dried thatch that does nothing to stop the rain but offers protection from the fierce midday sun.

Palo Verde, in western Honduras not far from the Pacific Ocean, has long been a smuggling point between Nicaragua and Honduras. The market sprang up soon after the 1979 Sandinista victory over former Nicaraguan dictator Anastasio Somoza, but merchants said its importance has increased in recent years as the Nicaraguan economy has deteriorated.

Access to the market is controlled by Honduran soldiers who check the Nicaraguans for weapons. The soldiers pass the time keeping the Nicaraguans from escaping into the interior of Honduras and listening to songs by Kenny Rogers or Pink Floyd blaring from a huge boom box.

The goods most in demand from the Nicaraguans are pesticides and antiparasite medicines for cattle.

"They get them from the people of the [farming] cooperatives and bring them here to sell," said Marco Solivares, another Nicaraguan refugee in Honduras who sells at the market.

The most sought-after product is a Swiss-made insecticide used to control pests on cotton plants. At Palo Verde, bottles of it can be bought or traded for 50 percent less than it sells for in Honduran shops.

Cosmetics and women's underwear are the biggest draw for Nicaraguans, and the path from the market to the river is littered with wrappers from face creams and finger nail polish bottles.

On their return to Nicaragua, the women put on layer upon layer of clothing. Though they would not be able to conceal the goods in a rigorous body search, the women said they would attract less attention from the Sandinista guards if they were empty-handed.

The Honduran soldiers who patrol the border at Palo Verde turn back any Nicaraguans who want to go past the market. "They can go there and buy everything they want," said Honduran Sgt. Pedro Bogardo Cruz. "At least 10 come every day asking for permission to stay . . . I am not going to let one Nicaraguan past. Not one."

In spite of the soldiers' efforts, many Nicaraguans manage to slip into Honduras, where they compete with Hondurans for scarce resources and jobs.

The estimated 250,000 refugees in Honduras worry government authorities so much that Foreign Minister Carlos Lopez Contreras appealed for international relief earlier this month in a speech to the United Nations General Assembly.

At Palo Verde, the problem takes on a human dimension. One Nicaraguan mother accompanied by two draft-age sons pleaded with Bogardo to let them visit relatives in a Honduran town near the market.

"If you are of a good heart, you will let us pass," the mother said.

"Yes, I would like to let you pass, but that's not my job," he said. "If any more Nicaraguans enter our country, it will bring us problems . . . Look, you know why. Go back to Nicaragua."

The mother, from Chinandega, said afterward that she had planned to return to Nicaragua but had intended leaving the boys with relatives so they would not have to serve in the Sandinista Army.

While there was no tension apparent at the market during a visit by reporters, the crossing into Honduras is not without risk.

Nicaraguans slip down to the river's edge before dawn, avoiding Sandinista patrols, and cross at first light. The Nicaraguan side is littered with land mines, which have killed and maimed dozens of people over the years.

The return to Nicaragua is more dangerous, and many fear being caught by guards who will confiscate their belongings and, in some cases, jail them for smuggling, several Nicaraguans said.

While Honduran soldiers come to the river's edge, Sandinista border guards are nowhere to be seen, although during the reporters' visit, a burst of automatic rifle fire was heard from the Nicaraguan side of the river.

The vendors say the Sandinistas do not want to stop the flow of people across the river. Not only can the Sandinistas keep themselves supplied with hard-to-find goods, but the free flow of people allows them to move spies in and out of Honduras, according to the vendors and the Honduran soldiers.

November 11, 1988

Angola on 5 Eggs a Day—A Bird's-Eye View of a Barter Economy

DAVID B. OTTAWAY

This is the story of Luanda's golden eggs.

It is also a story of a war-battered economy in transition from socialism to a free market that is so scrambled that eggs are far more valuable to a foreign visitor than the local currency, the kwanza.

I arrived in Luanda at the start of a recent weekend after the banks had closed. There was no way to exchange dollars legally into kwanzas, and thus no way to buy gas for a rented car that came with a nearly empty tank.

"No problem," a friend said. "Let's go to the Intermarket."

This is a supermarket that caters to the better-off of Luanda, those who have dollars or other hard currency. The Italian-provisioned supermarket's wide variety of goods—clothes, household items, food and alcohol—are priced in kwanzas, but all transactions are made in hard currency. One dollar at the store is worth 30 kwanzas of merchandise at the official exchange rate.

"We need to buy some beer," my friend said.

No beer.

So my friend suggested that we buy eggs instead. There were newly arrived crates of them on sale.

We bought six dozen.

The eggs were priced by the half-dozen—47 kwanzas for that number, or about 26 cents an egg. The total bill came to 564 kwanzas, or $18.80, which seemed a high price to me.

With six dozen eggs in the back seat, my friend set off for a condonga, one of Luanda's many black markets, which is a misnomer since they are very open. Practically the entire city shops at them.

A couple of hours later, he returned to the hotel with a full tank of gas, and 4,600 kwanzas in change.

"What happened?" I asked in no small wonderment.

He explained that he had sold the eggs.

"I found a lady at the market and asked her for 150 kwanzas," he said. "She refused, but she offered 100 kwanzas. So I sold her the eggs at that price."

"One hundred kwanzas for a dozen eggs, or for six?" I asked, remembering that the eggs had been sold in units of six but packaged in cartons of 12.

"No," he laughed, "100 kwanzas for one egg." That's $3.33 for an egg that I had paid 26 cents for.

"How much can she possibly sell them for?" I asked with growing disbelief.

"She told me she would sell them for 150 kwanzas an egg"—about $5.

In this one transaction, I learned just how out of whack the Angolan economy has become. I had converted $18 dollars into 72 eggs, which then hatched 7,200 kwanzas, or $240 at the official rate—enough, it turned out, to fill the car with gas and carry me through a week's stay in Luanda, with 3,000 kwanzas left over.

How was this possible? How was it possible that Luandans could afford to purchase eggs at 150 kwanzas apiece when salaries in the government sector range from 5,000 to 35,000 kwanzas a month, about $160 to $1,160 at the official exchange rate?

When I left Luanda, after interviewing Finance Minister Aguinaldo Jaime and talking to scores of residents and diplomats, I still did not understand the price and value of those eggs. But I had a feeling that they had taught me a lot about the sad state of Angola's economy.

In October, Jaime explained, the government carried out Operation Troca, or exchange, obliging everyone to turn in their old kwanzas for new ones. But the banks only gave back five kwanzas in cash for every 100 handed in. For the remainder, each person was given a government IOU.

The idea, said Jaime, was to sop up the mountains of kwanzas the government had printed to finance its deficit over the years and bring the ratio of money supply to the gross domestic product down from 150 percent to 40 percent. The banks took in about 90 billion kwanzas out of an estimated 150 billion in circulation.

"There was too much money around, and people really didn't have a need to work," he said. "We have got to give a real value to people's salaries to energize them to work."

At first, the reform seemed to work, even though the government backed out of an IMF-urged devaluation of the kwanza at the last moment. Prices dropped dramatically because Luandans did not have the kwanzas to purchase even basic food items.

For example, beer, which serves as a major item in barter trade on the condonga, fell in price overnight from 30,000 kwanzas for a case to 6,000—$1,000 to $200 at the official rate. In early December, beer prices were still relatively low, at least by Luandan standards, varying anywhere from 150 to 300 kwanzas a can ($5 to $10).

But eggs were up to their old value, apparently indicating that Luandans again had sufficient kwanzas to purchase them at the same outrageous prices as before.

But, as several Luandans stressed, much of the buying and selling on the condonga is not done with kwanzas but through barter—with beer, cigarettes and precious goods such as eggs serving as prime items for exchange.

On the whole, there was scant evidence that the government was succeeding in instilling any confidence in the kwanza among Luandans two months after the great troca. Most restaurants and all the main hotels would not take kwanzas for payment. About the only need a visitor had for kwanzas was to buy gasoline at state-run stations, or the local party-owned newspaper.

Jaime said the government has big plans for 1991 when the economy will be opened up to the free market and when 200 small- and medium-sized state companies will be privatized. Government expenditures are supposed to be cut way back, forcing even some of Angola's embassies around the world to be closed, and 7,000 government employees are expected to be laid off to pare down the bloated civil service.

The economy is in such disorder, according to Jaime, that no state company— or the government—can draw up a budget or make a plan that means anything. "Our national accounts are in a state of disarray," the minister said. "In Angola, it's difficult to give figures for anything." He attributed much of the mismanagement to the civil war, which after 15 years has been closing in on this capital in the form of sabotage of water lines, power plants and, most recently, the oil refinery. This means that factories, like homes, are often without electricity or water for hours, if not days, resulting in highly erratic production.

As for when the government will take the big jump to devalue the highly overvalued kwanza, Jaime was not saying. Angolan businessmen were betting on early January for an announcement.

But back to the eggs.

The manager of Intermarket later explained how he came by them, thus revealing more about the workings of the Angolan economy. The pricey eggs were not imported from Italy or Portugal, as my friend had surmised, but came from Portuguese-run farms around Lubango in southern Angola.

He bought then for a mere 15 kwanzas per half-dozen, about 50 cents, or eight cents an egg. But he did not pay for them in kwanzas.

Instead, he gave the farmers credit in dollars, calculating the value of each half-dozen eggs at 50 cents. He then allowed the farmers to choose items from a shopping list of goods he was importing—more barter trade.

As for those eight-cent eggs, they went by truck to the port of Namib and then by boat to Luanda, where eventually someone shelled out $5 for one of them—not exactly chicken feed.

December 12, 1990

Nice Food—If You Can Get It

In Moscow, Barter System Fills
Mouths of the Connected

FRED HIATT AND MARGARET SHAPIRO

The White Cottage farm on the outskirts of Moscow still sends pigs to slaughter every day, but there's no pork in the stores. The cows of the huge Gorki dairy still give milk, but cheese is a rarity here. The nets of the Soviet fleet teem with fish, but the Moscow Port Cold Storage refrigerator rooms stand half empty.

This is the mystery of the Moscow food chain; its solution is a tale of corruption and improvisation and ruthless Darwinian competition that has created a pervasive sense of lawlessness. There is food in the Soviet Union—less than in the past, to be sure, but still available to those who have the money, connections and savvy to navigate the anarchy.

Young entrepreneurs with cash and daring bribe store directors with extra rubles or calculators to get meat at the back door. Factories, no longer fulfilling their state-dictated plans, instead barter their television sets or shoes for food to distribute to their workers. Warehouse directors, instead of shipping food to shops, trade their vodka for meat, meat for sugar, sugar for milk.

Ordinary customers, meanwhile, wait for hours in front of shops, edgy and suspicious but powerless to protect themselves. These are the unfortunate Muscovites who produce nothing concretely tradable—civil servants who prospered under the old system, teachers, writers, nurses, bus drivers. The most vulnerable among them, pensioners and children, already pick through the central city garbage dump as they face the prospect of a hungry winter.

This is the Moscow food chain at a critical moment of transition, as the old economic system based on fear and orders from the top breaks down and the country fragments. Sugar is not delivered, potatoes rot in the fields, and processing plants decay or run out of fuel. Meanwhile, leaders talk about free-market reforms and privatization, but apparatchiks still cling to power, forcing food to pass through layer upon layer of bureaucracy.

And all along the food chain people take their cut, skimming off the choicest—for themselves, for friends, for barter—and sending the rest on until it arrives, a skimpy, pathetic remnant, at the ordinary stores.

"Unless we have a person watching at every link of the chain, from the producer to the purchaser, the goods will be lost," said Victor Semenov, general director of the White Cottage farm, which produces pigs and vegetables. "The people at every part of this chain will pursue their own interests at the expense of ordinary buyers."

The result is a house-of-mirrors world where a bent form of capitalism is taking shape in the shadows, where ordinary people struggle to stay a meal or two ahead, and where money is often worth next to nothing, fulfilling in an unintended way Karl Marx's prophecy that communism would lead to a moneyless society.

"We've reduced our country to a feudal state over 74 years," said Ella Yudrina, deputy head of the city organization responsible for food supplies in Moscow's Kievsky district. "No one is interested in money, only barter. It's a very bad omen for the future economic level of our country."

'The Black Entrance'

Maxim Valetsky, 26, is not going hungry, yet his very success shows how seriously askew the system in the Soviet Union is today. In his small Moscow flat, dozens of cans of vegetables are stacked under a tarp on the balcony. Cans of milk are crammed into a cupboard beneath the kitchen window. Three refrigerator-freezers are stuffed with cheese, chicken, beef, butter, chocolate, even batteries and antibiotics. His larder, a testament to his anxiety about the future, would inspire envy and wonder among his neighbors. "In company, I wouldn't say that I still eat cheese," Valetsky said.

But even for the Valetskys, feeding themselves and their 5-year-old daughter is a constant challenge. He works 14 or 16 hours a day as an independent businessman and sales representative, earning perhaps 10 times the average monthly wage. His wife works almost as many hours, putting together the convoluted deals necessary to get for her family the foods that no longer appear on store shelves.

The cheese, for example, began with a rumor: A cafeteria in a government office had some blocks of cheddar. The Valetskys, trading on past favors, were able to purchase some scarce medicines from a friend working in a state pharmacy, where drugs are almost never openly for sale. They offered the medicines to the cafeteria manager, who agreed to trade the cheese—but only if the Valetskys also bought a consignment of scarves that the manager had earned in an earlier deal.

"So now I am giving scarves away," Valetsky said, shrugging his shoulders as he sipped coffee—also not available through ordinary channels—at his kitchen table.

When the local meat store gets a shipment, the Valetskys get a telephone call; for a few extra rubles per kilogram above the fixed price, the clerk sells them everything out the back door, or what the Russians call "the black entrance." About 30 or 40 women get their provisions the same way, with the clerk pocketing some of the bribes and passing more up the ladder to his director, to whom Valetsky's wife brings gifts from time to time. Valetsky said he believes little meat is sold these days to legitimate, front-door customers.

Six months ago the Valetskys bought only meat at the back door; now they buy everything but bread that way, because so little is put on the shelves to be sold at the state prices.

"I feel guilty that I cannot live in another way," Valetsky said. "I am not proud of it . . . But I want to live, and so I do. I wonder how the other people manage."

Lately, as the gap widens between him and "the other people," Valetsky has begun worrying about social disorders, about someone seeing his wife at "the black entrance." "People are becoming more and more anxious every day," he said.

Indeed, one day this month in southwest Moscow, scores of shoppers, alerted by a suspicious "customers' committee" that had watched the local grocery day and night for months, overran blockades and stormed the store, looking for meat, vodka and sugar they believed was being hidden in the basement and smuggled out the back. The search was fruitless, and the shoppers returned to their lines and their self-compiled waiting lists of more than 5,000 names in chronological order.

But the newspaper Trud saw the small riot as an ominous sign. "It seems we have come to the moment when everyone fears everyone else," the labor newspaper commented. "In the 165th police station, they told us, 'Everything is under control.' But will police power be sufficient for long?"

Depleted Depots

The breakdown in the distribution system is painfully visible in the middle of the Moscow food chain at the filthy, ramshackle, two-story building from which the government long supplied food to the 58 government groceries in the city's Kievsky district.

Cold storage rooms once filled with milk, eggs, meat, fruit and other necessities now store cartons of canned salmon sent by Germany as "humanitarian aid." Upstairs in other sparse rooms were stacked bags of partially processed rice, some sugar and bars of soap from India. The depot's only precious commodity, butter, was reserved for children and people who donate blood.

"Even a year ago, we got more than this. This year, right before our eyes, the quantities have been reduced," said depot employee Vladimir Fyodorov as he trudges through mud two inches deep to watch the unloading of low-quality boiled sausages and of frozen beef kidneys in ripped, dirty cardboard boxes. Until recently, few Muscovites deigned to buy such meat, Fyodorov said; now it sells out swiftly.

This depot, like thousands across the country, is bare in part because the harvest was smaller this year, a result of bad weather, spoilage and disabled, crumbling farm equipment. The nation can afford to buy less fodder overseas, so beef and pork production has fallen off. With grain supplies low, chickens are being slaughtered, and the number of eggs has dropped; Moscow gets 5 million instead of

10 million a day, said Elionora Borodina, a city bureaucrat who still tries to direct where and how food will be distributed in Moscow.

Economy in Chaos

The former 15 republics of the Soviet Union, each going its own way, no longer fulfill old state-mandated plans, often refusing to ship food beyond their borders. Ukrainian sugar, for example, no longer reaches Russia, Borodina explained, and the newly independent Baltic republics are looking for new markets for their meat and fish. New "customs posts" between republics take their share of food that does get shipped, as do highway and railroad robbers. To fill their freezers for the winter, Valetsky and two friends plan to drive south and buy 400 pounds of beef—and then drive back, revolvers at the ready, without stopping.

Many producers, anticipating the free-market economy that Russian President Boris Yeltsin has promised but set no date for, simply hold goods off the market, waiting for a better price. Many others trade for food but not for rubles, which constantly diminish in value as the government speeds up the printing of money.

The persistence of fixed prices feeds a thriving black market. One former bus driver said he quit to earn a far more handsome living speculating in vodka, which officially is sold not only at a fixed price but also for ration coupons alone.

When a shipment of 80 cases of vodka arrives at a neighborhood store, the director immediately claims 20 cases for himself and his staff to barter for food and other necessities, the speculator explained. The director sells 40 cases more, at twice the low state price, to the former bus driver and other speculators, who double the price yet again before selling the bottles on the street or out of their car trunks. Only 20 cases remain for the customers lined up in front of the store, many of whom wait for hours yet never manage to use their ration coupons. At one liquor store recently, 4,000 customers had signed the informal daily list reserving their places in line for vodka purchases.

Such scarcity breeds theft. At the Moscow Port Cold Storage facility, for instance, director Oleg Ivanov said boxcars sometimes arrive open and empty of the fish that was loaded onto them in Murmansk or Vladivostok.

But losses to theft are not his major problem, Ivanov said. The Soviet fleet is catching about as many fish as ever, he said, but now wants to trade fish directly for sugar, for ball bearings, for whatever it needs to feed its crews and keep its ships afloat. And when Ivanov does receive fish, such as the frozen perch that were falling stiffly out of their burlap sacks onto the truck's muddy floor the other day, he too trades much of it to a local store for meat and other provisions for him and his workers.

"It's really a pity that a country like ours, one-sixth of the world and with enormous resources, has come to this," said city administrator Yudrina, itemizing for a visitor how severely food stocks in the Kievsky region have plunged in the last year.

She said she believes the freeing of prices will improve the situation, but added: "There is a time factor. The people who made the [August] coup are still sitting out there and waiting, waiting until things get bad."

November 24, 1991

Russia Backs out of Polish Barter Pact

Natural Gas Deliveries to Warsaw Cut 40% without Explanation

BLAINE HARDEN

Two weeks after signing a huge barter deal with the Polish government for food and drugs, Russia is reneging on a pledge to supply Poland with natural gas.

Without official explanation, natural gas technicians in Warsaw were informed late last week by their Moscow counterparts that Russia is cutting pipeline deliveries of gas to Poland by about 40 percent.

"Of course we are upset. It could be dangerous to Polish industry. It is very hard to determine the reasons for this," said Mieczyslaw Ratajewicz, a director of the Foreign Trade Ministry and one of the officials who helped to put the agreement together.

Ratajewicz suggested that political and administrative confusion in the former Soviet Union lies behind Russia's inability to keep to its part of the barter agreement, whose value was put at $2.8 billion.

"It seems to me that the people who deliver the natural gas probably don't know that we have signed the agreement," Ratajewicz said.

The Russian government had agreed, in a protocol signed in late December, to meet Poland's need for natural gas this year. In return, Poland promised to deliver $500 million worth of food to Russia, as well as pharmaceuticals and coal-related products.

The transaction, which also includes a commitment by Moscow to meet half of Poland's needs for crude oil, is the largest barter agreement that Russia has signed with an Eastern European country.

The agreement was hailed by Polish trade officials as a "solution" to chronic energy problems.

A 40 percent cut in imports of natural gas would cause industrial and perhaps consumer shortages, according to Aleksander Findzinski, director of Poland's state-owned gas company.

"Information which we have received is very worrying. We are trying to intervene at a higher level, but this is very difficult due to lack of competent answers from the Russian side," said Findzinski.

"Officials with whom we have talked are pretending that they know nothing of the Polish-Russian protocol and its provisions."

Poland relied on the former Soviet Union for all imports of natural gas. Finding an alternate supplier is impossible in the short term because Poland has no facilities for unloading ships containing liquefied natural gas, and the country's only gas pipeline originates in Russia.

Several Eastern European countries have joined Poland in recent weeks in signing trade agreements and barter deals with the republics of the former Soviet Union.

Most of the agreements are to provide food and machinery in return for oil, natural gas and raw materials.

January 8, 1992

17 Counterfeiters

Counterfeit Shoe Ring Uncovered
Cheap Imitations Made in South Korea

BILL MCALLISTER

First there was phony Chanel perfume, then Gucci bags and Rolex watches.

Now, the Justice Department claims to have uncovered a counterfeit ring that has been turning out thousands of fake Nike, Reebok, Puma, Adidas and L.A. Gear athletic shoes.

A federal court in Phoenix yesterday unsealed an 18-count indictment charging 18 individuals with creating "a worldwide conspiracy" to make and import into the United States thousands of counterfeit high-priced athletic footwear in violation of various trade and copyright laws.

The indictment charged that a maze of companies based in South Korea controlled the operation, which sold cheap Korean-made shoes with phony brand names to retailers throughout the United States, Mexico, South America and the Caribbean.

Investigators said they have seized more than $4.5 million in assets, including bank accounts, vehicles, precious metals and gems, as the illegal proceeds of the shoe operation.

The sealed indictment, returned Wednesday in U.S. District Court in Phoenix, was the product of a 4 1/2-month investigation that began when Mexican customs agents refused to allow 40 cartons of Vans brand shoes into Mexico.

The shoes were part of a larger shipment that investigators said were exported by the Mi Ju Trading Co. of Pusan, South Korea, and were being shipped to Mexico through the United States.

When U.S. Customs Service agents reexamined the shipment, they discovered that the Vans were counterfeit and not manufactured by the Southern California firm that owns the brand.

That discovery triggered the inquiry and, said U.S. Attorney Stephen M. McNamee of Phoenix, led to an unusual amount of cooperation among the makers of Reebok, Converse and Vans shoes, staunch competitors in the booming sports footwear market.

Fake footwear has become a major headache for shoemakers, prompting them to file a number of civil lawsuits in an effort to curb the pirating of their products.

The U.S. International Trade Commission has estimated that U.S. businesses are losing $8 billion to $20 billion a year to the makers of counterfeit products, a problem that Commerce Department officials have said continues to be difficult to police.

The Korean operation was said to be headed by a businessman identified as Dae Yun Hwang, president and chief executive of Royal Trading Corp., Mi Ju Trading Corp. and a number of affiliated businesses.

In addition to Hwang, those indicted included employees of two groups of Southern California businesses, which were alleged to be American sales agents for the counterfeit shoes, and others in Boston, Cincinnati and San Juan, Puerto Rico, as well as in Mexico and Chile.

A New York investigator said some of the counterfeit shoes were easy to spot while others were difficult.

The Vans, which are made in America, probably were the easiest to spot, he said. "Any Vans that said they were made in Korea, they're bogus," he said.

Those indicted face charges of making false statements about the goods they were importing, trafficking in counterfeit goods and money laundering.

Conviction on the latter offense carries a maximum sentence of 20 years in prison, a $500,000 fine or triple the amount of money involved.

December 30, 1989

Fighting Trespassing on "Intellectual Property"

U.S. Tries to Prevent Overseas Copying of Everything from Music to Microchips

JOHN BURGESS

Eager to safeguard the dwindling number of economic fields in which it retains world dominance, the United States is pressing hard in foreign capitals for better protection of "intellectual property"—things like computer software, movies and recorded music, books, pharmaceutical formulas, consumer brand names and microchip designs.

Since 1985, U.S. negotiators have brought this message to some 30 foreign governments, sometimes threatening sanctions to make them crack down on unlicensed copying. Now it is pushing the General Agreement on Tariffs and Trade (GATT), the Geneva-based organization that polices trade, to enact international standards and find ways to enforce them.

Many governments have tightened controls in response. But in parts of the developing world, the campaign is running up against well-entrenched industries founded on copying and armed with political connections at the highest levels. It is also clashing with deeply held beliefs that what Washington calls piracy is a legitimate means by which a bit of the wealth and learning of the industrialized world is passed to the poorer countries and raises living standards there.

In industrialized countries, the United States runs up against profit-motivated obstruction, but also good-faith differences in philosophies of the details and mechanisms of protection. And as technology advances in fields such as genetic engineering and million-bit microchips, courts are finding it harder and harder to answer a basic question of litigation in this field: How much must you change an object to make it a new, unprotected innovation rather than an unauthorized copy?

U.S. Trade Representative Clayton K. Yeutter recalls that when he left government service at the end of the Ford administration, hardly anyone in Washington had ever heard of the notion of intellectual property. He returned to government two years ago to find it one of the hottest buzzwords in town. "Intellectual property issues have become central to congressional debate on trade policy," says Sen. Patrick Leahy (D-Vt.).

The main reason is money. In this era of record trade deficits—the United States recorded $170 billion in red ink in 1986—products in the intellectual property category are among the charmed few that consistently run a surplus.

The world has little appetite these days for American automobiles, steel or television sets. But it can't get enough of its movies and television programs, buying $2.5 billion to $3 billion worth in 1986, according to the Motion Picture Association of America. It uses U.S. medicines and pharmaceuticals as well, with $3.1 billion worth sold abroad in 1986.

The United States continues to lead the world in the development of technology—the writing of computer software, the designing of computer microchips and the development of life forms through genetic engineering. Fields such as these bring in billions of dollars more in direct sales and licensed production overseas.

In days past, Washington tended to look on piracy abroad as a nuisance. Now it is seen as a threat to U.S. economic vitality and one of the most serious of trade barriers facing U.S. manufacturers, on the assumption that piracy in a foreign country means that legitimate U.S. products will be shut out.

"We get down to technology as the principle determinant of our competitiveness," Yeutter said at a recent Washington conference on intellectual property organized by the American Council for Capital Formation and the Center for Policy Research.

Timothy J. Richards, an international trade specialist at the law firm of Dewey, Ballentine, Bushby, Palmer & Wood, estimated in a presentation to the conference that U.S. companies lost about $25 billion in foreign sales in 1986 due to piracy. Figures of this sort are highly speculative, however, since no one knows the true scope of piracy and how many people would have bought non-pirated originals, which are typically many times more expensive than copies.

The issue began taking form in the late 1970s. In 1982, federal legislation for the Caribbean Basin Initiative, the United States' effort at building a cooperative sphere with that region, picked up the issue, largely in response to pirating of satellite-broadcast entertainment by resort hotels there. In 1984, a trade bill was passed by Congress that included provisions making the safeguarding of intellectual property a consideration in granting developing countries preferential tariff treatment.

Also that year, Congress passed a law extending proprietary protection specifically to the design of computer chips. The law gives protection to foreign designs if authorities here judge that the country of origin is making good-faith efforts to protect foreign chips in its own market.

With measures such as these as leverage, U.S. trade negotiators have been pressing foreign governments to tighten laws and enforcement. They report generally good responses in many Pacific Rim countries.

There are rarely simple solutions, however. Singapore is an example. "The pirates are pretty much out of business in Singapore," says Emery Simon, an intellectual property specialist at the Office of the U.S. Trade Representative. "What they've done is move across into Malaysia and Indonesia."

Historically, patents and copyrights have been a point of friction between rich and poor countries. In the 19th century, when Britain was the world leader in technology and popular culture, it complained that the U.S. gave insufficient protection. Its complaints had little effect, however; American companies wanted freedom to capitalize quickly on British innovations and bring them to market.

Today, pharmaceuticals offer an extreme example of the issues at hand. An American company may spend 10 or 12 years and millions of dollars developing and testing a new drug. It therefore feels it has a right to recoup part of this investment by going abroad and selling, at a "reasonable price," the drug itself or the rights to make it.

But in the Third World, where standards of public health are decades behind those of the United States, policy-makers see things in a different light. Why should the local people be denied the better health that the drug could bring because they can't afford the price the American company would want to charge? In Brazil, Chile and Argentina, patent laws protect only processes for manufacturing a drug, not the final product. Anyone who can arrive at the same drug by a different process than the U.S. inventor is free to do so.

It is not only the Third World that makes these arguments. In recent negotiations with Canada, the U.S. objected to provisions in its laws that provide for compulsory licensing of new drugs to Canadian companies, which pay a 4 percent royalty to the American company. The United States argued that that figure was way too low; Canada said the idea was to keep drug prices low. It has now agreed to change the system as part of a larger trade agreement.

Arguments of national welfare are applied to computer software and virtually every other technology. By having access to low-cost software—that is, copied software—local companies can function more efficiently, speed national development and have a fighting chance in the world economic race.

Similar thinking applies to foreign-developed pesticides and foreign-authored textbooks. In South Korea, illicit copies of American textbooks are common in university classrooms. South Korean officials have argued that students couldn't afford books at all if they had to buy the original versions.

"We consider that all countries must have rights to access to technology in order to improve the living standards of their people," says Mauricio Cortes Costa, economic counselor at the Brazilian Embassy here. "A patent is not given with the sole object of protecting the innovator."

Rather, he contends, reflecting a common view in the Third World, it serves to create a relationship between innovator and society, with both sides having responsibilities. As for using patents or copyrights to stop the international flow of technology, he said, "the ultimate effect would be to interfere with many countries' economic development—and this must not be allowed to happen."

P.S. Sahai, minister of commerce at the Indian Embassy, voices a similar concern: "Any protection to the patentee should not be at the cost of the public."

Enhancing public health and industrial development are typically cited by Third World governments in excusing piracy. But piracy also occurs in industries devoted to simply making quick and easy money by replicating imported music, TV programming and brand-name products.

In many Third World countries, granting protection is seen as eradicating local jobs and caving in to bullying from the United States, whose trade deficits garner little sympathy. No government wants to take that political heat.

In Thailand, a center of film and music piracy, analysts say that opponents of Prime Minister Prem Tinsulanond recently used Prem's alleged excessive flexibility with the Americans on this issue to try to force the calling of new elections.

The intellectual property issue has also added tension to the already deeply troubled U.S.-Japan trade relationship. U.S. officials feel that the snail-paced consideration that Japan's patent office gives applications results in foreign companies getting no real protection. They have also pushed for greater protection of U.S. computer software and a crackdown against pirated video movies, which the Motion Picture Association of America estimates cheat U.S. companies out of about $160 million in sales a year. This type of piracy is declining, the association says.

These days the United States is increasingly less willing to listen to arguments that the quest for development and a dignified standard of living legitimizes such behavior. "That's really an indefensible way to run a society," declared Yeutter. "I don't see how any nation in the world can defend piracy as a means of keeping consumer costs down."

Typically, the United States makes the argument that it is in a country's own interest to protect foreign products. Doing so will make foreign companies willing to introduce their newest developments there. It will also result in reciprocal protection to innovations that the country's own companies eventually devise and allow them to make money from exports. Some countries embrace this logic; others bow only under the threat of sanctions.

In November, President Reagan took the unusual step of actually applying sanctions, slapping steep tariffs on a range of products from Brazil to protest the country's software import rules.

Brazil has refused to protect foreign software. It has also banned sale of a common product line of the U.S. company Microsoft Corp., saying that local software could do the job just as well. The United States contends that Brazil's software is just a copy of Microsoft's and that the U.S. company is losing sales.

U.S. manufacturers have also moved to take legal action against unauthorized reproduction through the Commerce Department and the International Trade Commission. Earlier this year, Texas Instruments won rulings against a number of

South Korean and Japanese companies that it alleged had improperly appropriated the design of chips. It lost cases filed against other companies, however.

The United States's own clout in the battle is diminished by the fact that it has never joined the largest international agreement on copyright, the century-old Bern Convention, which has 76 countries as members. Three bills are before Congress to make the changes that would bring the United States into line with Bern—one conflict, for instance, is that the United States does not protect architectural works, while Bern does.

Joining the convention, said Rep. Robert Kastenmeier (D-Wis.), sponsor of one of the bills, would bring "enhanced political credibility in our global effort to strengthen copyright norms, to suppress piracy and to secure in all the countries of the world a realistic minimum standard of protection for creative works."

December 3, 1987

Polish Copyright Pirates Peril U.S. Trade Ties:

Mosbacher Warns Warsaw on Unlicensed Books, Tapes, Software

BLAINE HARDEN

Poland's pirates are everywhere, plying their trade in bookstores, video shops and software bazaars.

As Poland lurches through uncharted seas of capitalism, this country's post-Communist entrepreneurs are plundering the West's creative property.

U.S. Secretary of Commerce Robert A. Mosbacher warned the Polish government this month that until something is done about the pirates, Poland cannot count on American investment or trade.

Consider these pirate raids:

At the beginning of this year, G&G Publishers of Warsaw bought the rights to Alistair MacLean's novel 'Circus" and printed 150,000 copies. Before the books hit the stores, however, another Polish publishing house forged a contract with the author, printed 50,000 copies of the same book and sold them all.

Every weekend in central Warsaw, there is a big outdoor computer software bazaar. Word-processing, spreadsheet and game programs, no matter how expensive they might be in the West, sell for an average of about $1 per floppy disk. The U.S. mail-order discount price for a popular word-processing program, such as Word Perfect 5.1, is about $250. The price of the same product at Warsaw's software mart is about $6.

An estimated 60 percent of the videocassette tapes rented in Poland are pirated, according to Rapid Associates, an organization of Polish authors, producers and distributors. The association has been authorized by the Polish government to investigate and levy fines against video shop owners who rent pirate tapes. Last month, someone tossed a firebomb through an office window at Rapid.

"The argument that we hear from the pirates is that they are helping the Polish population to make contact with the cultures of the world," said Krzysztof Teodor Teoplitz, president of Rapid.

The legacy of four decades of communism encourages such reasoning. In the old Poland, legal contact with Western films, books and technology was severely restricted by the Communist bureaucracy. Until the late 1980s, a Pole returning home from vacation with a Western book about, for example, the Soviet KGB, faced arrest at the border.

This, of course, did not cut Poles off from Western culture. Rather, it piqued their interest and sanctified all manner of video smuggling, underground publishing and illegal copying of computer programs. Through the Communist looking glass, such fiddles were patriotic, even heroic endeavors.

A good Polish anti-Communist was likely to have been a skilled copyright thief, or at least to have depended on one for intellectual succor. Poland was not alone. Across the old East Bloc and in the Soviet Union, an argument can be made that homegrown pirates of Western culture were key actors in the collapse of communism.

The thief-as-hero legacy does not die easily, despite scolding from the U.S. secretary of commerce. In this week's Polish parliamentary elections, there is a political party that stands foursquare for piracy. The platform of Party V—whose members are owners of videotape recorders—declares that all cultural goods are the property of the people.

"That one person could own the rights to a film or a novel, this is not quite natural yet in the Polish way of thinking," said Teoplitz, a well-known Warsaw journalist.

To change Polish thinking on intellectual piracy, Rapid Associates has hired private investigators who sniff around video shops in search of knock-off cassettes. When they find a fake, the investigators flash an ID stamped with the insignia of the Polish Interior Ministry and invite the pirates to come down to the main headquarters of Rapid.

The revised role of the Interior Ministry is itself a telling measure of how Poland has changed in the past two years. Eight years ago, police from that hated institution murdered a Roman Catholic priest for his anti-Communist activities; now the ministry is working with private eyes to help pop star Madonna protect her video rights.

"We have negotiations daily with about 30 or more pirates," said Teoplitz. "We meet the guy, and we say: 'Because of your activities, our client (who has purchased a distribution license from a Western company) has lost such and such amount of money. You should pay it back to him.' "

For a videotape of a popular film, Rapid estimates that the pirate should pay about $200 for every six-month period that the tape has been in circulation.

But if the pirate does not want to pay, he faces no criminal penalty. Under current Polish law, the only recourse for a licensed distributor is to file a civil suit—and wait for months or years as the case winds its way through a court system run by judges who know little about western copyright law.

Prime Minister Jan Krzysztof Bielecki, in the wake of Mosbacher's weekend rebuke, has promised to appoint a team of experts to adapt Polish copyright law to international standards, and the Polish parliament has begun considering a bill to license trade in video and audio tapes. These two moves, presumably, will result in criminal penalties for pirates.

Publishers in Poland, meanwhile, doubt whether teams of experts are needed to draft a proper law on copyright theft. "You don't need to be a genius at law. You don't have to be inventive at all to fix the situation. You simply make the same law as in Britain and the United States," said Krzysztof Adamski, senior editor for foreign literature at G&G Publishers.

Police refuse to arrest pirate publishers or confiscate their goods, Adamski said, adding that there is nothing to stop pirates from continuing to publish illegal titles, even after they are sued in civil court. While his Warsaw-based publishing house was suing the Gdansk-based publisher of MacLean's "Circus," the first illegal printing of 50,000 copies sold without restriction.

Not everyone agrees, however, that Poland, Eastern Europe and the Soviets should be forced to pay Western prices for intellectual property. There are responsible businessmen here who argue that the West must understand that East Europeans are too poor to pay full price.

"The average Pole earns about one-tenth what the average American earns. So the prices of software should come down by a factor of 10 to fit Polish conditions," said Stanislaw Kern, a technical director at Hektor Computer, a large computer retailer in Warsaw.

Kern said that if prices are reduced substantially now, they could be increased gradually over time as Polish living standards rise. In the process, he said, a legal and regulated system of distribution and sales could develop.

Western software distributors have a choice, Kern said. They can allow their products to be sold legally, albeit at a very low margin of profit, or they can fume helplessly as their products are sold by Polish pirates at $1 a disk.

October 21, 1991

18 Regional Integration

When it Comes to World Trade, Blocs are in

HOBART ROWEN

Conventional wisdom among economists of all nations is that multilateral trade produces a higher standard of living than is possible under competitive regional blocs.

Moreover, the world trading system operated in the 1980s on an assumption that high technology and instant communications would bring the world together under the Geneva-based General Agreement on Tariffs and Trade.

But this textbook analysis has been pushed aside by the pragmatists. Experience showed that geography and ethnic unity still count. Around the world, as former Treasury assistant secretary C. Fred Bergsten said, the message was that "even the United States is going regional."

Frustrated with GATT, the United States, normally the strongest backer of multilateralism, launched a North American free-trade pact with Canada and is now in the process of extending it to Mexico. Later on, other Latin nations will be invited to join as full or associated partners as part of President Bush's "Enterprise for the Americas" initiative.

Europe already has in force the biggest and tightest regional bloc, ready for further expansion. The Asian countries are seriously exploring the practicality of similar groupings.

On the trade front, "global" is out and "regional" is in.

The one thing that could slow the drift toward regional blocs would be a dramatic, last-minute revival of the GATT negotiations, known as the Uruguay Round. Recently, a belated, reluctant and tentative push by German Chancellor Helmut Kohl to generate a compromise has revived hopes that the round can be completed next year.

Over a four-year period, the negotiating parties in the Uruguay Round have failed to get a change in GATT rules to adjudicate disputes fairly. And the disappointment in GATT, as the chief symbol and operator of a multilateral trade regime, has been exacerbated by Europe's stubborn refusal to abandon a highly protectionist farm subsidy system known as "common agricultural policy."

244

But whether Kohl's new gesture will be vetoed by a stubborn President Francois Mitterrand of France remains to be seen. It depends on complicated internal European politics.

Even if, by some miracle, the Uruguay Round is successfully revived at this late date, multilateralism—at a minimum—will have to accept a two-track existence with regional blocs. Paradoxically, as John Yochelson pointed out last week at a Center for Strategic and International Studies conference, "The strengthening of economic regionalism has occurred at a time when the failure of communism and the spread of market-oriented ideas in the developing world would have opened up a historic opportunity to extend the global marketplace."

Yochelson suggests that one reason for the trend toward regionalism in Europe and the Americas is that Japan, Korea and other Asian countries have been the competitive winners in the 1980s. "They own the surpluses, we have the deficits," he said.

In Asia, the problem is seen from the reverse perspective. Promoters of a regional bloc in Asia are motivated by a fear that unless the many Asian countries get together, they will be outmaneuvered in a battle for markets by North America and Europe.

Japanese elder statesman Saburo Okita—often referred to as the father of the postwar Japanese economic miracle—cites the Asian developing countries' contention that "the international economic system is structured to the advantage of the industrial countries and that they are underrepresented in it."

Almost a year ago, Malaysian Prime Minister Mahathir Ben proposed the formation of an East Asian economic group that stirred enormous interest in Asia, but—typical of Washington's parochial view of the world—got little attention here.

Yet Okita said that the Asian regional grouping suggested by Mahathir, with the addition of coastal China, would equal North America or Europe in both gross national product and population by the year 2000.

Many Latin nations, including Mexico, Peru and Chile, are eager to be associated with an Asian bloc, seeing unique opportunities available in the fasting growing part of the world to help stimulate their own economies. They know a good thing when they see it: Growth rates in Korea, Taiwan, Singapore and Hong Kong averaged 8 percent annually, against 3 percent for the global economy from 1980 to 1988.

Back from a trip to Japan, Yochelson reports that the pragmatic Asians, who had concluded the United States was the sales market "of choice" in the 1980s, believe that in the '90s their own expanding backyard will offer more opportunities than the United States, where economic growth may be minimal.

An Asian regional bloc, to be sure, is far from a fait accompli. Asia is composed of disparate economies from rich to poor, widely separated by culture and history, most of whose citizens hate Japan. Japan itself is ambivalent: It has huge markets outside of Asia to keep nurturing. And the United States, not invited by Mahathir to join, lobbies hard against an East Asian economic group, preferring to be included in a differently structured Pacific bloc, if there is to be one.

So Mahathir's grand vision may never be realized, although some other grouping may be developed. From either the Western or Asian perspective, the reality is that the trend of the '80s toward multilateralism has been reversed and the bloc system will grow.

My colleague John M. Berry reported in September that at least a few influential economists in a group gathered by the Kansas City Federal Reserve Bank accepted the inevitability of trading blocs as a second-best system, arguing that second best is a good deal better than nothing at all.

That may or may not be true. But it looks as if we are going to find out in the '90s what the price of regional blocs will prove to be in terms of protectionism, higher consumer costs and in other areas not even visible today.

November 3, 1991

Europe Seeks an Economy of Scale

Twelve Nations Work to Build
a Real Common Market by 1992

ROBERT J. MCCARTNEY

In an ambitious effort to forge a more united Europe and compete better economically with the United States and Japan, 12 West European nations already have approved nearly half of a revolutionary program to scrap barriers to travel, trade, employment and investment that have separated them for centuries.

The members of the European Community (EC) are seeking to create through negotiations something that has eluded statesmen and military conquerors since Charlemagne: a single European market, in which national boundaries would be no greater impediment to economic activity than state borders in the United States.

Approved in principle four years ago, the project aims by the last day of 1992 to establish an identical economic environment for businessmen, workers and consumers across a giant region stretching from Scotland to Spain and from Portugal to Greece. With 322 million mostly middle-class consumers, it would be the developed world's largest single market.

The 12 EC governments have made significant progress on those parts of the program designed to harmonize industrial and technical standards and eliminate barriers to the free flow of money and financial services within the community. Of the 279 formal, legal directives by the EC Commission that form the core of the single-market program, 107 have now been adopted by the EC states. Tentative agreement has been reached on two dozen other directives, and some parts of the program already have taken effect.

Tough talks lie ahead, however, on those planks which call for abolition of customs and immigration checks at internal EC borders and the narrowing of tax policy differences among member states.

A major dispute also is brewing over proposals to create a single West European currency unit and a single EC central bank. Adoption of a single EC currency is not a part of the 1992 project, but is viewed by many experts as a logical and perhaps vital step to be taken in the mid-1990s to ensure that the full benefits of the 1992 program are realized.

"We have completed about 45 percent of the program. Of course, that has been the easiest part of the project, and now we have to face the most difficult issues.

But we have a very strong political commitment to meet the 1992 objective," said Michel Ayral, a senior planner for the 1992 project at the EC Commission in Brussels.

The program creates major opportunities for U.S. and other non-EC businessmen by making it easier to operate in Western Europe once they are established here. But it also poses big challenges for outsiders.

Non-European governments and businesses fear that the community will become a "fortress Europe," with free trade internally but new commercial barriers against non-EC members. Protectionist sentiment is particularly strong in France, Italy and Spain, and a showdown is expected between those countries and free-trade advocates Britain and West Germany.

Attempting to allay U.S. concerns, European officials indicate privately that any EC trade barriers after 1992 are likely to be aimed principally at Japan, which is viewed in Western Europe as a bigger trade threat than the United States.

But foreign firms are not the only ones worrying. Many West European companies that currently enjoy various degrees of state support fear that they may not survive the elimination or reduction of protectionist regulations and subsidies that have long sustained them.

"The single market will be able to fulfill the expectations placed in it only if, in European-wide competition, it is the efficient companies that win and not those that have easy access to state subsidies," said Alfred Herrhausen, chairman of West Germany's largest bank, Deutsche Bank AG.

The EC's own planners admit that the project will eliminate hundreds of thousands of jobs in the short term, as fresh competition drives inefficient firms out of business. Labor unions have expressed skepticism over the planners' argument that the plan, by stripping away regulations, will reduce company costs, spur economic growth and eventually create millions of new jobs. The unions also doubt claims that the new competitive environment will help hold down consumer prices.

Competing With Japan, U.S.

The 1992 plan is explicitly designed to create a more dynamic economy in Western Europe, helping the EC compete more effectively with the United States and Japan.

"Behind the project is the feeling that a fragmented Europe would not be in the game anymore vis-a-vis the United States and Japan. The governments have become aware that their market base is too small," said Michel Petite, a senior staff official at the EC Commission, or executive body.

The EC's economic growth rates have consistently lagged behind those of the United States and Japan. EC leaders have worried that without major new steps to maintain the economic vitality of their industries, their countries would fall further behind in the international standings of the 1990s.

The European Community

BRITAIN	Population: 56.8 million GDP: $662.6 billion. Prime minister Margaret Thatcher fears that planned scrapping of border controls may make it harder to keep terrorists and other criminals out of the country.
IRELAND	Population: 3.5 million GDP: $29.1 billion. One of the poorer Economic Community members, Dublin is to receive substantial economic adjustment aid under the 1992 plan. Ireland already gets large sums for training young workers.
DENMARK	Population: 5.1 million GDP: $101.4 billion Many Danes still favor leaving the EC. Denmark is pulled in two directions: toward fellow Scandinavians outside the EC and toward the continent and the Community.
NETHERLANDS	Population: 14.7 million GDP: $214.6 billion The Dutch expect to benefit greatly from the 1992 plan because of a strong presence in trucking and shipping—industries where costs should drop when customs controls are dismantled.
BELGIUM	Population: 9.9 million GDP: $138.5 billion As hosts of Western Europe's "capital" in Brussels, the EC Commission, or executive body, and its thousands of "Eurocrats," Belgians tend to benefit when the Community prospers.
LUXEMBOURG	Population: 0.4 million GDP: $6.2 billion. This tiny grand duchy, the EC's smallest member, hopes that liberalization of banking rules will help it thrive as a financial center.
WEST GERMANY	Population: 60.1 million GDP: $1,118.8 billion. Efficient manufacturers are looking forward to strong expansion southward. Highly regulated insurance industry here fears British and other competition.
FRANCE	Population: 55.6 million GDP: $879.9 billion. Of the major capitals, Paris is most enthusiastic about Western European integration. Outsiders see the French as too sympathetic to creation of a protectionist "Fortress Europe."
PORTUGAL	Population: 10.2 million GDP: $26.1 billion. Lisbon hopes a combination of fresh competition and EC adjustment aid will give its economy a needed injection of dynamism.
SPAIN	Population: 38.7 million GDP: $288.0 billion. Iberia expects to get a major influx of northern European manufacturing companies, banks and other firms that will take advantage of relatively low wages and under-exploited markets.
ITALY	Population: 57.3 million GDP: $751.5 billion. Some high-powered Italian entrepreneurs see great opportunity to move north after 1992. Others fear added competition will hurt Italy, already saddled with a staggering budget deficit and cumbersome bureaucracy.

continued

GREECE	Population: 10.0 million GDP: $47.0 billion. A backward administrative structure and less-developed economy are expected to make it particularly hard for Greeks to adjust to the post-1992 world.
EEC TOTALS	Population: 268.3 million GDP: $4,263.7 billion
UNITED STATES	(for comparison) Population: 241.6 million GDP: $4,435.8 billion

"The EC is trying to avoid being in the position of the bicycle, which falls down when it stops," said Paolo Cecchini, a prominent adviser to the EC Commission.

The vision of a quantum leap in economic and social integration has generated an enthusiasm for West European unity unseen since the 1960s. The progress achieved so far has rekindled faith that Western Europe can make the necessary changes to avoid slipping behind other regions of the world.

West European companies already are scrambling to position themselves for what promises to be both a more open and a more competitive market. Companies have launched a wave of takeovers, similar to the one begun several years ago in the United States, to make sure they have an adequate presence throughout the EC.

West German banks, for instance, have bought smaller banks in Spain and in other EC nations where national regulations have made it difficult for foreigners to operate. Such regulations are now doomed under the 1992 plan.

British companies have staged numerous raids on firms based across the English Channel, with the aim of ensuring that they are well-positioned on the continent to take advantage of more open markets there after 1992. U.S., Japanese and other non-EC companies also are buying new subsidiaries in Europe, expanding current operations or otherwise preparing for the post-1992 world.

Everybody wants to preserve the rich diversity of cultures within the community, in which more than 10 languages are spoken. But, inevitably, the project appears destined to erode each nation's distinctiveness and speed up growth of a uniform West European lifestyle.

Some critics charge that the resulting lifestyle is likely to be similar to that of the United States. The 1992 plan, it is alleged, will accelerate the "Americanization" of Western Europe. Large-volume discount department stores and fast-food chains will find it easier to expand into sleepy farm areas in southern Spain and Italy.

In any case, by the end of 1992, if all goes according to the master plan, life in Europe will be much less regulated and national markets more integrated than ever before.

For instance, a Bavarian autoworker who always bought insurance from a West German company will find it much easier to shop around and perhaps get a cheaper policy from a British or Italian firm.

A Greek lawyer, eager to work for a Paris firm, will not be required to attend French law school. His diploma from an Athens university will be enough to qualify him.

Television sets, cement and baby rattles produced in, say, Spain will be made under safety and performance standards accepted by all 11 other EC states.

For most Americans, the most impressive part of the plan is likely to be the proposed abolition of border checks at internal EC frontiers. In theory, a vacationer touring Western Europe by car four years from now will breeze past abandoned immigration and customs booths when crossing from one EC state to another. After entering any of the 12 member countries, the vacationer should be able to visit the other 11 without having to show a passport or open a suitcase for inspection.

The abolition of such border checks is at the heart of the program and already has been approved in principle. Nevertheless, some governments are resisting it.

In particular, British Prime Minister Margaret Thatcher is skeptical that her country can keep out terrorists and other criminals without some form of immigration checks. Some EC officials believe that Britain may retain some border controls, while the other 11 go ahead and scrap them.

Something for Everyone

The project represents a grand compromise between the EC's northern, wealthier countries such as West Germany and France, and its poorer, Mediterranean members, including Italy, Spain and Greece.

The better-off, northern countries hope to take advantage of the opening of the market to aggressively expand their business activities in southern Europe.

The less-developed, southern EC countries—while worried about penetration from the north—hope that the increased competition will give their economies a needed dose of dynamism. They also feel they must go along with the program, or risk seeing themselves cut off from the most prosperous part of Europe.

In addition, the wealthier EC members have agreed to give tens of billions of dollars to the four poorest EC countries—Spain, Portugal, Greece and Ireland—to help finance structural investments designed to bring their economies up to the level of their better-off neighbors.

"It was recognized in the mid-1980s that what was needed was a comprehensive plan, so everybody benefited in some way and had a stake in the whole," said Adrian Fortescue, director of the EC Commission's general secretariat.

"It also was recognized that a time scale was needed, the discipline of a target date," he added, explaining why the 1992 deadline was adopted.

The European Community, which was created by the Treaty of Rome in 1957, long ago abolished tariffs and other direct trade barriers within its borders. Now it intends to go a step further and get rid of all indirect or hidden hurdles that restrict commerce. Thousands of differences among the 12 members' industrial standards, commercial regulations and other laws and policies are to be eliminated.

Close to adoption, for example, is an EC-wide measure fixing the maximum permissible noise for lawnmowers. Any company that makes lawnmowers for one EC country is to be able to ship them to the 11 others without having to worry about making changes to satisfy differing national rules.

The plan will not abolish all economic differences within the community, however. Despite a harmonization of technical standards, for instance, at least three different kinds of electrical plugs will continue to be used in the EC. A study found it would cost $80 billion to adopt the same kind of plug throughout the community.

Each member country also will keep its own currency, although France, West Germany and some other members are pushing to adopt a single EC monetary unit sometime after 1992. Eight EC countries—all except Britain, Spain, Portugal and Greece—already have linked their currencies to one another within the European Monetary System.

The plan's architects at the Brussels-based EC Commission say that the plan will work only if there is a psychological leap of faith in the value of European union, an increase in the degree to which people identify themselves as "citizens of Europe" rather than of their individual countries.

This shift in consciousness is needed in particular to make possible the abolition of border controls that is the plan's centerpiece.

"It's a question of confidence. The Danes, for instance, have to be convinced that Greek border checks on people entering the EC will be as good as those in Denmark," said Ayral, the Commission planner.

The other major dispute currently threatening the plan concerns handling of value-added-taxes, which are roughly equivalent to sales taxes and are a major source of revenue for many EC members. The plan foresees abolishing the large bureaucracy that now collects such taxes at internal EC borders and bringing roughly into line the various tax rates of EC member states.

These tax collections now account for 90 percent of the paperwork at the borders. Internal EC border formalities as a whole cost about $45 billion, and the plan aims to abolish those costs and pass the savings on to EC companies to make them more competitive.

But France and some other countries are resisting the tax plan, partly to preserve their revenues and partly to preserve special, national tax breaks of various kinds.

In historical terms, the 1992 project represents a shift from the EC's expansionary phase in the 1970s and early 1980s to a period of consolidation. For about 15 years ending in the middle 1980s, the EC was preoccupied by the addition of new members—Britain, Ireland and Denmark in 1973, Greece in 1981 and Spain and Portugal in 1986.

"Enlargement became an excuse for paralysis," Fortescue said.

The Community Grows

May 9, 1950	French Foreign Minister Robert Schuman makes a proposal to place Europe's coal and steel economies under a common European authority.
April 18, 1951:	A treaty creating the European Coal and Steel Community (ECSC) is signed by Belgium, France, Italy, Luxembourg, the Netherlands and West Germany—known as the Six.
March 25, 1957:	Treaties creating the European Economic Community (EEC) and the European Atomic Energy Community (Euratom) are signed.
April 8, 1965:	The Six sign a treaty merging the ECSC, EEC and Euratom into the European community.
July 1, 1968	A joint customs union is formed. Remaining industrial tariffs among The Six are abolished. A common external tariff is created.
Jan. 1, 1973	Denmark, Ireland and Britain join the Community. Free trade agreements with European Free Trade Association countries begin to take force.
June 7-10, 1979	In the first direct elections, citizens of the nine member states vote for 410 members of the European Parliament.
Jan. 1, 1981	Greece joins the Community.
June 14-17, 1984	In the second direct elections, citizens of the 10 member states vote for 434 members of the European Parliament.
Feb. 1, 1985	Greenland, which joined as part of Denmark, leaves the Community.
June 29, 1985	EC heads of state or government endorse a "white paper," outlining a strategy for creating a true common market by 1992.
Jan. 1, 1986	Spain and Portugal join the Community.

In addition, the EC was deeply divided throughout the 1970s and early 1980s by bitter disputes over its budget and agricultural policy. Chronic battles over these issues—especially between Britain and the rest of the community—fueled widespread cynicism throughout the EC.

Finally, the two "oil shocks" of the 1970s, and the recessions that followed, encouraged individual countries to erect subtle trade barriers of various kinds to protect their domestic industries during hard times.

By the mid-1980s, however, protectionist pressures were subsiding as the world economy recovered. The British cut a deal with the rest of the EC in 1984 on how to divide up many of the community's bills.

Jacques Delors' Dream

The stage then was set to move ahead and focus on making the enlarged EC more efficient. In January 1985, Jacques Delors, an ambitious Frenchman committed to the ideal of European unity, took over as EC Commission president and began looking for a theme for his stewardship.

Delors considered trying to push for increased cooperation within the EC on defense or monetary affairs. But he concluded that the EC member governments were not yet ready for major progress in those areas.

Instead, Delors settled on the idea of seeking to create a single, internal market. He drew up a now-famous white paper outlining the broad goals of what became the 1992 plan. The project's emphasis on making markets more competitive was inspired in part by the deregulation policies of the governments of Britain's Thatcher and President Reagan.

At an EC summit in June 1985, EC leaders approved the program in principle. EC Commission staffers in Brussels, nicknamed "Eurocrats," began drawing up the lengthy, detailed list of proposals to make the program a reality.

one significant legal hurdle still remained. Throughout its history, the EC had required unanimous consent from its member governments to adopt any new EC legislation. That made it possible for any single country to block agreement, and encouraged individual governments to blackmail the rest of the Community to get their way.

To ease the decision-making process, the EC in 1987 adopted the first major revision of its charter, the Treaty of Rome. No longer can a single nation veto an action.

Under a new, complicated voting formula, opposition from at least two large members, plus one or two small ones, is now needed to block a bill. Without that change, the 1992 program would be far behind schedule, EC officials said.

March 19, 1989

Along Border with Mexico, People and Goods Move Freely

STUART AUERBACH

Guillermo Ochoa stands with his feet on both sides of the U.S.-Mexican border. He was born in Mexico, educated in the United States and serves on boards of banks in both countries.

"I'm not unusual. Along the border there are a lot of people like me," said Ochoa, 44, who develops industrial parks in both Texas and the neighboring areas of mexico around Ciudad Juarez, El Paso's sister city.

From afar, the 2,000-mile-long border between the United States and Mexico appears to be a formidable boundary. But up close, the barriers become fuzzier. Despite the vast economic differences between El Paso and Juarez, residents here say they have more in common with Juarez than Dallas or Houston.

"These communities (El Paso and Juarez) have been together and will be together for a long time," said Ochoa.

"This is really one community. The boundary is almost irrelevant. Whatever problems they have in Juarez we experience here," said Deborah Kastrin, another developer.

As Washington and Mexico City consider negotiating a formal free trade agreement, goods and people already move freely between El Paso and Juarez in formal and informal ways.

"Socially, the border doesn't exist. So many people have families on both sides . . . " said C. Richard Bath, director of Inter-American and Border Studies at the University of Texas at El Paso. "But it's a real border when it comes to law enforcement, immigration, customs and drugs."

Without any formal agreement, for instance, El Paso's mosquito control unit goes across the border to work in Juarez. "Mosquitoes don't know any boundaries. Helping them with their mosquito problem helps us," said Travis Johnson, a lawyer and former county judge here.

West of here, the fire department in Columbus, N.M., scoots across the border if a fire breaks out in neighboring Las Polomas. Both towns share the same Lion's Club, with meetings alternating between the two countries. San Diego and Tijuana, the largest communities on the border, are considering building a common airport on the border to serve both cities.

In El Paso, the industrial development group draws members from Juarez; banks get as much as 15 percent of their deposits from Mexican businesses, which need the dollars to pay bills in the United States; and the El Paso Ballet has changed its name to the Ballet of the Americas to draw financial support from the Juarez community.

Some Americans live in Juarez because of the low-cost housing there and commute to work in El Paso. They are joined each day by at least 115,000 Mexicans who cross the border here legally, some to work and many more to shop. Retailers estimate that two in five cars parked on a weekend at the Cilio Vista Shopping Mall, on the east side of El Paso near the border, come from Mexico.

"The retail business in El Paso is probably one of the strongest segments of the economy because of Mexicans who come over to shop," said developer Kastrin.

Thus Mexicans crowd through the downtown streets, stopping in stores that display more signs in Spanish than English. Geneva Loan & Jewelry Co., a pawn shop, displayed a new typewriter in its window with a for sale sign advertising "con ñ y acento," meaning that the typewriter has keys for Spanish accent marks.

At dusk one evening last week, Silva's Super Market at the foot of Stanton Street, strategically located at the El Paso end of the bridge over the Rio Grande, was thronged with Mexican shoppers heading home with U.S.-bought groceries. They carried plastic bags packed with rolls of toilet paper, fresh dairy products, canned evaporated milk and American junk food—all cheaper here. Others carried electronic goods, clothing and appliances.

For their part, American shoppers cross over into Juarez to buy meats and beautiful hand-carved furniture, which are cheaper there.

Besides the legal crossing, uncounted thousands more Mexicans move over the fenceless border illegally each day, generally people who work as maids and gardeners for wealthy El Paso residents. The flow is so heavy in the early morning and at dusk that residents here drive especially carefully down Interstate 10, the main highway that dips close to the border as it runs through the city, for fear of hitting an illegal worker crossing the highway.

Poor Mexican women in the last days of their pregnancies cross over the border to have their babies born in the United States, qualifying them for U.S. citizenship. The women generally go to midwives, who charge $600 to $750 a delivery.

Many children in Juarez are sent to El Paso schools. Some go to private schools, others pay tuition in the school system and still more are believed to enroll by using the U.S. addresses of relatives.

But the biggest impetus toward blurring the boundaries comes from the 26-year-old maquiladora, or twin-plant, program. In Mexico, factories manufacture labor-intensive components for cars, electronic equipment, television sets and other products; in the United States, the products go to warehouses and service facilities. Components made in maquiladoras pay U.S. tariffs only on the value that was added in Mexico, generally just the labor costs that amount to a bit over $6 an hour. These plants are leased by U.S. or other foreign manufacturers.

The plants have put money in the pockets of workers in Juarez, which now suffers from a labor shortage in a country where unemployment is a national problem, and added $229 million last year to the El Paso economy in salaries paid to support workers and managers here.

There are about 1,500 of such plants in Mexico, adding up to a $12 billion cross-border industry. The San Diego-Tijuana area has the largest number, 550, but the 293 plants in the El Paso-Juarez area employ 180,000 people, more than twice as many as in San Diego-Tijuana. The maquiladoras—with American and, more recently, Japanese managers moving daily from El Paso to Juarez and Mexican workers earning higher-than-average wages and learning U.S. manufacturing techniques—have accentuated the cross-border ties.

"Every time we have had a boom on the border it has been because of an economic slowdown in the United States. Managements look at their costs and find that maquiladoras make real sense," said Ochoa, who has had a hand in developing 200 twin-plant projects that are responsible for 80,000 jobs in Juarez.

"I think the border is the next major industrial center for a North American common market," said Donald A. Michie of the Texas Center for Economic Development of the University of Texas at El Paso.

"There is a definite bullishness in this area. I feel this area is going to reverse decades of poverty existing on the border through industrialization."

May 13, 1990

Trade Blocs Friend or Foe?

In Asia, If it Looks Like a Trade Bloc . . . Some Say Japan and its Neighbors have the Earmarks of One

JOHN BURGESS

The countries of Asia don't call themselves a trade bloc, and they have no special trade treaty. But Japanese trade and aid and investment in the region sometimes make them look like one, according to some observers.

In Singapore, Thailand and China's coastal cities, tens of thousands of people report daily to Japanese-owned factories to make products that range from electronic components to textiles and automobiles. Japanese government loans and grants—$4 billion was given to Asia in 1989 alone—finance such things as power stations and irrigation systems.

Do these broadening economic ties constitute a bloc that makes Asian countries favor one another's products at the expense of outsiders?

Those who believe it does note that the Japanese plants scattered about Asia, the results of $42 billion in Japanese investment in the region, have no trouble selling their goods to Japan. Also, Japan's foreign aid often requires that the Asian recipients use it to import equipment from Japan.

"An economic entity is developing which has many of the appearances of a bloc," said Clyde Prestowitz, who heads a Washington think tank called the Economic Strategy Institute. But he suggested it was not due to some sinister design by Japan, but was part of the general decline of American economic influence in the world. As the United States has become a borrower in the world, Asian companies have overtaken U.S. companies as investors in the region.

But Japanese officials and many American analysts deny there is a bloc or other form of invisible resistance to non-Asian goods. Hiroshi Hirabayashi, a counselor at the Japanese Embassy here, has likened the region's postwar economic order to a "V" formation of geese, with Japan flying in the forward position and leading the others toward affluence.

Many analysts see forces stronger than these working to pull the supposed Asian bloc apart. Experts say that many Asian countries are uneasy that so much of the investment in their countries is Japanese and would like more from the United States to balance it.

Memories of World War II aggression linger in these countries. Indeed, Japan's new Asian zone of influence closely follows the borders of its wartime

"Greater East Asian Co-Prosperity Sphere." Asia's countries have widely diverging standards of living, political systems and world views, making bloc-building difficult. Edward Lincoln of the Brookings Institution in Washington notes that they have no unifying fear of a powerful neighbor, such as that which linked Western Europe during the Cold War.

Moreover, Japanese investment in Asia over the last five years is a mere fraction of its interest in the United States and Europe.

Japanese investment in its neighboring Asian countries is about the same as that in Latin America. Does that mean, skeptics ask, that Latin America and the United States are part of a Japanese trading bloc?

A.F. Jacobsen, chairman of St. Paul-based manufacturer 3M Co., said his company sees no informal bloc. "I've traveled the region and have never heard anyone talk about it. Our people seem to be able to develop and get business." 3M has 17 subsidiaries in the region.

But he suggested that Asia may respond with barriers if it fears North America and Europe are building walls around themselves. He called on the United States to include Asia fully in multilateral trade agreements to make sure things stay as they are.

June 2, 1992

Japan's "Asian Bloc"

More Illusion than Reality—Behind the Rhetoric, Trade Statistics Show Nation's Ties are Far Stronger to North America

PAUL BLUSTEIN

An hour's drive on the highway leading east from Thailand's capital vividly documents Japan's growing economic power in this part of the world.

Nearly every car whizzing by is a Toyota, a Honda, an Isuzu or some other Japanese make. Every couple of miles, another Japanese-owned factory looms, making the likes of Daikin air conditioners, Mitsubishi electrical equipment, Hitachi wire, Nissan auto parts and Yamaha sports equipment.

Similar scenes can be found in Malaysia, Indonesia and other nations in East and Southeast Asia, the result of Japan's unprecedented, $28 billion investment in the region over the past five years.

But although Japan's economic forays may recall anxious memories of its military reach for dominance over Asia 50 years ago, the reality does not quite measure up to that image, according to a range of experts and a solid array of trade statistics.

Moreover, if any sort of economic "bloc" of nations is in the making, economists say, it is one that stretches across the Pacific Ocean to include not just Asia, but North America as well.

"One can't get away from the fact that there is increased trade within Asia, but even more dramatic and even more important is the increase in cross-Pacific trade," said Peter Petri, a Brandeis University professor who has written extensively on the subject. "There have now been established such close links across the Pacific that I cannot imagine anytime in the near future a viable Asian bloc that doesn't include the countries on the eastern side of the Pacific."

Among those links, for example, is the $109 billion that Japanese companies have poured into North America to erect factories and buy businesses over the past five years—a figure nearly four times the amount invested in Asia.

Such a conclusion may seem surprising, for both the Western and Asian press have been rife with speculation that an Asian bloc is in the works. Helping to fuel the talk was the proposal last year by Malaysian Prime Minister Mahathir Mohamad for the creation of an East Asian Economic Group (EAEG) that would

260

include Japan and the other Asian nations of the Western Pacific, while excluding the United States, Canada, Australia and New Zealand.

Further heightening the perception of a bloc in formation is the fact that this year, Japan's trade with its Asian neighbors will exceed its trade with the United States for the first time in decades. Meanwhile, the closing of U.S. military bases in the Philippines and the planned withdrawal of one-tenth of the 135,000 U.S. troops stationed in Asia have reinforced the view that before long, Japan will be stepping into a role as the region's natural leader.

But almost unnoticed among these highly publicized developments are some powerful trends working in the opposite direction. A close look at these trends suggests that, despite Japan's dominance as a supplier, investor and aid-giver in Asia, the American role in the region will remain preeminent for the foreseeable future—unless, of course, the United States decides on its own to retreat into protectionist isolation.

"Japan can't replace the U.S. in terms of wielding influence in this region," said Sanjoy Chowdhury, chief regional economist for Merrill Lynch & Co. in Singapore. "I think more and more people are realizing that."

Here are some of the reasons:

The explosion of commerce across the Pacific has given the United States a semi-permanent importance as the largest single customer for Asia's export machines, just as Asian countries are major customers for U.S. manufactured and agricultural products.

"To talk about Japan as the hub of Asia really isn't accurate," said Robert Broadfoot, managing director of Political and Economic Risk Consultancy Ltd., a Hong Kong-based firm. "Japan is a very large supplier to many of the countries of the region, [but] which is more important, your supplier or your market? You can debate that all day."

Not that the U.S. role is being limited to that of customer. "We now export more to Singapore than to Spain or Italy," Secretary of State James A. Baker III noted in a recent speech.

In 1980, two-way trade between the United States and the Asian Pacific countries (including Japan, China and Australia) totaled $113 billion—almost exactly the same as two-way trade between the United States and Western Europe. Last year, U.S. trade crossing the Pacific exceeded $300 billion. The figure is roughly one-third greater than either transatlantic trade or intra-Asian trade.

Dig beneath the surface, economists add, and it becomes clear that Japan's growing trade with Asia represents less of a disengagement from the American market than might be assumed. Much of what is happening, according to Petri, is "triangular trade," in which "components and equipment are exported to Asian nations by Japan, and final products go from the Asian countries to the European and U.S. markets."

Japan's neighbors, ever mindful of Tokyo's past imperialism, are showing a firm resolve to keep a lid on Japanese power in the region.

Throughout capitalist Asia, a constant refrain can be heard: Even after the end of the Cold War, the United States must remain as the region's military superpower—in part because of fears about resurgent Japanese militarism.

"If the U.S. withdrew its forces," said Kook-Chin Kim, dean for research at Korea's Institute of Foreign Affairs and National Security, Japan would surely increase its military," because of having lost the protection afforded by the U.S. presence. The result, Kim said, would be "a very dangerous situation" as other nations raced to counter the new potential threat from Japan. "Every country in this region appreciates the role that the U.S. plays," he said.

One country—Malaysia—seems to be putting itself unabashedly in Japan's orbit, in part because of Prime Minister Mahathir's zest for thumbing his nose at the West. The Malaysian government even asked the Japan External Trade Organization (JETRO) to perform a study identifying what products Malaysia should specialize in to attract Japanese investment. (The answer: computer peripherals and fax machines, among others.)

But other Asian nations treat Japan with considerably less warmth, the most notable example being South Korea, which this year opened its stock market to foreign brokerage firms but pointedly excluded all Japanese securities houses.

Moreover, Asian leaders have shown little enthusiasm for Mahathir's proposal to create an exclusive group of Asian nations because to do so would begin the process of cutting themselves off from America and handing regional leadership over to Japan.

Even though Mahathir's proposal has been watered down to a mere "caucus" for discussing regional matters, "It's a crazy idea" to start down the road of Asian exclusivity, a Korean diplomat said. Only if Europe and the Americas split into protectionist blocs would it make any sense, he added.

American culture and values are spreading, not receding, in Asia.

Much attention has been paid to the growing popularity in places like Bangkok and Kuala Lumpur of Japanese pop culture crazes such as karaoke (sing-along bars) and manga (comic books). But for sheer impact on Asian public opinion, nothing can beat the fact that the region's elite youth are flocking to attend U.S. universities in record numbers—229,800 in the 1990-91 academic year, well more than double the number enrolled a decade before and six times the number enrolled in Japanese universities.

Beyond that are some more intangible factors. The Japanese working in Asia are widely denounced for failing to promote local people to top management positions, for refusing to share their companies' technologies, and for generally being clannish. U.S. businesses, by contrast, are regarded as much more open and integrated with their communities.

It is undeniable, however, that Japan's ability to shape events in this part of the world is far greater than 15 years ago, when a visit by then-prime minister Kakuei Tanaka sparked riots in Bangkok.

This increasing influence is a natural consequence of the magnetic pull that Japan's economic success has in creating a role model for some less successful economies. It is also a natural consequence of the benefits that Japanese investment has brought. malaysia, for example, has gone in five years from being an exporter primarily of rubber, palm oil, crude oil and tin to an exporter primarily of manufactured products such as air conditioners.

What worries many Americans in the region is that U.S. companies have for the most part stood idly by while Japanese competitors have sunk their roots into some of the most dynamic economies of the world. A few American high-technology companies, such as Motorola Inc., Intel Corp., Advanced Micro Devices Inc. and Texas Instruments Inc., have established new Asian manufacturing operations in recent years, but they are the exception rather than the rule.

"We used to own the auto market out here," lamented Bob Martin, the head of Colgate-Palmolive Co.'s Thai operation. "Now you can't even see an American car. This is where per capita income is increasing; this is where the market is booming. How can the U.S. auto industry not be here?'

And there is evidence that Japanese companies are starting to embark on a new strategy to capitalize on Asia's rapidly growing markets. When they first began erecting factories in the region, they were motivated by a need to secure cheap labor, to compensate for a surge in the value of the yen starting in 1985 that was threatening to render their products uncompetitive. Now, the same companies are investing more with an eye to serving an increasingly prosperous local customer base.

For example, Daikin Industries Ltd., an air conditioner maker, announced last week that it will expand its Bangkok plant so that it can manufacture 180,000 units a year, triple the current level. The company said it would ship about half of those air conditioners to Japan, but half will go for the local Southeast Asian and Australian market.

But a number of veteran observers shrug their shoulders over the Japanese surge. "Japan is the new boy on the block in terms of foreign investment," said Broadfoot of Political and Economic Risk Consultancy. "The average U.S. company has got about 21 percent of its production outside the United States, and the average German company has about 17 or 18 percent of its production outside Germany. The average Japanese company has only about 6 percent of its production outside Japan. They're rushing to catch up now, and everyone is saying, 'We're being taken over.'"

But the U.S. presence in Asia was well established before the Japanese surge began and there are some signs of a selective revival. Broadfoot and other analysts predict, for example, that the highly competitive U.S. service industry will become increasingly active in Asia over the coming decade; an example is National Medical Enterprises, which is already running medical operations in Singapore, Malaysia and other countries.

"The U.S. and Europeans invested in this region a long time ago," Broadfoot continued. "Take a look, for example, at Hong Kong. Look at the U.S. Chamber [of Commerce] versus the Japanese Chamber. The U.S. Chamber has about five times the membership." That partly reflects the fact that American companies have been in Hong Kong longer, he said, but it also reflects the large non-American membership of the group, "because the organization is localized. Look at the Japanese membership—it's just Japanese names, which shows what one of their problems is."

December 8, 1991

Competitiveness 19

U.S. Firms Lag Japanese in Spending

Study Fuels Debate on Competitiveness

STUART AUERBACH

For the first time since World War II, Japan last year spent more money than the United States in adding new factories and equipment to make its industries more productive, the Council on Competitiveness said in a study this week.

The report on the council's third annual "competitiveness index" fuels arguments that America is failing to keep pace with other industrialized nations. It showed that the United States lags behind other industrial nations in investing in new plants and spending for nonmilitary research and development.

As a result, the report said, the standard of living in the United States has increased at a slower rate than it has in other industrialized countries.

"America is looking like an aging athlete—still on top but trying to ignore all the younger talent that is breaking into the lineup," said Kent Hughes, president of the council.

The council was founded four years ago by a group of business leaders, union officials and academics who were concerned that the Reagan administration was ignoring signs that America's once dominant position in the world was eroding.

While President Bush sounded the competitiveness theme in his State of the Union message this year, his administration has been split over how to tackle the problem.

"For years, the United States has had the luxury of relying on its big post-World War II lead and the strength that came from a continental economy to sustain its competitive advantage. Now the big lead is gone and the competition is more intense," said Hughes.

The "competitiveness index" compares the United States in six key areas with six other industrialized nations: Canada, France, Britain, Italy, Japan and West Germany.

The index noted that the rate of U.S. investment in plant and equipment has lagged behind other industrialized nations. Japan, for instance, has spent an average of 17 percent of its gross domestic product on plant and equipment every year since

1972, while the United States spent 12 percent. The others—all participants in next month's economic summit in Houston—have spent 14 percent.

For last year, Japanese investment jumped to a record 23.6 percent of its gross domestic product and its actual dollar spending exceeded U.S. investment by $36 billion despite the fact that the U.S. economy is twice as large as Japan's.

"The end result of Japan's concentrated spending is an industrial base that is one of the most modern, efficient and competitive in the world," the report said.

Furthermore, the report said that U.S. spending on roads, railways, airports and bridges—the infrastructure of an efficient transportation system that is crucial for a continent-wide economy -has been more than halved between 1965 and 1985.

While the United States leads in total spending for research and development, its principal economic competitors, Japan and West Germany, each spent 50 percent more on non-defense research. The council said that figure is a better indicator of future commercial competitiveness, especially in the post-Cold War era in which economic concerns are expected to be more important than the tanks, missiles and military bases that have symbolized power since the end of World War II.

Other "troubling trends" mentioned in the report:

Because its productivity growth rates have sagged in 1972, the United States "has squandered" a once-commanding lead over the rest of the world. U.S. productivity is now just 30 percent greater than other industrialized nations compared to an 87 percent lead 18 years ago. In Japan, the average worker has more than doubled his productivity since 1972 and that country is quickly closing the gap with the United States.

Wages of U.S. manufacturing workers have remained stagnant over the past 20 years while the wages of its major competitors have increased. The average salary and benefits for an American worker have gone up by little more than $1,000 since 1972 while manufacturing employees in West Germany earned $7,500 more and Japanese workers $5,000 more.

June 29, 1990

The Art of a Deal in East Europe

Czechoslovakia, a Fistful of Marks—But Few Dollars

MARY BATTIATA

As Czechoslovakia's point man for foreign investment, Zdenek Drabek keeps three big envelopes on his desk at the Economics Ministry here. One holds the business cards of potential German investors. Two hold those of visiting Americans.

The American envelopes are stuffed with cards, even though U.S. investment here lags far behind that of the Germans. The German envelope, paradoxically, is nearly empty.

"The Germans almost never come to see me," Drabek said. "They know they can make deals by going directly to the factories. But the Americans think they have to come here first. They come and say, "Where should I invest? Who should I see?"

To the growing concern of some Czechoslovaks, Germany is now the most important and powerful foreign investor here, with the lion's share of foreign investment and million-dollar mega-deals. It is snapping up stakes in everything from car manufacturing to electronics.

Germany's industries and entrepreneurs, taking advantage of next-door-neighbor status and long historical and cultural ties here, now account for nearly three-quarters of all foreign investment in Czechoslovakia, according to government estimates.

Germany and Austria together account for more than 60 percent of the total number of deals made and 80 percent of foreign capital invested, according to the Czechoslovak foreign trade office.

Meanwhile, American investment, which Czechoslovakia had expected would play a major role here, trails that not only of Germany and Austria but of Switzerland and France as well, Drabek said.

"Americans often find it more difficult to do business here," said Alex Seippel, an American investment banker who represents Bankers Trust in Prague. "They're not sure they're welcome. They secretly suspect the Czechs would rather have the Germans as partners. They're put off by the lack of laws."

The triumphant march of German capital here since the fall of communism in 1989 is part of a broader arc of German economic influence now emerging across eastern and central Europe, from Yugoslavia to the Baltics.

While most diplomatic observers view Germany's growing economic clout here as benign and inevitable, Czechoslovak politicians lately have begun to express misgivings openly.

"This year, our government suddenly realized that German investments are simply dominating," Drabek said. 'The question now is, is this consistent with our own interests? And if it is not, what do we do about it?"

According to a recent survey published by the British-based Czechoslovak Financial Review, 80 percent of the people questioned in the Czech republic—as distinguished from this:hybrid country's Slovak republic to the east—said that German business has too big a stake in Czechoslovakia.

Even as most Czechoslovaks welcome German capital and know-how as a source of jobs and future prosperity, the rise of the German mark and the parade of confident German executives through Prague's best restaurants and hotels stirs old anxieties and painful memories of how Germany's economic preeminence throughout the region between the world wars was followed by Nazi aggression.

Nationalist politicians here now complain openly about a German "economic anschluss," or annexation. Lately, there has been talk in parliament of erecting barriers to slow German investment.

Even mainstream politicians, such as the Czech republic's Prime Minister Petr Pithart, have voiced concern about "excessive German investment" in the Czech lands—Bohemia and Moravia. Pithart recently announced that all major new German investment projects will be subject to government review.

That means a bid by Germany's Daimler-Benz to take over Czechoslovakia's two big truck manufacturing companies will be assessed for political as well as economic considerations, although many analysts say the Daimler-Benz deal is better for Czechoslovakia than a competing bid by French car maker Renault.

Czechoslovak officials say there is nothing sinister about German success here. "The fact they are here is not because they're doing dirty tricks," Drabek said. "It's simply because they're very competitive, and they know us very well."

In fact, German company representatives never left, traveling in and out of Czechoslovakia throughout the communist years, Drabek said. "They were dealing with our factories for the last 40 years. Even if they weren't doing business, they were coming and going and talking." German investors also benefit from an array of German think tanks and institutes devoted to the study of central and eastern Europe economies, trade and politics.

While deals are struck at the factory level, any proposal involving foreign capital here also must make its way through at least three layers of bureaucracy—the federal government, the Czech republic, and the new Economic Council of the Czech republic. It is a maze that favors German and other companies with Prague offices that predate the 1989 revolution.

"You can't put together a deal in two or three days," said Peter Singer, Prague representative of Dow Chemical Corp., which is nearing completion of a $100 million deal to buy a state-of-the-art Czechoslovak chemical plant. Dow Chemical has had an office here for 25 years, but it is an exception among American companies.

"The bottom line," Drabek said, "is the Germans have a natural advantage here, and they are better informed . . . The American ignorance about this part of the world is very visible."

While the experienced Germans march directly to factory managers' offices armed with sophisticated market studies, the typical American investor, without benefit of long experience, too often behaves like "Alice in Wonderland," in Pithart's words.

"The typical American businessman comes here a bit like an American tourist," said Seippel of Bankers Trust. "He says, 'I'd like to do a deal here, but I don't know who to talk to, I don't know anyone.' The Germans just come and do it. They don't take it personally if they're kept waiting outside the minister's office for an hour. Or if they do, they don't show it. The Americans think the Czechs ought to be bending over backwards for them."

The Czechs soon may be doing just that. Drabek and many other government officials say the answer to German dominance is more energetic encouragement of American investment. Prime Minister Marian Calfa said recently that the government must make a fresh effort to court American and other non-German investors.

Part of that effort will be to improve an irregular bidding process. Potential American investors often are discouraged by bidding rules that shift according to the whim or appetites of individual factory managers.

"We have provided very clear rules of tender, but each enterprise does it its own way," Drabek said. "They have to learn that you do not change your mind after you've already selected the company."

After a slow start, American investment may be approaching cruising speed, according to U.S. commercial analysts. An inaugural meeting of the American Chamber of Commerce in Prague last week drew more than 200 representatives from 100 U.S. companies. American corporate offices are springing up all over the capital.

Shirley Temple Black, the U.S. ambassador to Prague, recently told a group of American executives that with 25 large deals now "in the pipeline," she expects American investment here to reach at least $5 billion by the end of the decade.

Critics say the slow U.S. start has somewhat squandered two years of goodwill—the feeling widespread here immediately after the revolution that anything American was best.

American executives hope the new misgivings about German dominance will restore that advantage. All other points in a deal being equal, Singer said, Czechoslovaks tend to favor an American partner.

Nonetheless, Germany's advantages, plus the disappearance of the Soviet Union as an economic counterweight, are expected to make it the undisputed economic powerhouse here.

While large deals, such as Volkswagen's stake in the Czechoslovak car maker Skoda, make headlines, about two-thirds of the estimated 4,000 deals involving foreign capital are small or medium-sized ventures, Drabek said, citing, for example, a Czech on one side of the border pooling resources with a German to buy a $30,000 truck.

Even in the former Sudetenland—the portion of Czechoslovakia from which hundreds of thousands of ethnic Germans were expelled after World War II—Czechoslovaks voice misgivings about muted German demands for restitution of lost property, but they continue to welcome German investors who pour over the border intent on restoring western Bohemia's crumbling spa towns.

February 10, 1992

Education and Employment 20

A World to the Wise

High School Students Get Crash Course in Global Economic Competition

PETER BAKER

Homework time in classroom 118 at McLean High School and teacher Gina Bottoms asked students to pull out their assignments and read some of their answers aloud.

"I have something interesting," announced senior Kristi McCullough. "I had a Ralph Lauren blouse that was made in Hong Kong and a Ralph Lauren dress that was made in Singapore. Isn't that weird?"

"I have a knee brace from West Germany," said Meera Trehan, sporting a cast on her leg.

"It's weird—every single brand of eye shadow I had was made in Italy," exclaimed an astonished Erin Barnes. "Every single brand!"

First impressions aside, Bottoms does not teach a class in fashion design, sports medicine or cosmetics. She teaches two periods of international trade and marketing, the first such high school course in Virginia—and possibly a harbinger of things to come. If a plan left by the administration of former governor Gerald L. Baliles comes to fruition in the 1990s, every student in the state eventually will have to take such a class to graduate.

Bottoms's class and its possible statewide expansion illustrate the increasing emphasis schools nationwide are placing on international education.

Stemming from the fear that the United States is rapidly losing ground in the global marketplace, states are looking for ways to graduate more internationally literate students—more conversant in foreign languages, more acquainted with different cultures and more versed in international business.

In few places is that more evident than Virginia.

"In Virginia, we have resolved that the next generation of Virginia business leaders should be able to understand their competitors, wherever those competitors may live," Baliles said in a December speech to a group of Fairfax County educational, political and business leaders. In a recent class session at McLean,

Bottoms and her students went over the homework assignment from the night before—find 25 items in your house and identify where they were made. The students discovered, sometimes to their chagrin, that everything from paper clips to hot rollers are made overseas.

"I don't have anything on made in the United States," said a clothes-conscious Kristi McCullough.

From there, the class launched into an animated discussion of the trade deficit, the 1973 Arab oil embargo, the gold standard and other topics seemingly more likely to put students to sleep than arouse their intellectual curiosity.

Now in its second year at McLean, the course aspires to teach students about world markets, the global economy, basic macro- and micro-economic concepts, cultural differences among nations and how domestic and foreign markets are "penetrated," according to its syllabus.

It also features field trips to such places as the World Bank and a week-long excursion next month to the Dominican Republic, which will be paid for privately. ("Unless you've been to a developing country, you just can't understand it," said Bottoms.)

In many ways, the class is symbolic of what Baliles tried to infuse in public education during his four years as governor. A plan drafted by his top education advisers and left for the state Board of Education to study would revamp graduation requirements and include international trade and marketing on the class schedule of every student in the state.

Proportionately more students in Virginia now take a foreign language class in high school than in any other state, and the governor has established special summer foreign language academies in Russian, Japanese, Chinese, Korean, French, German and Spanish. And last fall, thanks to a federal grant obtained by Rep. Frank R. Wolf (R-Va.), a handful of elementary schools in Fairfax and Arlington began pilot half-day immersion programs in foreign languages for youngsters.

But while Virginia may be among the most aggressive, it is not alone in this emphasis. In recent years, the term "global education" has become a common buzzword in academic circles across the country.

Several years ago, the state of Maryland began special international programs at two schools, Richard Montgomery High School in Montgomery County and Glenelg High School in Howard County. The interdisciplinary program offers students an "international baccalaureate" for completing an intensive academic course load with a global focus.

"We had our first graduating class last spring and, of course, colleges were clamoring all over the kids," said Richard Montgomery Principal Thomas E. Quelet. "They really wanted those kids . . . Those kids could move wherever they wanted to go."

But because of the cost, there are no current ambitions to expand the program to more schools around the state.

In Virginia, where a similar program exists at Falls Church's George Mason High School, officials are now taking the opposite approach with the new high school class—rather than immersing a few, the state wants to give every student a sampling.

"It's a class everyone should take," Meera Trehan said of her period with Bottoms at McLean. "Nothing against calculus and stuff like that, but it's a real day-to-day class . . . My sister came home from MIT, and I was explaining everything that was going on to her. I knew more about it."

Still, the McLean students are taking the class because they want to, not because they need it to graduate, and many of them from this affluent community have personal backgrounds that make the course especially relevant.

One student walked into class last semester and told the teacher that his father had just been contacted by a Russian about building paper plants in the Soviet Union. Others have traveled extensively or lived overseas as part of diplomatic or military families.

When the students recently got into an impromptu debate about whether Germans like American cars, several got into a one-upsmanship contest after Margaret Buxton insisted she knew what she was talking about because "I lived there four years."

"I was there five years," rejoined Erin Barnes.

"Well, I lived in Europe for eight years," piped in Elizabeth Bizic.

The real challenge for the course may be not in how it plays in McLean but how it plays in such economically depressed areas as Pulaski County, in the southwestern part of the state.

Although educators agree that international marketing is crucial even to the students from rural backgrounds, the trick, they said, is making the students agree.

"You would have to look for ways to make it very relevant to their lives . . . like how many foreign products are at the local level and what has that done to the job market at the local level," said Pulaski County Assistant Superintendent Phyllis E. Bishop. "We're still very much into manufacturing and we're still in an economic decline, so to be interesting to the students of this county we'd have to bring it to the local level."

March 5, 1990

Schools Learn to Go Global

MBAs Take on Curricula with International Flavor

STUART AUERBACH

It's not on their resumes, but Marnie Moore fled drug war bullets in Colombia, while classmates John Rosser watched the Berlin Wall being torn down and John Wallace learned how to live with Brazil's 50 percent monthly inflation—all in the process of getting a business degree from the University of South Carolina.

Some 67,000 students will graduate this month from American universities with master's of business administration degrees, but only a handful are specially trained like Moore, Rosser and Wallace to be the shock troops for U.S. companies trying to compete in an increasingly international business environment.

In the process of working overseas, moore, 24, Rosser, 26, and Wallace, 29, gained a special appreciation of what it is like to operate a business abroad. With Brazil's high inflation, for example, Wallace found that everyone tries to spend cash quickly, while it has value, and banks don't make loans. "You have to do a lot of cash management," he said.

Despite the growing realization during the past decade that corporate America must become more international, business educators and executives agree that the 2,000 U.S. business schools have lagged in giving their graduates a global perspective—a vacuum a number of business schools now are moving rapidly to try to fill.

"There's a lack of preparation' for the globalization of business, said Robert Parker, dean of the business school at Georgetown University.

Since 1974, long before globalization became part of the rhetoric of America businesses, South Carolina has offered a master's degree in international business that requires students to learn a foreign language and spend six months working for a U.S. company overseas. Even now, South Carolina is one of the few U.S. business schools to offer specialized study in international business and the only one to require an overseas internship and foreign language ability for an MBA.

"If we are going to do something about the U.S. trade deficit and raise the competitiveness of American industry, we have got to have people who really know international business, who have experience overseas and who speak a foreign language," said Jeffrey S. Arpan, director of the international business program at South Carolina.

The university's stress on the international business environment is being emulated by other universities around the country. Ten years after South Carolina started its program, the University of Pennsylvania's famed Wharton School established the Joseph H. Lauder Institute, which offers an MBA combined with a master's degree in international relations. Its new dean, Thomas P. Gerrity, plans to put an emphasis on the global marketplace, and Jerry Wind, the founding director of the Lauder Institute, now heads a faculty group revising the entire Wharton curriculum to make it more responsive to international trends.

Many other schools are seeking ways to make their courses more international to better reflect the current business environment:

Duke University's Fuqua School of Business is trying to inject an international perspective into every course it teaches. "We used to be national business schools. Now we are facing the era of global business schools," said Fuqua Dean Thomas Keller.

New York University's Stern School of Business participates in an international student exchange with 17 schools around the world and attracts an unusually large number of foreign students—almost one-fourth of its student body.

Michigan State University is starting undergraduate and graduate programs in international business.

Georgetown University changed its entire curriculum last year so that each course is taught with a global perspective.

The University of Virginia's Darden School of Business has been adding international courses, including a second-year requirement that studies industries in a global context.

"The full thrust has just really happened over the past four years. It is growing steadily. The interest is really very high," said Darden public relations director Elaine Ruggieri.

"Everyone's scurrying to do it," said Richard Scott, a professor of international finance at the University of Virginia's largely undergraduate business school, the McIntire School of Commerce.

He said McIntire is trying to inject a greater appreciation of global business trends in its curriculum and noted that the faculty "is slowly coming around" to the need to keep abreast of what is happening in the world instead of just the United States.

"It is probably the students that are driving the interest, not the faculty," said South Carolina's Arpan.

Wine, the Lauder professor of marketing at Wharton, said that many business school faculty members "don't recognize the importance" of international business and prefer instead to stay within the narrow academic disciplines in which they find it easier to do research.

"The problem is that international business doesn't fit into an academic mold," said Thomas H. Naylor, a professor of economics at Duke who used to teach international courses at Fuqua.

While corporate America has picked up the rhetoric of the global business environment, government officials and academic specialists noted that many U.S.

companies still plan as if they were operating in a vast continental market, without foreign competition.

"U.S. businesses are not prepared for globalization. Some of them are not even aware of how significant it is," said Arpan. "They still look at the domestic market as insulated from foreign competition. You have got to position yourself in a global market even if you are really a domestic company because foreign companies are selling here. That is a what a lot of U.S. companies have not understood. It is their Achilles' heel."

"You can see the firms that are slow in moving are losing ground and companies with strong international operations are being saved by them," said Wharton's Wind.

Odd Mikkel Lauritzen, 28, a Norwegian student in the South Carolina program, was amazed at how little attention was paid to international business during his internship this year at Westinghouse Electric Corp., which is a premier U.S. competitor in the world. "The strange thing was the lack of upper management commitment to international business," he said, noting that foreign sales accounted for almost one-forth of Westinghouse's total sales.

"CEOs [chief executive officers] are beginning to know the need, but they are not doing anything about it," said Georgetown's Parker. "Recruiters are asking for the same skills they have always asked for. The extra [international] skills are seen as a net plus, but not a basic. Over the next five years, I think it is imperative that they be regarded as an imperative."

W. Randolph Folks, one of the founders of the South Carolina program, noted an "ambivalence" on the part of recruiters. "I can't tell you how many times I heard it said, 'We don't recruit for international,'" he said.

Folks said that South Carolina graduates "will be stars" in any business situation "because they have a global perspective."

Nonetheless, South Carolina graduates have little trouble landing jobs, with about one-third of them hired by the companies they worked for during their overseas internships.

Marnie Moore, who worked for Colgate-Palmolive Co. in Cali, Colombia, before being chased by the drug wars to the company's Mexico City branch, will join Colgate-Palmolive's global marketing program after she graduates on May 11. Fluent in Spanish, Moore expects to be assigned overseas after the two-year training program.

Similarly, Diane Avore, 26, landed a job with Safeguard Corp., the Philadelphia holding company that she worked for in Paris. She still hopes to live and work in Paris, but for now Avore said she is content to stay in Philadelphia, helping her company introduce a new line of computer, business and office supplies made in France and aimed at American architects and engineers.

May 6, 1990

D.C. Firm Helps Others Get Business Abroad

Global Access Ltd. Hires Retired Foreign Service Workers

MOHAMMAD HANIF

Retired Foreign Service employees don't have to spend the rest of their years reminiscing about remote countries and exotic cultures. And American companies seeking important information about foreign markets don't have to go beyond Washington.

Global Access Ltd., a D.C.-based company, has established a network of retirees from the government's foreign affairs community that is designed to help American companies solve business and government problems in foreign countries.

"When people retire from government service after 25 or 30 years . . . they still have a lot of good years ahead of them," said Ashley Hewitt, founder and president of the company. "They also have a vast knowledge about cultures, languages and the way business is done in different parts of the world. We are trying to recycle their experience and reinvest it into helping American business."

Presently, Global can offer the services of 60 experts who have served in senior positions with the departments of state, defense, commerce, Treasury, agriculture and the CIA. "We plan to have about 100 associates by the end of this year and about 150 by next year," said Hewitt.

At the core of the company, however, are only three permanent staff. The associates are called in according to the requirements of a project and then paid on a daily basis.

Since its formal launching in March of this year, the company says, it has taken on about 12 clients, mostly small to mid-size companies seeking a new foreign market.

Its clients include companies like Celadon Group Inc., a New York-based trucking and logistics company that is the largest American carrier in Mexico.

"I wanted to explore some business opportunities in the Middle East and they did a very good job of it," said Len Bennet, president of Celadon. "What they are selling is their ability to get to the right people. It's very important for the businesses entering a new country to be endorsed, and since they have served in these countries they can be very helpful."

One of Global's more ambitious projects is a joint venture with Celadon in Mexico, where they plan to establish a business center equipped with state-of-the-art communications and conference halls where representatives of U.S. state governments could rent space at reasonable rates.

Global's group of associates works not only as a resource but also as a network that helps in locating the right experts for a project.

"We were approached by a businessman and he asked what can we do for him in Papua New Guinea," said Hewitt. "Within 48 hours we were able to locate two ex-ambassadors who were more than willing to work with us." Hewitt said Global takes care to avoid any suggestion of improper influence peddling or abuse of contacts cultivated during government service abroad.

"What we are selling is our expertise," he said. "We brief our clients in the beginning about the legal and moral limitations here and abroad. If one of our associates happens to know someone in Poland, there is nothing wrong with using that contact. We will use our background, our knowledge, even our influence to advance the interests of American business abroad."

Hewitt acknowledges that veteran civil servants aren't always good in business. "What they lack is in business acumen," said Celadon's Bennett. "That's because they have never done business before. But they are quick learners. It's a great concept and they are doing very well for a start-up."

September 23, 1991

In Hungary, Faith and the Free Market:
Church Preaches the Gospel of Capitalism to Frenzied Believers

PETER MAASS

As thousands of Hungarians chanted "Amen," pastor Sandor Nemeth preached the gospel of Milton Friedman.

"God created you so that you may have material blessings and a successful life," Nemeth roared to his evangelical congregation. "God is a god of growth. Renouncing growth means renouncing God."

The chorus of amens echoed again from the walls of the packed sports stadium where Nemeth was delivering one of his twice-weekly sermons to followers who sway from foot to foot, sing "Hallelujah" at the top of their lungs and weep tears of happiness like there's no tomorrow. Many of them take scrupulous notes as Nemeth preaches his supply-side religion.

"Forget about socialism," the paunchy pastor, 41, admonished a crowd of about 4,000 converts the other day. "You have to work hard. If you can't do something right, try it again. No one will listen to your whining and crying."

As Hungary turns the corner from communism to capitalism, more and more people are being drawn to the Faith Church's hybrid lessons in fundamentalist spirituality and free-market economics. Founded by Nemeth in 1979 with fewer than a dozen members, the Faith Church now claims 15,000 members and ranks as Hungary's fastest-growing religion.

"This type of religion is more emotional than intellectuall" said Miklos Tomka, head of the Hungarian Catholic Church's Religious Research Center. "Hungarians are very tired of ideologies but they have a great emotional need. The Faith Church provides this emotional help."

Across Eastern Europe and the disintegrating Soviet Union, people are looking to religion as a source of strength during difficult times. The Catholic Church,

279

Unification Church, Protestants, Hare Krishnas, Baptists—all are recruiting believers and battling each other in near-virgin lands behind the fallen Iron Curtain.

The most striking aspect of Nemeth's Church, aside from its success, is the raw energy that it generates in a dour country where enthusiasm is rare. Hungary, despite its relatively good economic performance, still has the world's highest per capita suicide rate.

But at the Faith Church, the faithful leap and shout with the energy of traders on the Tokyo stock exchange when Nemeth starts preaching or when the 10-piece band plays rousing revivalist tunes led by a thumping drummer and electric guitarist. Overcoats, obligatory when the service begins in the unheated hall, are shed as the temperature quickly rises.

Nemeth is generating born-again capitalists by assuring them that the once-forbidden accumulation of wealth is good. Most of his followers are young and wear Western clothes, flashy bracelets or gold tie clips. Some of them drive to the sermon in BMWs. The church's office in the fashionable heart of Budapest has a joint-venture decor of glass tables, leather couches and plush carpets.

"We want to convince our (church members) not to envy the rich but to become like them," Nemeth said in a post-sermon interview punctuated by the easy laughter and charm that are at odds with his frumpy, Bible salesman looks. "It does not mean we should give up taking care of the needy. But at this present time, we have nothing to give the needy. We must let people live and prosper so that they have money to give."

The message is getting out to all sectors of society. Two prominent members of Parliament are in the Faith Church, which has close ties to Hungary's leading opposition party. Faith Church members were some of the most diligent precinct workers in the Alliance of Free Democrats' general election campaign last year.

Nemeth and his church enjoy a political halo because they struggled against communism, and this helps explain their popularity. The Catholic Church, still the dominant religious force in Hungary, is burdened by its open collaboration with the country's communist regime.

Even rock stars are joining up. One of Nemeth's high-profile devotees is Tomas Pajor, lead singer and guitarist of a religious band called "Amen." Before joining the church, Pajor headed a new wave band called "Neurotica" whose act included the beheading of chickens.

"For me and many other people, we can feel and know God in this church," said Pajor, 28, who has given up the drugs and profanity of punkdom for a new life of marital fidelity, clean shirts and penny loafers. He no longer slays chickens.

Peter Morvay, a youthful businessman dressed for the service in a crimson suit, was a troubled university student when he joined the church a few years ago. He had been informing on his fellow students for the secret police, which in the waning days of communism enlisted his services with threats of expulsion—and the promise of a scholarship in the United States.

He finally told the secret police to get lost, apologized to the people he had informed on and joined the Faith Church. He is not burdened by his checkered past, thanks to Nemeth's insistence that all sins can be forgiven entirely if a person accepts Jesus Christ into his heart. Catholic-style prayers, repentance and sacrifice are not necessary.

"There is no reason to feel guilty," Morvay said with a smile.

December 23, 1991

It's an Ad Ad Ad World

PETER CARLSON

I have seen the future and it is Goofy.

It's Goofy and it's Mickey and it's Minnie and it's Donald. The future of American business and American culture—is there any difference between the two anymore?—will be much like the present in the world of Disney. This is the world in which Disney movies shown on the Disney Channel star Disney characters who appear at Disneyland and Disney World and in Disney News magazine and in endless permutations of Disney Wear in Disney Stores everywhere. In other words, the future is this: the commercialization of just about everything in just about every conceivable way.

Disney was there first, but everybody else is catching up fast. The future is already here.

All of this hit me like a revelation while I was browsing in the Fashion Centre, a massive four-tiered mall that squats like a big bullfrog atop the Pentagon City Metro stop. I chanced upon the Disney Store and marveled at just how far American merchandisers can go when not constrained by any parameters of moderation or good taste. In the center of the room was a gargantuan mountain of stuffed Disney toys piled below a huge screen that showed Disney characters singing Disney songs. Around this altar stood row upon row of Disney merchandise: Mickey Mouse earrings and Goofy golf balls and "Happy Birthday Disneyland" jigsaw puzzles and tapes of "Disney Sing-along Songs" and Mickey Mouse neckties and Mickey Mouse cookbooks and "Mousercise" exercise videos and a "Mickey-matic camera" and "Little Mermaid" sheets and towels and curtains and refrigerator magnets and "101 Dalmatians" raincoats and wallets and the "Chef Mickey" line, which includes spoons and cups and ice cream scoops and corn holders and pizza slicers and oven mitts and even the "Mickey Mouse Egg Ring," which enables you to "fry Mickey-shaped eggs."

As I wandered through this wonderland, Baloo, the bear in Disney's version of "The Jungle Book," was up on the video screen singing—believe it or not—"the bare necessities, the simple bare necessities . . ."

Which is, of course, about what you'd expect in a Disney Store, I thought, as I fled the place in terror. Then I noticed the store next door, which was called the Museum Company. Ah, some art to uplift my kitsch-battered soul! But as I wandered around inside, I found myself gazing at the "Masterpieces" coloring book and a game called Art Rummy and Monet waterlilies jigsaw puzzles and Degas playing cards and ArtDeck: The Game of Modern Masters and cocktail napkins from "the collections of the Metropolitan Museum of Art" and a "Picasso-Mobile" and neckties with paintings by Klee and van Gogh and the "Museum of Modern Art Clock Kit" ("batteries not included") and plates made from Robert Mapplethorpe photos (the flowers, not the penises) and reproductions of Rodin's "Thinker" ("Large Thinker $185, Small Thinker $95") and Andy Warhol note cards, with a little ® after his name, indicating that the late pop artist is a registered trademark.

Which is appropriate, when you consider that he became famous by painting Campbell's soup cans, I thought as I moseyed into the store next door, which is called the Nature Company. Standing guard at the entrance was a giant inflatable plastic penguin, selling for $24.95. Inside were grasshopper statues, crystal hummingbirds, coffee mugs with pictures of toucans, plastic ladybug rings, endangered species T-shirts ("20% off"), a $199 watch with pictures of insects perched where the numbers usually sit, fish earrings, parrot neckties and rubber pig noses like the ones Hogs fans wear at Redskins games.

That's when it hit me: It's all Disney. The Nature Company and the Museum Company sell the same stuff as the Disney Store—T-shirts, neckties, coffee mugs, games and assorted gewgaws. The only difference is the theme—nature or art or Mickey Mouse.

In fact, our world has become a Disney World. It's a world of theme stores and theme parks. A world of cash-ins and tie-ins and endless licensed products. A world where movies become breakfast cereals, where celebrities become board games, where a fast-food chain spawns a line of clothing, where the advertising and entertainment industries have merged, where movies contain advertisements and so do public bathrooms, where dead celebrities endorse products that didn't exist when they were alive, where environmentalism is used to sell cars and booze, where radical groups run mail-order businesses.

It's a world where everything is commercialized, even an athlete's moment of ultimate triumph:

"Michael Jordan and the Bulls, you've just won your first NBA Championship," the interviewer says. "What are you going to do next?"

And the players, still sweating, still flushed with victory, dutifully reply: "We're going to Disney World!"

The Positive Cure for All Female Complaints

Of course, the United States has always been a commercial society, a capitalist country built on crafty real estate deals, with pieces purchased from France and Mexico and Russia. "The business of America is business," said Calvin Coolidge, the only president born on the Fourth of July.

America is the land of the carnival barker and the snake-oil salesman, the birthplace of P.T. Barnum and Sammy Glick and Lydia Pinkham's Vegetable Compound, which was widely advertised a century ago as "the Positive Cure for

All Female Complaints." (Now it can be told: The secret ingredient was booze.) America is the home of the Madison Avenue hustler, the "Hidden Persuaders" and ad execs like Bruce Barton, founder of Batten, Barton, Durstine and Osborn, the most mellifluously titled ad agency in history. Barton was also the author of The Man Nobody Knows, a book portraying Jesus Christ as "the founder of modern business" and His parables as "the most powerful advertisements of all time." Barton read a lot of meaning into Jesus's remark that "I must be about my father's business." He took the word "business" quite literally. The book was a big bestseller in 1926, which was—not coincidentally—during the administration of Calvin Coolidge.

Advertising is as American as a Washington's Birthday cherry pie sale, as patriotic as a thousand little flags fluttering over a used car lot, as Republican as a campaign commercial starring Willie Horton. Advertising gave this country Betty Crocker and Aunt Jemima, the Marlboro Man and Spuds McKenzie. It gave America "Buy Now, Pay Later" and "Satisfaction Guaranteed" and "Money Talks, Nobody Walks" and those amazing late-night speed-rap commercials for gadgets that guillotine vegetables:

They slice!
They dice!
They chop!
They shred!
And much, much more!

The United States has always been a commercial society, but in the last decade it got really commercial. From 1982 to 1990, the amount spent on media advertising doubled, going from $66 billion to more than $130 billion. Which doesn't include various non-media advertising, like direct mail ads—63 billion of them in 1990—and those annoying recorded ads recited over the phone by automatic dialing machines. Meanwhile, another barometer of commercialism, the licensing industry—which turns brand names and famous names into bedsheets, breakfast cereals and countless other products—rose from less than $5 billion a year in 1977 to more than $66 billion in 1990.

Perhaps this tidal wave of commercialism began with the advent of Ronald Reagan, the only former advertising pitchman (GE, Chesterfield, Van Heusen shirts) ever elected president. Reagan hung a portrait of Coolidge in a place of honor in the White House and promptly ushered in an era of conspicuous consumption and no-holds-barred greed—superb growing conditions for a bumper crop of commercialism. He also began an era of budget cuts for public institutions—from public broadcasting to public schools—which led those institutions to go begging for corporate contributions, which inevitably came accompanied by advertising.

But we can't blame it all on the president. Advertising experts cite other factors too: The mass media outlets that once reached virtually everybody—the TV networks and the big magazines—lost their captive audiences, and advertisers were thereby forced to chase their customers into ad "niches" all across the landscape. Meanwhile, computer data banks enabled advertisers to reduce human beings to socio-demographic stereotypes and then bombard them with the appropriate catalogues—52 per year for every man, woman and child in America.

But the most important factor in the flood of advertising is, according to advertisers, the flood of advertising. It's a phenomenon the ad biz calls "clutter"— so many ads that individual commercials get lost in the electronic undergrowth. "The current climate of ads is that people aren't watching commercials," says Richard Gore, a partner in Entertainment Marketing Group, a New York-based promotion firm. "They switch channels. So advertisers are looking for new forms— everything from blimps in the sky to benches in the playground."

All of this led to the current era of unsurpassed commercialism—a New! Improved! variety of commercialism that is 99 and 44/100 percent ubiquitous! An extra-strength commercialism more powerful than anything you can get without a prescription! A king-sized commercialism suitable for late-night speed-raps:

It turns presidents into pitchmen!

It turns home wreckers into hucksters!

It turns rock anthems into jingles!

It turns the Statue of Liberty into a deodorant ad!

And much, much more!

Missing Kids and Carpet Cleaning

"This broadcast of 'Morning Edition' is made possible in part," says the announcer on WAMU, "by the National Agricultural Chemicals Association on behalf of the makers of crop-protection chemicals, who serve mankind with science through agriculture."

" . . . by the Compaq Computer Corporation, providing high-performance business, personal computers and systems around the world . . . "

" . . . by *People* magazine, a place to meet the fascinating as well as the famous . . . "

As ads go, they're pretty inoffensive, certainly no match for the ear-shattering blasts of Crazy Eddie. You'd hardly notice them if they weren't on WANU, which is one of hundreds of radio and television stations deemed by the Federal Communications Commission to be "noncommercial." At least they used to be noncommercial. In the early '80s, the Reagan administration began slashing the budgets of the Public Broadcasting Service while the FCC started permitting public stations to air "noncommercial credits" or "enhanced identification credits" or "recognition opportunities," which is what commercials are called when they're on noncommercial stations. The FCC guidelines permit the advertisers—uh, "underwriters"—to mention their products, even to show them on TV, as long as they don't say how great they are or how much they cost or urge people to run right out and buy them. Which makes for some amusing court battles, like the one that ensued when the FCC objected to a Cincinnati public radio station that aired a Jiffy Lube ad offering a "discount on air conditioner recharging with a Pennzoil oil change and 14-point lube check." The FCC didn't like the word "discount." Too promotional.

But why pick on poor public broadcasting? These are tough times for the noncommercial. In America these days, everything serves as an advertising vehicle, even human tragedy. Every week the mailman brings me a postcard bearing a picture of a missing child. You could break your heart looking into those big, sad eyes. Or you could turn the card over and check out the ads for 40 percent off on carpet cleaning.

Ads are everywhere. There are ads on the towers of ski lifts and ads in pinball games and ads on the backs of supermarket receipts and inside credit card bills. There are ads for dinnerware on boxes of Land O'Lakes butter and ads for beer and cigarettes in the "Knife & Fork Menuzine," a hybrid menu-disguised-as-magazine that is used in many restaurant chains. Ads for Fuji and Ford float across the heavens on blimps. Laser beams projected ads for Doritos and BMWs onto clouds over San Francisco. Absolut vodka hired an "artist" to create a 20-acre ad for Absolut that is visible to planes flying out of Kansas City International Airport. And the Atlantic Monthly magazine invited 200 subscribers to a party featuring political prognostication by contributing editor William Schneider—combined with a preview of the 1992 Toyotas.

Meanwhile, In-Stall Ad Systems puts ads in public toilets, a venue once limited to crude scrawls urging, "For a good time, call ..."

Even federal agencies now carry advertising: The Smithsonian museums recently agreed to display the logos of corporate contributors. This spring the Department of Defense began soliciting corporate sponsors for events on military bases. "They can put their logos on fences, softball backstops, softball uniforms, lots of things," Anthony Figlia, coordinator of Fort Meade's Commercial Sponsorship Program, told the *Washington Post*. "Signs near the porta-johns could say, 'Porta-johns sponsored by the So-and-So Company.'" Right now, Americans seeking ad-free zones can flee to the national parks, but that won't work for long. The National Park Service recently announced plans to relax its ban on displays recognizing corporate contributors. "People are tuning out TV and radio and print media," a service spokesperson explained. "Seeing corporate names in an uncluttered environment has become desirable."

Advertisers irked that "people are tuning out TV" have taken to putting TVs where they can't be tuned out. The best-known example is Channel One: Whittle Communications gives free video equipment to schools that promise that every day they will force all students to stop their readin', writin' and 'rithmetic and watch 10 minutes of low-voltage pseudo-news interspersed with two minutes of ads for jeans and junk food. Meanwhile, Ted Turner's new Checkout Channel sends news nuggets and ads to TV sets propped up over supermarket checkout lines, and Time Warner's PrimeTime Video does the same for people standing in line at Six Flags amusement parks. And other companies put ad-spewing TVs in railroad stations, airports, malls and doctors' offices.

And then there's VideOcart, a shopping cart equipped with a little video screen. As shoppers proceed down the aisles of the 40 American supermarkets that currently carry VideOcart, sensors in the stores' ceilings follow their progress, triggering ads appropriate to their location. "As you're standing opposite the Coca-Cola display, you'll see a Pepsi ad," says Bob McCann, VideOcart's executive vice president. "This represents for the manufacturers an opportunity to reach out to the shopper just as he's ready to make a brand decision."

And VideOcart has another feature that manufacturers will no doubt love: "You cannot turn it off," McCann says.

Diet Pepsi, Underwear and a Bed of Nerds

Nerds are not an impressive sight. On the box, they're pictured as cuddly cartoon creatures, but the little candies themselves look more like pastel-colored pebbles or particularly painful kidney stones. Most people wouldn't see them as potential bedsheets. But Shirley Henschel did.

Henschel is the founder of Alaska Momma, a Manhattan-based licensing firm. Back in the mid-1980s, the makers of Nerds told her that plans were afoot to turn the little balls of sugar and artificial flavors into a children's TV show, like the Smurfs, and they asked her to spin off a line of Nerd products. As it turned out, Nerds did not become a TV show, alas, but Henschel did manage to license more than 60 Nerds products—Nerds breakfast cereal, Nerds clothing patterns, Nerds squeeze dolls, Nerds soap, Nerds jewelry, Nerds watches, Nerds comforters and, yes, Nerds bedsheets. And much, much more!

Such is the power of the licensing industry, that midwife of commercialism, the business that spins fame into gold. Licensing has been around for decades—remember Davy Crockett coonskin caps?—but it exploded in the '80s. Led by such mega-licensees as the Teenage Mutant Ninja Turtles ($900 million in sales in 1990), New Kids on the Block ($800 million) and the Simpsons ($750 million), licensing was a $66 billion industry last year, five times as big as it was a decade earlier. "It has grown tremendously," says Arnold Bolka, former editor of the Licensing Letter, the bible of the industry. "I guess it's a form of identification, a form of expression, to wear a Coke beach jacket or a Turtles T-shirt or for a woman to use a Bill Blass fragrance or for kids to wear Air Jordans. It says, 'I like this' or 'I'm like this' or 'I want more of this' or 'In your face,' depending on the product."

In the last few years, the licensing business has performed some amazing feats of alchemy:

It turned McDonald's into a line of McKids clothing.

It turned Robin Hood and Batman into breakfast cereals.

It turned rapper M.C. Hammer into dolls, games, backpacks and pencil cases.

It turned the Rolling Stones into a line of clothing.

It turned Donald Trump and Morton Downey Jr. into board games.

It turned "Saturday Night Live" into greeting cards, calendars and a computer game.

It turned the California Raisins ad campaign into a kids' TV show, a line of toys and a college bowl game.

It turned the Diet Pepsi ad jingle "You Got the Right One Baby, Uh-Huh" into jackets, hats, T-shirts and boxer shorts.

It turned Christie Brinkley, Florence Griffith-Joyner and Pee-wee Herman into dolls.

It turned Looney Tunes characters into a line of frozen dinners.

And much, much more!

The next stage in the licensing explosion is retail stores devoted entirely to a line of licensed products. Hey, why sell them wholesale and let somebody else pocket the markup? The Disney Stores were the pioneers, opening their first outlet in 1987 and their 110th this year. Now Coca-Cola has followed Disney's lead, with four stores in Florida and one due to open soon in Manhattan, all of them vending Coke's 99 licensed products and its line of Coke clothes. Meanwhile, Sesame Street and Hanna-Barbera have launched retail chains. And filmmaker Spike Lee has been threatening to franchise Spike's Joint, the store that sells T-shirts, books and other memorabilia from his movies.

If a licensee can't have its own store, it can at least have its own catalogue. PBS, the semi-noncommercial TV network, does. It's called Signals, and it proves that licensed products aren't just for lowbrows. Signals sells "Mr. Rogers' Neighborhood" sweatshirts and "Mystery" coffee mugs and "Celebrated Generals of the Civil War Collector Cards." It peddles "This Old House" ties and "This Old House" hammer-shaped chocolate bars. Also chocolate golf balls, chocolate dinosaur eggs and a "Happy Hanukkah" mug filled with gold-covered chocolate coins. Speaking of solemn religious holidays, Enesco, a leading manufacturer of knickknacks and gewgaws, has announced its annual line of licensed trademark Christmas ornaments. There are Cheerios ornaments and Wheaties ornaments and Baskin-Robbins ornaments and Coke ornaments and several McDonald's ornaments, including one that shows a little tyke curled up in a Big Mac box beneath a holly wreath, a Christmas stocking and the words "McHappy Holidays."

It sells for $17.50—the perfect gift for people who feel that Christmas isn't commercial enough.

Madison Avenue and Hollywood Merge

NEW YORK (AP)—In a long-expected move, the entertainment and advertising industries officially merged yesterday. The president of the new mega-conglomerate, Bill Cosby, vowed to "erase forever the outdated boundaries between these two great American art forms . . . "

Actually, I made that up. But sometimes you'd swear it was true. Like when you're watching the movie "Days of Thunder," for instance. The movie, which starred Tom Cruise as a stock-car racer, was not a cinematic masterpiece, but it was a great ad vehicle. All the race cars constantly wore the logos of their corporate sponsors, and so, most of the time, did the actors. Much of the plot, in fact, is about man's age-old struggle to find a corporate sponsor. When Mello Yello finally agrees to sponsor Cruise, its electric-yellow logo is plastered on his Chevy Lumina race car, on his helmet and on the uniforms of his pit crew. Meanwhile, Cruise's main rivals are sponsored by Exxon and Hardee's, and their cars, pit crews and helmets are similarly decorated.

When the movie opened, in the summer of 1990, it was hyped in more than $35 million worth of advertising by—you guessed it—Mello Yello, Chevy Lumina, Exxon and Hardee's. Mello Yello consumers were offered a tape about the making of the movie. Chevrolet promoted the Lumina with a movie-related ad campaign. Exxon touted the movie in booklets distributed at its gas stations. And Hardee's sold toy Luminas painted to advertise Hardee's and Mello Yello and Chevrolet. This carefully organized, color-coordinated "cross-promotion" was wonderfully symmetrical: The movie advertised the products, the products advertised the movie, and everybody was happy.

Except, perhaps, the audience.

This orgy of back-scratching began back in 1982, when E.T. ate Reese's Pieces candy, inspiring millions of Americans to do the same. After that, a whole industry arose to serve as matchmakers for these "product placement" deals. "Imagine the impact of your customers seeing their favorite star using your product in a feature film," Silver Screen Placements said in its ads." ... Both YOUR COMPANY'S NAME AND PRODUCT thereby become an integral part of the show, conveying both subliminal messages and implied endorsements ..."

Who could pass up such an offer? Not Domino's Pizza, which paid an undisclosed sum to have its pie delivered to the Teenage Mutant Ninja Turtles. Not Philip Morris, which reportedly paid $350,000 to ensure that James Bond smoked Larks—and used a Lark pack to conceal a tiny detonator—in "Licence to Kill."

And not Black & Decker, which paid $20,000 to have its drill used by Bruce Willis in "Die Hard 2," only to sue for $150,000 when that scene was cut from the movie.

But the Oscar for most shameless shilling goes to "Mac & Me," a 1988 "E.T." knockoff featuring Mac, an alien who literally lives on Coke and whose little human buddy takes him to a birthday party at McDonald's, where everybody drinks Coke while Ronald McDonald sings the company jingle until the bad guys chase Mac into Sears, which just happens to sell McKids, the McDonald's clothing line, and ... well, Mac ends up taking the oath of American citizenship—while wearing a McKids T-shirt.

These days, paying cold cash for product placements is becoming passe. Now studios want something more valuable than money—advertising. They want cross-promotional tie-ins, like "Days of Thunder" got. And they get them. In "King Ralph," John Goodman dined at Burger King, and the food chain repaid the favor by promoting the film in a $10 million ad campaign. When Huggies were featured as Diane Keaton's diaper-of-choice in "Baby Boom," their manufacturer touted the movie in a TV ad, a contest and a coupon offer. And in 1988, Forbes and Fortune magazines got into a bidding war for the honor of being called "the bible" by Charlie Sheen in "Wall Street." First Fortune promised the producers a free full-page ad, then Forbes offered two free pages, and finally Fortune matched it, winning the promo and prompting Malcolm Forbes to lament in print: "We were out-slicked a wee bit ..."

Meanwhile, rock-and-roll, which once promoted a countercultural mix of illicit sex, illegal drugs and adolescent rebellion, now advertises Jovan fragrances and Alberto VO5. And much, much more!

It began in 1981, when Jovan sponsored the Rolling Stones tour, which seemed quite bizarre at the time. After all, Stones tours were more closely identified with drug busts and arrests for public peeing than they were with pleasant fragrances. Back in the '70s, the Stones hired underground filmmaker Robert Frank to make a documentary about their tour, and the result, "[Expletive Deleted] Blues," was deemed too obscene for release. But under the Jovan banner, rock's bad boys behaved like choirboys, thus consummating the marriage of rock and advertising.

Today, Lite Beer sponsors Luther Vandross, Bud Lite sponsors Jan and Dean's oldies tour, Bacardi sponsors Gloria Estefan, British Knights sneakers sponsors M.C. Hammer, and Alberto VO5 sponsors the Moody Blues. Meanwhile, Eric Clapton and Steve Winwood sing in Michelob ads, Huey Lewis sings a Bud jingle, and rapper Ice Cube recites this little ditty on national TV: "Get your girl in the mood quicker ... with St. Ides Malt Liquor."

Courageous rockers have lined up on both sides of the last great ideological debate in America—Coke vs. Pepsi. George Michael, Robert Plant, Whitney Houston, the Pointer Sisters and Run-D.M.C. stake their reputations on Coke, while Madonna, Robert Palmer, David Bowie, Ray Charles, Tina Turner and Lionel Richie stand firmly behind Pepsi.

As rock music becomes more commercial, the great rock songs of the past become commercial jingles. The Beatles' "Revolution" became an ad for Nike sneakers. "Fun, Fun, Fun," the Beach Boys' ode to youthful mischief, became an ad for Kentucky Fried Chicken. "Let the Sunshine In," the hippie anthem from "Hair," became a mustard ad. "Whole Lotta Shakin' Goin' On," Jerry Lee Lewis's erotic classic, became an ad for paint. Screamin' Jay Hawkins's wonderfully demented "I Put a Spell on You" became a Perrier ad. And Bob Marley's "Lively Up Yourself" became an ad for the Hair Cuttery.

The Hair Cuttery? Did they ever see Bob Marley's hair?

But the Grammy award for crass commercialism in popular music goes to country singer Barbara Mandrell. After signing a multimillion-dollar deal to serve as a pitchwoman for No Nonsense pantyhose, Mandrell promptly entitled her next album ... that's right: "No Nonsense."

Home-wrecker Hucksters and Presidential Pitchmen

Neil Cole had a problem. He was trying to sell his line of jeans, called "No Excuses," but there wasn't much difference between them and any other jeans. "Ninety percent of all jeans are the same," he says. "The difference between $50 jeans and $20 jeans is about a quarter."

What he needed was a good marketing gimmick. At a strategy session one day in 1987, somebody suggested that they hire Donna Rice, Gary Hart's close personal friend, to appear in an ad. Cole thought it was a brilliant idea, but he figured Rice would never go for it.

He was wrong. She did the ad, sprawling languidly across a chair while purring, "I have no excuses. I just wear them." A couple of years later, when model Marla Maples became famous as the "other woman" in Donald Trump's tabloid divorce battle, Cole hired her to do a No Excuses ad too.

Such is life in the age of the homewrecker huckster. Back in Nathaniel Hawthorne's day, Hester Prynne wore the Scarlet Letter; today she would wear No Excuses jeans. Either that or she'd be paid handsomely to wear nothing at all in a photo shoot for *Playboy*. Tai Collins, the beauty queen who rubbed Sen. Chuck Robb the right way, did that. So did Jessica Hahn, the church secretary who had a brief but meaningful fling with televangelist Jim Bakker.

"People criticize me for taking advantage of opportunities," said Hahn, after earning nearly $1 million for appearing in a 10-page *Playboy* pictorial. "But I believe God is opening the door, and you have to walk through it."

Which pretty much sums up the great American philosophy of cashing in, the process whereby fame is spun off into commercial endorsements, as-told-to autobiographies, made-for-TV movies, cameo appearances on sitcoms and after-dinner speeches to gatherings of Amway dealers or dental hygienists. It is, wrote columnist Ellen Goodman, "the process by which America turns every achievement into a hustle and every achiever into a hustler."

Goodman wrote those bitter words because she was "appalled" that another occupation had joined the rush to cash in: major American politicians. Geraldine Ferraro went from vice presidential candidate to Pepsi pitchwoman. Former speaker of the House Tip O'Neill popped out of a suitcase in a motel ad and asked, "Who says a politician can't save you money?" O'Neill also shilled for American Express, Lite Beer and Hush Puppies and then appeared in a Trump Shuttle ad with former White House aide Alexander Haig. Meanwhile, ex-president Gerald Ford promoted a series of presidential coins sold by the Franklin Mint and also hired himself out for speeches, ribbon cuttings and ceremonial service on corporate boards, including the board of Spectradyne, a company that provides, among other services, porno movies for hotel televisions. Ford's former press secretary Jerald F. Terhorst charged his old boss with the "huckstering and hustling and merchandising of the presidency."

But when it comes to merchandising the presidency, nobody rakes in the money like Ronald Reagan. After making $5 million on his memoirs, the Great Communicator took his now-famous trip to Japan to deliver two 20-minute speeches sponsored by Fujisankei, a huge communications company, which paid him $2 million plus an additional $5 million in expenses for his 20-member entourage, which included Julius the hairdresser.

At one point in the trip, Reagan tooled past the press corps in a golf cart, and a CBS reporter took advantage of the silence to holler a question: "Many people in the United States are critical of this trip and the money you're being paid. What do you say to that?"

In a gesture he made famous, Reagan cupped his hand around his ear, shook his head in amiable negation and mouthed the words, "Can't hear."

Green is Gold

The smiling young woman carefully separates her cans and bottles, then bundles up her newspapers. "Everything's changing," she tells the TV camera as she piles her recyclables into the trunk of her Toyota. "Wasting is out. Saving, conserving, all that stuff is in . . . "

She's an eager young environmentalist, doing her part for the planet by appearing in an ad for the Toyota Tercel. "It's simple," she explains. "New values, new car."

In 1970, at the first Earth Day, protesters ceremoniously buried a car, symbol of the evils of pollution. Now, in the age of commercialism, environmentalism is used to sell cars.

And booze too: A slick four-page magazine ad depicts an arctic landscape with wolves, polar bears and penguins. Atop an ice floe a sticker reads: "Lift and Listen." Lift it and you hear a portentous computer-chip voice say: "Every animal and plant on this page is in danger of extinction. And every day you make hundreds of decisions that affect their fate. To have peace on earth, we must first make peace with the earth. The importers of Absolut vodka invite you to take the future of the planet into your own hands."

Or at least in the hand that's not holding the vodka glass.

The caption reads: "Absolut Environment."

Environmentalism, with its creed of recycling, conservation and "less is more," once seemed like a threat to the ethos of ever-expanding consumption. Now the green movement has spawned a mutant child, the "green marketing movement," which produces videos, books, newsletters and seminars that teach corporations how to sell goods with environmental pitches. The title of one handbook pretty much sums it up: "Green is Gold." The message is: Don't try to beat the greens, join them. Consequently, recent Earth Day celebrations have lined up so many corporate sponsors—Procter & Gamble, Union Carbide and Hardee's, among others—that the Wall Street Journal noted: "Earth Day could easily be renamed Marketing Day."

These days just about every company has some kind of green-tinged hype. Kenner Products promoted a line of environmental Care Bears: "Bedtime Bear's priority is to stop noise pollution." A British airline promised to plant a tree for every passenger who flew between London and Los Angeles. A waterbed manufacturer promised to plant one for every $3,000 bed sold. McDonald's gave out millions of tiny seedlings. And Marla Maples's ad for No Excuses carried a green theme. "The most important thing we can do today is clean up our planet," she says as she throws out a couple of tabloid newspapers with stories on her and The Donald. But wait a minute: She's throwing them in a garbage can, not a recycling bin! What gives?

Even nuclear power plants are promoted with an environmental pitch. Recently the nuke industry took out full-page magazine ads illustrated with a photo of a pristine mountain lake. Nuclear power, says the ad copy, "emits no sulfur dioxide, nitrogen oxides or greenhouse gases." True enough. Unfortunately, the ad neglected to mention the fact that nuke plants produce tons of waste that will remain radioactive for millions of years.

But it isn't just businesses trying to move goods or services with green marketing. Environmental groups do it too. Today green organizations don't just sell buttons and pamphlets, they peddle jewelry, perfumed stationery and teddy bears—enough stuff to fill the fat mail-order catalogues that they send to their members.

Environmentalism is big business these days, and the phenomenon called "cause-related marketing" has turned the marketplace of ideas into a marketplace of T-shirts and gewgaws. The World Wildlife Fund, for example, sells tropical fish coasters and elephant Christmas cards and "Safari Shower Curtains" and endangered species plush toys. And the National Wildlife Federation sells butterfly-shaped bow ties and fish-shaped tote bags and fox-shaped light-switch covers and $195 statues of grizzly bears—"Raw Power in Porcelain." And much, much more!

Ironically, some of the most militant environmentalists are the most vigorous mail-order businessmen. Greenpeace, for example, is a gutsy group that's not afraid to take on big corporations or sail small boats into places where nuclear bombs are scheduled to be tested. It's also a group that peddles ladybug puppets, "Hugg-a-Planet" soft globes, penguin wrapping paper, dolphin key rings and the cuddly Greenpeace teddy bear.

People for the Ethical Treatment of Animals—is a militant animal rights group that has infiltrated laboratories, staged sit-ins in government buildings and rallied support for activists who "liberate" lab animals. It's also a group that sells PETA shoelaces, PETA pens, PETA watches, PETA dog leashes and the "Special PETA Product Pack," which includes PETA Choice laundry detergent, PETA Choice dish detergent, and Kiss My Face liquid soap—"over $60 worth of products for only $53!"

Obviously, the point of all these marketing campaigns is to raise money for the cause. But the underlying message is the same theme espoused by all advertising: All of life's problems can be solved by buying the right products. In the case of the environmental groups, the message seems to be: Buy enough endangered species T-shirts and you'll save the planet. As Jay Hair wrote in the Spring 1991 National Wildlife Catalogue: "Our environmental products are simple and user-friendly—you won't have to change your lifestyle to help change the world."

Meanwhile, at least one environmental group has moved so far into direct mail that it's crossed over into enemy territory. Last March, the National Audubon Society peddled its mailing list in an ad in *DM News,* a publication of the direct mail industry:

"The National Audubon Society's members are some of the industry's most consistently mail-responsive consumers. No wonder so many major retailers rely on this repeatedly effective audience to reach their marketing goals! ... It's easy to see why this list is so reliably responsive for quality offers such as publishing, fashions, gift catalogs, upscale general merchandise, fund-raising, club memberships, and home, family and child products and services of all kinds . . . "

Last August, *Harper's* magazine ran the full text of the ad, along with this editorial comment: "An estimated 5 million trees are destroyed each year to produce direct mail that goes unopened by recipients."

Is Anything Sacred?

No.

Nothing is safe from commercialization. Every aspect of life is, in a phrase frequently used in the licensing business, "ripe for exploitation." Including many of the things Americans hold most dear:

The Statue of Liberty: The centennial of the statue, back in 1986, set off an orgy of commercialism. There were official Statue of Liberty pocketknives, charcoal briquettes, dry-roasted peanuts and 100 percent polyester "Women's Bend Over trousers." Avon marketed 'Liberty Look' makeup by depicting the statue's restoration as a "monumental makeover." Sure deodorant used the statue to demonstrate the ability to hold one's arm aloft without worrying about unsightly stains. And U.S. Tobacco said this: "Just like Lady Liberty, smokeless tobaccos such as Copenhagen have also played a major role in shaping America's heritage."

Sports: College basketball coaches are paid $200,000 to require their players to wear certain sneakers. Millionaire baseball players charge money to sign autographs. Professional tennis players are now as ad-covered as race cars or America's Cup yachts. In the National Hockey League, referees are instructed to call penalties on players using equipment that displays the names of companies that have not paid the league for the privilege of advertising. Meanwhile, the Orange Bowl has become the Federal Express Orange Bowl, the Cotton Bowl has become the Mobil Cotton Bowl, the Sugar Bowl has become the USF&G Sugar Bowl, and the Sun Bowl has become the John Hancock Bowl. Not to mention the Sunkist Fiesta Bowl, the Mazda Gator Bowl, the Sea World Holiday Bowl, the Domino's Pizza Copper Bowl, the California Raisin Bowl and my personal favorite, the Poulan/Weed Eater Independence Bowl. And much, much more!

Martin Luther King Jr.: Every January, such black-oriented magazines as *Essence* and *Ebony* are thick with corporate ads praising Dr. King. "We at American Airlines salute the vision of people like Dr. King," says one. "McDonald's joins the community in dedicating ourselves to keeping Dr. Martin Luther King, Jr.'s dream alive," says another. "His truth is marching on," says Coors, while Du Pont salutes "Dr. King's courageous leadership." All of which are noble sentiments. But you'd tend to put more credence in these corporations' sincerity if they placed the same ads in magazines with a large white readership.

Schools: American public schools are full of corporate sponsored "teaching materials" that are packed with ads. Chef Boyardee, Nutrasweet and McDonald's distribute nutrition information. Colgate-Palmolive provides dental health posters for first- and second-graders. Procter & Gamble donates materials on economics, history, cooking and personal grooming. Needless to say, these materials frequently come bearing logos, ads and coupons. Meanwhile, one marketing company provides free ad-filled book covers to American schools and another puts up advertising posters called "GymBoards" in the locker rooms of 3,000 high schools. Why? "Kids spend 40 percent of each day in the classroom where traditional advertising can't reach them," said one industry ad. "Now, you can enter the classroom through custom-made learning materials with your specific marketing objectives in mind . . ."

The Dead: D.H. Lawrence rides the Metro these days, looking haggard and tubercular on a sign that reads, "What is Man's Deepest Desire?" Friedrich Nietzsche rides too, with a thick moustache and a morose expression on his face as he wonders, "Why does man exist?" Good questions, but the answers aren't forthcoming, only the information that "Bass [ale] helps you get to the bottom of it all." D.H. and Freddy are only two of many dead celebrities now endorsing products that may or may not have existed when they were drawing breath. James Dean appears in ads for sneakers. Buddy Holly shills for Maxell tapes, and Babe Ruth is used to sell everything from Zenith electronics to Chevrolets to Sears computers. Merchandisers love dead celebrities because they are a lot less liable than live celebrities to get busted for dope or statutory rape. Still, one suspects that Ernest Hemingway wouldn't want his prose read over footage of a writhing shirtless male in a TV ad for perfume.

Religion: Has God been commercialized? Is the pope Catholic? Does he have a 900 number? Yes. "Welcome to Christian messaging from the Vatican . . ." begins the $1.95-per-minute tape. Protestants may prefer browsing in stores like the Family Bookstore at Lakeforest Mall in Gaithersburg, which carries such items as religious punk music CDs; Heaven's Trail, a biblical Trivial Pursuit knockoff; a

Christian exercise video called "Fit for a King"; and a bear-shaped baby dish with the words "Jesus Loves Me" on the forehead. Jews can collect "Rebbe Cards," trading cards featuring pictures of the great rabbinic teachers.

Desert Storm: The Persian Gulf war, said Gen. Norman Schwarzkopf in his famous post-victory briefing, was "not a Nintendo game." At the time, he may have been right. But now it is a Nintendo game called "F-15 Strike Eagle," which is billed as an opportunity to "locate and destroy chemical warfare plants, blast entrenched positions . . . lead an assault force against the enemy's capital city . . . " Desert Storm has also spawned a couple dozen books, various videotapes, several series of trading cards and a bunch of bizarre little statuettes that look like pre-pubescent tykes in military uniforms. They're called the "Bless Those Who Serve Their Country" line, and they're sold for $32.50 apiece by Enesco, the people who gave us McDonald's Christmas ornaments.

The Collapse of Communism: When joyous East Germans tore down the Berlin Wall, Kenneth Cole shoes celebrated by putting a picture of the historic scene in an ad, along with this observation: "Now there's nothing to keep anyone from coming to our Semi-Annual Sale." More recently, the unsuccessful coup in Moscow spawned several ads for booze. "Da! Once you have a taste of freedom, you'll never go back," observed an ad for Pilsner Urquell, a Czech beer. And an ad for Stolichnaya vodka showed a picture of Russians defending their parliament building during the coup and the caption, "We're prouder than ever to be Russian."

That did it. *Adweek,* the advertising industry magazine, was appalled and indignant: "The lesson learned from the failed coup is that no subject, person or event is so important to world history that it's above being used for the purposes of self-promotional hype." Which is another way of saying that no, nothing is sacred.

The Pig is Us

This unceasing blare of commercialism makes Michael Jacobson mad as hell, and he blasts each new outrage with a volley of press releases.

When Barbara Mandrell signed on with No Nonsense pantyhose and then titled her album "No Nonsense," Jacobson banged out an angry press release calling the deal "a new low for the music industry" and Mandrell the "Sell-Out of the Year." Then he sent letters to hundreds of country music radio stations. "Don't give free advertising to No Nonsense pantyhose," he wrote. "If you play songs from the album, don't mention the title on the air."

For decades Jacobson, the executive director of the Center for Science in the Public Interest, has crusaded against deception in ads for food and alcohol. But last year he decided to broaden his targets and he co-founded the Center for the Study of Commercialism. Since then, the tiny but feisty nonprofit group has testified in Congress against computer-generated telephone ads, petitioned the Federal Trade

Commission to require warning labels on movies containing product placements and lobbied against the advent of Channel One in Washington public schools.

"Omnipresent commercialism is wrecking America," Jacobson says.

Ceaseless advertising warps our kids' values, he says. It creates demand for junk foods and fad products. It promotes individual greed over social concern. It accentuates class envy. It debases politics to the level of advertising. And it's bad for the environment. He advocates eliminating ads aimed at kids, banning billboards and taxing ads.

"Our system of advertising purposely promotes envy, creates anxiety and fosters insecurity," Jacobson and Catholic University law professor Ronald K.L. Collins wrote in the *Christian Science Monitor.* "The tragic end-product of this is kids killing kids in Baltimore and elsewhere in order to walk in their playmates' $100 name-brand sneakers."

Jacobson's group is not the only one battling advertising. This summer, the American Academy of Pediatrics urged the banning of TV food commercials aimed at children because they promote bad nutrition and obesity. Activists in Harlem and Baltimore have defaced dozens of billboards advertising tobacco and alcohol in inner-city neighborhoods. And in Vancouver, a group called the Media Foundation produces anti-commercial TV commercials. In a 30-second spot called "American Excess," the map of North America becomes a gross grinning animated pig. "A tiny 5 percent of the people in the world consume one-third of its resources and produce almost half the non-organic waste," says the voice-over. "Those people are us." The pig grunts and burps, and the voice says, "Nothing is destroying this planet faster than the way we North Americans live."

Even *Advertising Age,* an industry publication, has attacked the ubiquitousness of advertising: "What used to be a somewhat even battle between the exaggerations and lure of advertising and the prudence of authority figures at home has become dangerously one-sided."

Americans are "fed up with being bombarded by up to 3,000 marketing messages a day," observed *Business Week.* " . . . A consumer revolt against advertising seems to be taking shape."

A consumer revolt against advertising? Could it be? If so, it invites the question: Is there some way this trend can be commercialized?

Of course, the answer is: Of course. In fact, it's already been done.

Last year, Esprit, the hip clothing chain, put an ad titled "A Plea for Responsible Consumption" in an alternative magazine called the *Utne Reader.*

"We do need clothes, yes, but so many?" it asked.

"Today, more than ever," the long text continued, "the direction of an environmentally conscious style is not to have luxury or conspicuous consumption written all over your attire. This is still our message. We believe this could be best achieved by simply asking yourself before you buy something (from us or any other company) whether this is something you really need . . . "

The ad was inspired, company spokeswoman Susan Alexander told the *Post*, by polling data indicating that consumers wanted to buy from environmentally responsible companies. After seeing that ad, she said, perhaps "they'll come to us instead of someone else." And then there's tennis champion Monica Seles:

"I'm not going to sell out," she announces.

"I'm not going to Disney World," she says.

Pretty radical statements. Unfortunately, she utters them in an ad for No Excuses jeans.

Where No Ads Have Gone Before

We have seen the present and it is goofy. But what about the future of commercialism?

Gloomy, if you listen to the ad people, who have been moaning lately about how ad spending is increasing at a slower rate than the rest of the economy. The recession has certainly cut the amount of advertising in the traditional markets—newspapers, magazines and network TV—but such less-traditional forms as direct mail, event sponsorship and other promotions are booming. Which might explain why Advertising Age recently asked prominent ad agency media directors: "Where can advertisers boldly go where no ads have gone before?"

The ad men came up with some nifty ideas: ads on subway tokens. Ads on the backs of chairs in commuter trains. The Gateway Arch in St. Louis—perfect for a big banner ad! Ads on postage stamps. Pet food ads in vets' offices. The slot machines in Vegas casinos: Why should they show cherries and oranges? Why not boxes of Tide? Ads in those smarmy mailings that members of Congress send to their constituents. Upscale ads on polo ponies. Ads on the space shuttle and on the astronauts' uniforms ...

Maybe they were kidding. Or maybe they weren't. It's tough to tell. After all, skeptics once scoffed at the idea of ads in public bathroom stalls. Besides, Pete Riordan—a manager at BBDO Worldwide and the guy who came up with the polo pony idea—didn't sound as if he was kidding when he said, "I don't think there's any saturation point in the selling environment."

No saturation point! Ads without limit! The mind reels as it ponders a future of commercialism unchained: Richard Nixon sprawls languidly across a chair in a pair of tight jeans. "I have no excuses," he purrs. "I just wear them." ... Michael Jackson's new album, "Pepsi!," shoots to the top of the charts, displacing M.C. Hammer's "You Deserve a Break Today, Sucka!" ... For the benefit of C-SPAN viewers, ads hang from the rafters of Congress ... Disney unveils the new all-Mickey home ... Gov. Mario Cuomo announces that the State of New York will henceforth be known by its acronym, SONY, thanks to a generous gift from the corporation of the same name ... The Congressional Record begins accepting ads, and the Tobacco Institute immediately announces that it will sponsor the speeches of Sen. Jesse Helms . . . In the remake of "A Tale of Two Cities," Marie Antoinette utters the immortal line, "Let them eat Sara Lee cake."

And much, much, more!

Meanwhile, the smiling interviewer steps through the cheering crowd.

"Dan Quayle, you've just won the presidency," he says. "What are you going to do now?"

And the president-elect, still flushed with victory, dutifully replies: "I'm going to Disney World!"

November 3, 1991

Looking for a Better Label

Futurist Graham Molitor and His Global Collection of Ideas

CAROLE SUGARMAN

Call him Labelman. After all, anybody who has catalogued, dissected and analyzed thousands of food packages from all over the world deserves to be considered a super hero of sorts.

Labelman, a k a Graham T.T. Molitor, is a futurist, a one-person think tank prone to interrupt himself with "I'd love to do a paper on that!" A high-tech fortune teller with a résumé the size of the S&L legislation and a fascination with facts that most people reserve for sports trivia, Molitor runs Public Policy Forecasting, Inc.

Predicated on the idea that America lags anywhere from six to eight years behind the rest of the world in implementing consumer policies, Molitor's consulting business offers companies, federal agencies and academic organizations a crystal ball on international trends and their outcomes.

Last week, Molitor was working on the future of the ozone layer, but his 25 years of experience with the food industry, including stints as a lawyer-lobbyist for Nabisco and General Mills, keep him busy tracking various food industries. Candy, yeast and soft drinks are a few of the subjects Molitor has studied, often with the focus on foreign ownership and competition.

In his Potomac office—a home version of the Library of Congress—28-foot walls are lined with bookcases and sliding ladders. More than 30,000 volumes are indexed here, ranging from "The Logarithmic Century" to "All About Beer."

On one side of the room a huge glass window overlooks one of the three Japanese bonsai gardens and waterfalls surrounding the home. Nestled above is a library loft, complete with a trick bookcase that swings into the room behind it. This is not to mention space for the 120 periodicals he receives and peruses via speed reading, a photo archive with 40,000 slides used for multimedia presentations and a voluminous card catalogue filled with facts such as the languages required on food packages in Switzerland (German, French, Italian).

Molitor has looked at food safety standards around the world (he believes that the Soviet Union has the toughest pesticide policy—at least on paper) and likes to say that while "most Americans tend to think we do everything right—and first— it's not true."

A case in point is the food label. Molitor believes that Scandinavian countries—particularly Sweden—are way ahead of the United States. (When it comes to food and nutrition policies, his motto is that "everything that eventually happens in the U.S. happened six years ago in Sweden." In 1971, for example, Sweden was the first country to develop and implement national nutrition goals; the U.S. Senate Select Committee on Nutrition and Human Needs published its recommendations in 1977.)

Molitor's observations are particularly timely in light of recent efforts to revamp the food label in this country. Spurred by the increasing awareness of the connection between diet and health and the decreasing effectiveness of the food label to communicate useful information, Congress began hearings on a comprehensive food labeling bill earlier this month. The bill calls for mandatory and expanded nutrition labeling on all food products, including saturated and unsaturated fat and the calories derived from them, cholesterol, fiber and complex and simple sugars, and directs the National Academy of Sciences to recommend the manner in which the information should be displayed.

While Molitor doesn't believe any country has achieved the optimum label format, nevertheless, "there's a lot of experimentation going on. We ought to be able to take advantage of that," he said. "It doesn't [necessarily] mean we should copy."

If we ignore the global experience, however, Molitor predicts that Americans will make the same mistakes that other countries have already made: the label will become more complicated before it gets simpler. "It may initially go the way of providing a long laundry list," said Molitor, who believes that the current American food label is "very modest" and "not very useful." But Molitor supports symbolic formats such as pie charts, graphs or colors; complicated, overly specific depictions "turn people off."

When it comes to confusing the public, Denmark at one time had 13 different graphic formats that manufacturers could choose from to depict nutrition information, according to Molitor.

The Albert Heijn supermarket chain in the Netherlands unsuccessfully experimented with a format in the 1970s patterned after the five-ring symbol of the Olympic Games. Each of the rings designated a particular dietary component, shaded to represent the nutritional values of the food, but the terminology was unfamiliar to most consumers, according to Molitor.

Among the foreign food packages Molitor has amassed in his basement through more than 40 research projects is a French spongecake listing the weight of the ingredients in parts per million. The weight of the sugar in the cake is 37.9070 percent of the total; egg 18.3650 percent. A label for breath mints from Sweden details the type and amount of sugar in the tablets, listing glucose, fructose, sucrose, lactose, sorbitol, manitol and xylitol.

Other labels are simpler. A Swedish margarine company makes its tubs in two different colors—green and red. The green tub contains the firm's margarine with the more favorable ratio of polyunsaturated to saturated fats; the red tub has a less favorable ratio.

The label panel on a Danish package of vanilla pudding lists the country's quantitative nutrition goals for fat, carbohydrates and protein alongside the amounts of those nutrients contained in the pudding. A Nestle-owned company in Sweden pictured potatoes, peas and an orange on the label for its fish product, giving the nutrition information for the whole meal.

While nutrition labeling is mandatory only for certain products in Europe, according to Molitor, many countries do require percentage declaration for key ingredients. Thus, a package for Scottish butter cookies lists 28 percent butter; Belgium chocolate biscuits contain 12 percent chocolate and a German prune cake includes 83 percent prune cream.

Sweden is even experimenting with graphically depicting taste. On a can of Pripps Bia beer, pie charts show the percentage of bitterness and sweetness in the brew.

Western Europe has also done a lot of experimentation when it comes to label accoutrements such as approved seals and tags. In Norway, for example, a state-certified symbol can be used by manufacturers whose products are safe for diabetics.

And the Swedish government has just instituted a program that permits companies to use a seal if their products meet certain nutritional guidelines for fat and fiber. Thus, firms that make breads and grains with at least two-thirds whole-wheat flour and at least nine grams of fiber per 100 grams can apply for the seal; dairy products and margarine must have a specified fat maximum. The manufacturers do not have to pay the government to use the seals.

But labels, seals and package tags are not the only way to communicate nutrition information.

"I collect little odd ball stuff that strikes my fancy," says Molitor, pulling out a file entitled "Electronics." Among his many professional lives, Molitor was an undercover agent involved in electronic counter intrusion. ("There really are antennae in the toothpicks in martinis," he says.) In the file, Molitor has collected news clippings and advertisements for hand-held devices that detect everything from calorie counts to pulse rates and sunburns.

What's the connection? Molitor envisions consumers someday carrying computerized wands as they shop. The computers, programmed with a health profile of the shopper, could be scanned across the universal product codes on packages which would contain a nutrition profile of the food. The tiny computer screen would then light up, informing a shopper who has had a bypass operation, for example, whether the fat content in the particular food was appropriate for him.

Molitor also predicts that nutrition information will be accessible on home computers, and hopes that 800 numbers on food packages will be commonplace.

As far as the past and present, he is bothered when multinational companies make the argument that changes are too costly or that there is no room on the label.

They have been able to make these adaptations on their products sold in foreign markets, he says. "The standard arguments really don't hold up."

While informative labels are crucial, Molitor believes, their net impact—changing dietary patterns and decreasing disease—may not really be so great. "It isn't," says Molitor, "the end-all, save-all." Detailed sugar labeling in Sweden has not made substantial inroads to decreasing sugar consumption, for example.

And in countries that have established national nutrition goals—recommending a decrease in fat consumption and an increase in carbohydrates—the trends are just the opposite, he says. The reason? Molitor's conclusion, a factor that no study will ever be able to correct, is simple self-indulgence.

August 16, 1989

An Investment in American Citizenship

Immigration Program Invites
Millionaires to Buy their Way in

AL KAMEN

Lady Liberty may still beckon to the "huddled masses yearning to breathe free," but Uncle Sam now extends a special welcome to those who can pay cash.

Under a new immigration program that goes into effect Tuesday, 10,000 visas for permanent residence in the United States will be available each year for those who agree to invest at least $1 million in businesses here. Full citizenship will be available for them and their families after five years.

The program, part of the Immigration Act of 1990, is an unabashed attempt to attract wealthy foreigners—especially Asians and, most particularly, Chinese from Hong Kong who are worried about living under communist rule in 1997.

The response—100 applications so far—has been less than overwhelming. Officials at the Immigration and Naturalization Service say they are confident many more people will apply once final regulations are issued. But immigration lawyers and others are not sure, saying the program is too restrictive and expensive.

The plan is patterned after highly successful programs in other countries, especially Canada and Australia. Canada's program, which began in 1986, has brought in more than $3 billion a year and has created more than 40,000 jobs, Canadian officials said.

Australia's program, begun in 1982, brought in $1.3 billion in new investment last year, with about 10,000 settlers coming mostly from Asia, according to the Australian Embassy.

Those figures—and a sluggish U.S. economy—overcame the discomfort some lawmakers felt about the notion of a dollars-for-visas program.

Sen. Dale Bumpers (D-Ark.), who led the opposition, thundered on the Senate floor against "auctioning off our souls" by "allowing somebody into this country simply because he or she happens to have $1 million either inherited, made in the drug cartel, regardless of where the money comes from."

But Republican backers, such as Sen. Phil Gramm (Tex.), countered by quoting Calvin Coolidge that "the business of America is business" and the country needed entrepreneurs as much as any other category of immigrant. Democrats, such as Sen. Edward M. Kennedy (Mass.), insisted the program was not selling visas, but creating jobs because, in addition to the money, investors also would have to create 10 jobs to qualify for permanent residency.

The bill's supporters predicted that about 4,000 millionaire investors, along with family members, would sign up, bringing in $4 billion in new investments and creating 40,000 jobs.

Immigration lawyers and business promoters went into a feeding frenzy at the possibilities, shuttling back and forth to the Orient, conducting dozens of seminars and discussions with prospective clients.

But now, after all the congressional angst and the promotional activity, immigration lawyers and business brokers are not sure wealthy foreigners will bite.

One problem, said Harold Ezell, a former INS official and now an immigration consultant in California who is advising foreign investors, is that "INS dropped the ball," and has yet to publish regulations to implement the law. As a result, applications cannot be processed. Ezell is confident applications will increase. The Canadian offer is attractive, he said, "if you want to go to Canada and freeze your buns off."

Even when final regulations are issued, possibly in the next few weeks, there still may be uncertainties, immigration lawyers said. Immigration officials are debating whether to lower the ante to $500,000 for investments in rural or high-unemployment areas.

Entrepreneurs will receive a two-year provisional visa and, if still-to-be-decided criteria are met, a permanent green card may be issued, with citizenship three years after that. One-question unanswered, however, is what happens to the visa if after two years the business falls on hard times and employs only seven people or if other regulations aren't met.

"One million dollars is not chump change," said St. Louis immigration lawyer George Newman. "People with that kind of money didn't get it because they are idiots," he said, and they are not going to jump into the program without a clear idea of what will happen.

Newman said many of the inquiries he has received have been from European entrepreneurs. He said many have gone to Canada, but "the country of choice is the United States."

"The Canadian program has been a spectacular success," he said, "and we just sat here and let them do it."

Canada and Australia were also a lot easier to enter, said attorney Austin Fragomen of New York City. Even if all the uncertainties are cleared up, Fragomen said, "our program is not a competitive product" with the Canadian program.

Australia's program requires an investment of only $120,000. Canada's program requires $220,000 and no "hands-on" directorship of 10 employees. The U.S. requirements are obstacles, Fragomen said. "Who wants to run a McDonald's in the South Bronx?" he asked. "It's very difficult."

The other advantage with the Canadian program, said San Francisco investment banker Tony Angotti, is that Canada has a list of hundreds of preapproved investments, so that when people invest, they know that after three, not five years, they can be citizens.

"People tend to forget that for the wealthy the United States is not the only game in town," he said. "If you are Hong Kong Chinese, wealthy and worried about 1997, you've been concerned for some time and you already have a New Zealand [or other] passport. These guys are the first ones out" when trouble is coming, he said.

Irvin Philpot, office manager of a Palm Beach, Fla., holding company called Global Group, said ads he has placed worldwide have generated substantial responses, "but we're not getting as many people that have a million in liquid cash that we had hoped for." To have that much, he said, "you've got to be worth between $10-$12 million."

Philpot, who has submitted four applications for the visas, said he was looking for investors in any of 27 companies, including fast-food franchises, light bulb manufacturing or taxi and limousine companies.

The response has been cautious, he said.

September 29, 1991